M  O F  L I B Y A  Kufra

AL·UENAT

Massif de

PIC TOUSSIDÉ

Zouar

T I B E

FREN

Moussor

assakori

AMY

| DATE | | |
|---|---|---|
| APR 21 '83 | | |
| | | |
| | | |
| | | |
| | | |
| | | |
| | | |
| | | |
| | | |
| | | |
| | | |
| | | |
| | | |

© THE BAKER & TAYLOR CO.

# MIRAGE OF AFRICA

"It is near Fort-Archambault that live the *négresses à plateau . . .*" *p. 110*

# Mirage of Africa

---

### ALAN HOUGHTON BRODRICK

With 33 illustrations

**GREENWOOD PRESS, PUBLISHERS**
WESTPORT, CONNECTICUT

Library of Congress Cataloging in Publication Data

Brodrick, Alan Houghton.
    Mirage of Africa.

    Reprint of the 1953 ed. published by
Hutchinson, London.
    1.  Africa, North--Description and travel
--1951-       2.  Brodrick, Alan Houghton.
I.  Title.
[DT190.2.B68  1979]    916.1'04'3        79-139
ISBN 0-8371-5186-4

First published 1953 by Hutchinson & Co. (Publishers) Lt
London

Reprinted with the permission of Hutchinson Publishing
Group Ltd.

Reprinted in 1979 by Greenwood Press, Inc.
51 Riverside Avenue, Westport, CT 06880

Printed in the United States of America

10  9  8  7  6  5  4  3  2  1

*Pour*

MONSIEUR LE MIRE

*en*
*Souvenir amical*
*et reconnaissant*

*Il y a un allégement pour le cœur qui s'abandonne au pur voyage, pour l'âme en migration, ne fut-ce pour une saison brève, loin des maisons des hommes, un éventement d'ailes, une fraîcheur de résurrection.*

JULIEN GRACQ: *La Terre Habitable.*

# LIST OF ILLUSTRATIONS

"It is near Fort-Archambault that live the *négresses à plateau* . . .    *Frontispiece*

FACING
PAGE

"One dancer is veiled white and the other blue-black"    16

". . . the tunnels, dark alleys of a maze . . ."    17

". . . the expanse of flat roofs . . . from whose corners rise the famed horus . . ."    32

". . . the track over the Hammada-el-Homra—a petrified sea rippled with murderous lines of stones . . ."    33

"The walls are crowned with teeth, rows and rows of them . . ."    36

"Here are huts and a line of plaited wattle fencing"    37

"In the real Black African villages . . ." (Moussoro)    44

". . . the ill-famed Kourizo Pass . . ."    45

". . . the people of Douirat . . . have more houses than families"    48

". . . the fairyland of the Sissé Needles, jutting upwards from meadows of saffron sand"    48

"The hair . . . plaited in rope-like strands . . ."    49

"An Egyptian painting . . . so lively and living . . ."    64

". . . buried cities of the ancient Sao, where are found earthenware . . . statuettes . . ."    65

"Near Ghat is such a graveyard, but it is unwalled and slopes down . . . dotted with cairns . . ."    68

"From Matmata in the north . . ."    69

"*Méharistes*, the Camel Corps, Tuareg far from their homes . . ."    76

"Below . . . is an arid dale of crumbling arches and dilapidated masonry"    77

". . . we stand at the arched gateway and survey the dunes . . . a Door on Dreams"    80

7

FACING
PAGE

"Men slumped in the miserly shade. A hungry land"          81

". . . the *Limes*, the Outpost of Empire . . ."          96

". . . the forepart of a stupendous saurian, a dragon of the
    wastes"          97

"Ksar Lemsa is an unrecorded treasure . . ."          97

"The effect is that of an edifice set upon an artificial hill"          112

"The camels stroll and nibble as they please . . ."          113

"I . . . prepare to daub a little . . ."          128

". . . the Capitoline Temples, luminous and majestic"          129

". . . neatly framed in Diocletian's Arch we may observe
    the functional outline of a lofty derrick"          144

". . . the most obvious man-made objects remain . . .
    uprights . . ."          145

"The Trees of Life"          160

". . . the fish between two cups. But it is something quite
    other . . ."          161

". . . fat amorous bull-frogs are reposing from the heat of
    the day"          176

". . . Ksar Lemsa has a familiar outline . . ."          177

# INTRODUCTION

North-West Africa, or what the Arabic-speakers call the *Maghreb*, has changed much since the time I wrote my *Parts of Barbary*, published in 1944 and long out of print. However, in this book there is not much mention of the tensions and of the shifting, elusive political expressions of North Africa, although it is impossible to write about the region unless something is said of why and how what is happening on this section of the arc of Islam is reverberating along the whole.

It seems to have become the fashion among some English-language writers to adopt a marked, and in some cases, a quite unreasonable, hostility to the French as the masters of their North Africa. It is true that most, if not all, of these authors are ill-equipped to offer their readers anything but a subjective impression uninfluenced by long experience, much study or, in not a few cases, ability to speak fluently a language essential for the formation of understanding or judgement based upon it.

This sounds rather presumptuous but I know that few who are fitted to appraise will disagree with what I say. I should like, therefore, right at the start of this book to make my attitude quite clear. In *Mirage of Africa* I have felt as free to comment, to criticize and on occasion to condemn, as I have when writing anything else, but perhaps I may be allowed to state that my sympathies, on the whole, lie with the French in North Africa. Any considerable weakening of their position would be a disaster not only for the peoples of the *Maghreb* but also for the general strategical situation of Western Europe. This does not mean that there should not be, that there will not be, notable changes in administration and in the relations between the French and the peoples of the *Maghreb*, but it does mean that irresponsible and unfair attacks on the French achievement in North Africa are much to be deprecated.

*Mirage of Africa* neither covers the same ground nor does it treat, essentially, of the same subjects as *Parts of Barbary*. Instead of making our way from east to west and then back again we drive southwards to the sands, the heart of the Sahara, and beyond to the savannas of the Sudan and the fringes of the great forests. In fact, our subject is very largely that of the water-

9

shed—though it is a fossil one—between White Africa and Black
Africa, the area where are the paintings and engravings of a
most ancient African art, which is prolonged in a curious way
right down the eastern side of Africa and round through South
Africa to South-West Africa. In subject, in technique and in
style not a few of these prehistoric African pictures show such
close resemblances to those of western Europe, and particularly
of Spain, that it is hard to avoid the conclusion that there was
direct contact between the arts of the two regions.

Within the last few years I have published several books
dealing either wholly, or in part, with prehistoric paintings, and
I know from what readers were good enough to write to me that
the magnificent memorials of a remote past interested them. The
pictures throw into life a whole phase of man's pilgrimage on
this earth, a beam of light shoots through the darkness of distant
ages. Art is always topical, it is man's creation of his own
special world.

The Spanish prehistoric pictures of the Levant figured
prominently in my book *Pillars of Hercules*, but in this volume an
attempt is made to show what we know or can reasonably deduce
concerning the mysterious prehistoric arts of Europe and Africa.
If, however, the 'Written Rocks' are a main theme of *Mirage of
Africa*, there is something about the mirage, too, and even about
Africa as a rather old hand saw it in 1951 on his twelfth voyage
to what was once known as the Dark Continent.

A. H. B.

Tunis 1951.
Paris 1952.

*Si le monde n'est que ce qu'il paraît être, au point où l'ont mené la science et la philosophie scientifique de ce temps, il est absurde pour la raison, révoltant pour le coeur.*

RENÉ GROUSSET.

THIS Monbazillac is quite remarkably good. It's true we are in the Dordogne and it is a vintage of the country; still, even here labels are often deceptive—nowadays.

Another glass. I can't get anything like this at my hotel though there's a wonderful cellar there; no, the Monbazillac is soothing me too much. Let's say an excellent cellar, an honourable cellar. Moreover, my pitch has been queered by an eminent Irish man of letters. Since I was last in this part of the world, he has set a new standard. God bless him, he enjoys well-merited prosperity.

Punctually an hour before meals he calls for a double *fine champagne*, repeats the order every fifteen minutes, then sits down to an elegant repast and tastes with it wines—no, not the wines of this countryside, but wines from the great vineyards, sumptuous vintages, Romanée-Conti, Mouton-Rothschild and I know not what.

Every day, three-quarters of a bottle of fine, old brandy and just as cocktail, *apéritif*, glorious appetizer.

About me are benches and tables for beano or barbecue. Two or three hundred feasters could gather under these garden-trees among the gravel. Perhaps on high days and holidays customers do spill over into this wine-grove, but I am here always alone. The regular customers foregather inside the pub that is also a greengrocer's shop.

The *patron* does not serve me, nor does his wife. They are an upstanding couple, but a little taciturn for the south, if we can call the Dordogne the south. I am waited on, most graciously, by the daughter of the house. Without my making more than a vague gesture, she knows when to bring clean glasses upon a silvered platter. Their shape is odd, though they are, I suppose, champagne-glasses of a sort; flat, broad-bowled ones used for the sweet champagne French countrymen and provincials favour. These glasses are delicately chased and I do not like chased glasses at all; still, they are clean and thin. Now, if the *patron* served me with *flûtes* or slender goblets which are right and proper for dry champagne, then I should get a good deal more Monbazillac in each glass.

I am always at home in these pleasant valleys, never more alluring than when autumn mists evaporate in benignant sunshine and leave you with the scent of walnuts and new wine. I feel that, in a measure, I was enriched and edified here where now I have had no home for nearly twenty years. I am never an alien, never was, indeed, a newcomer since I was denizened in this land before its peculiar treasures had been revealed in full. They were almost unknown a half-century ago, only fifteen years since they were less rich than they now are.

A half-century, fifty years, everything has swept along so quickly. Some physicists tell us that the Middle Ages came to an end in 1900.[1] Now, Heaven help us, we've got quantum mechanics, three-value logic, Principles of Uncertainty and Complementarity and what you will . . . two sorts of truth—we had always suspected that, in fact we feel there may be three or four sorts of truth. Let's be modest.

Another glass of wine, they are so small. The bottle stays with me upon the table but it is an absolute, unwritten law that I should not help myself. Each glass must be a fresh, clean one. Such refinement. But, then, that's how the *patron* keeps a tab on me.

The daughter fills my glass to the brim but never a drop does she spill. She is most adroit. This Monbazillac costs 25 francs, that is to say about 3*d.* a glass; as we've noticed, the glasses are not large, but the wine is princely. I had thought for a moment when I heard the stuff was obtained through a special traveller, I had imagined that he might be the son of my old bailiff at Fayolles, but, bless us, the young fellow's a big businessman nowadays, and he's not so young, either; getting on for sixty.

So the mathematicians are chagrined, their house of mathematical analysis cards has toppled over. The mathematicians, so it seems, must become non-mathematical, that's the dictate of fashion. Such a bore. Instead of protean reality, give us the solid, impregnable rock of fiction. What's true—or more or less true—on one scale, isn't true on another. The infinitely small, we are told, holds the secrets of the universe. But you and I, well, we live

[1] 12th December, 1900, publication of Max Planck's quanta theory. 1905 Einstein's union of time and space and deduction of the identity of matter and energy. The whole edifice of classical physics came tumbling down.

on one scale all the time, and what do we care if liquid helium[1] climbs up if, let us see, if liquid Monbazillac does not?

It is clear, never sticky, though fruity, too sweet, maybe, for some tastes; but so strong, so full of sunlight as to admit of no criticism. A noble drink indeed. The silent daughter's deportment is slightly bowed as that of one retiring reverently from partaking of the Eucharist. Her gait is a jerky shuffle, you would say that she must stumble at each step, but no, she is agile, agile as a sleepwalker. Through the trees comes swaggering along the best-looking girl in the town, side-set eyes, her sparkling glance twinkles through the leaves; an erotic wake follows her . . . yes, of course, we all know that, the job is not to find out what the world is but to fabricate a satisfactory language to describe what we think we see—satisfactory, that's it, or satisfying . . . now we feel better, let's reach for that popular and more or less medical review: leading article, *Est-ce que les gros sont plus virils que les maigres?* "Are fat men more virile than thin men?" It's absorbing reading, especially for, let us say, well-built men; the last paragraph is really illuminating even to my benighted understanding; everything that has gone before depends entirely upon what one understands by 'fat' and 'thin' in this connection. Quite so.

Another glass of Monbazillac. Perhaps the revelations of this awful half-century, the new views of our surroundings, are not so startling as new views of our own selves and not of what we think we see. After all, things exist because we see them, or, at least, if we could not see them they would not exist for us. So, everything perceived is a vision procured by an instrument, ourselves. But men not only observe, they make. What we know about men's creations in the remote past has been accumulated mostly in the last fifty years. Some engravings on bone and statuettes of women were recognized during the last century. The gorgeous painted cave of Niaux has been known for generations, the prehistoric pictures were glanced at but no one paid attention to them; the decorated cavern of Altamira was discovered in the 1870's but its significance was ignored. Not until 1897 did Rivière find at La Mouthe, just up the river from where we are sitting,

---

[1] At least, it seems, at about 2° above absolute zero helium changes its habits and finds its own level over any obstacles. In fact the liquid gas steps clear out of classical physics.

a grotto whose mouth was blocked and sealed by undisturbed ancient deposits. The entrance, then, bore the indication:

"Nothing inside here is less than ten thousand years old." I was always dreaming, years ago, that I might find a painted cavern on my own land. Had there not been the splendid revelations of the Trois-Frères and the Tuc d'Audubert on private property down by the Pyrenean foothills? Anyway, why not? In those days we had not found Lascaux; but not so far away, in fact quite near, merely twenty miles off, lay Les Eyzies and the Vézère Valley: and then, there are engravings in caverns, still nearer. Needless to say, I never found anything, but there were places I thought most promising. Limestone formations, hill-slopes and, below, a broad, smiling valley watered by a little stream. Here were the chestnut woods; there had been cuts but some old giants survived, for the chestnut trees in this Dordogne grow to enormous size. The woods stretched out and away; some parts of them I never visited. It is always rather amusing and old-fashioned to own something one has never seen. What's ownership? Well, hard to say, but an owner's a man who is playing the game strictly according to rules. Good enough.

Where the ground went broken the chestnut-trees grew thick in little glens, dells and dales, all on a small scale, of course. Neighbours here were few and the woods so situated that we never gathered the nuts, though sacks and sacks could have been filled; the fruit might have fed the poor, but there were no poor who would answer to the name, though they would have been eager to claim the pauper's privileges had he had any in those far-off days before social services.

Amid the tall bracken showed mossy boulders, and here and there a chink or cranny in the rocks, but I found no entrance to marvels and would stroll back through sparser woodland where the mushrooms were plentiful; yellow *girolles* that we in English call by their less-known French name chanterelles (though that means most often in French a decoy-bird)—perhaps this is a hint to be on the look-out for the false *girolle* that is poisonous. Mushrooms abound and you soon acquire a stock of mushroom-lore . . . when we got the oak-woods, here and there were fat, luscious *langues de bœuf* projecting from the tree-trunks, and below, sumptuous *cêpes*. This was where the wild strawberries never failed until late summer. There were other strawberry plants nearer the house but they did not yield so bountifully for there were truffles thereabouts. The subterranean fungus and the strawberry do not flourish well as neighbours.

The other day I went down to Cabrerets, outside of this region and in the old Quercy, but not more than thirty miles away. The sights of Cabrerets are two, the Castle and the Cave, though the delightful Célé stream gliding between deep wooded banks is one too. The cave they call Pech-Merle; it was discovered as short a time ago as 1922. A silly inscription has been placed over the cavern's entrance. 'Here Primitive Man sacrificed to his Gods.' What, we may ask, is, or was, a primitive man? and how do we know that the Pech-Merle artists had Gods or offered up sacrifices?

Tendentious terminology, otherwise nonsense.

The cave is magnificent and splendid just as a cave, rich in its stalagmites and stalactites. Then there are the prehistoric paintings, the famed dappled or spotted horses with a red pike swimming near them, engravings of mammoth and oxen, bisons and human figures, some obscene and copulatory, but human figures with caricatural heads and faces, or masked, or beast-headed; naked females with sagging breasts; blobs of black and red paint; then figures and outlines made to fit into the natural curves and contours of the rock-face. Did the shape of the rock suggest that of the animal, did the artist complete the unfinished figure, did he draw the image out of the stone, or did he select the curves and lines to help him in his creation? No doubt, as in all things human, there was a criss-cross of motives, impulses and undefinable acts, but it implies rather more sustained thought to visualize a scene or a figure and then search for what will aid in realizing them, than it does to let the natural shapes lead on to an artificial end.

There are men's footprints in the clay now hardened to the consistency of stone; all about you the richly coloured calcite glistens and glows under the electric lights each bulb of which, lighted, perhaps, for a few hours each week during half the year, quickens a green smudge of lichen. Everything is waiting to live. From the ceiling's height drops a dark column, dull against the glittering pillars, arches and vaults, for it is no concretion but a symmetrical bundle of tree-roots that hang down, seeking sustenance, it may be thirty feet from the roof.

A new gallery into which you slither over red clay and under two pendant paps of stalactite that, thousands of years ago, men touched up with black pigment so as to make the swelling breasts display nipples and areolas. Once past the protecting dugs you may straighten up while you gaze at engravings and paintings, composite, apocalyptic beasts, animals of the chase. . . .

Out into the light of day, you will want to explore the castle; it is an attractive 15th-century fortress perched high up upon a knoll commanding the course of the Célé stream. The delight of our European prehistoric sites is that they are embedded in a richly historic countryside. What is called prehistory—and almost any word with the adjunct 'pre' is chilly; prefabricated, pre-digested and the like—is a tale of ages stretching bleakly back in time; a story that can easily leave us cold. It is strange, puzzling. Yes, of course, ancient stone implements can be made to talk, but what they say, we know, can be but a feeble squeak like the gibbering of Homeric ghosts. But we all respond to the appeal and the voice of prehistoric art, we are all under the thrall of the magic pictures which revive the past and immortalize it. When we can touch our prehistory while we are sheltered in historic surround-ings, why, then we are reassured.

This Cabrerets Castle, now, is a relic of the Hundred Years' War; within its walls are the witnesses of remote antiquity and of contemporary antiquity; the castle belongs to a Mademoiselle Murat, descendant of the King of Naples' brother who, by the protection of the *Enfant chéri de la Victoire*, was gratified with the title of *comte* and a large country-house, just near here, at La Bastide, where their father kept the local pub. Sense of continuity.

In the old chambers and thick-walled halls is an exciting collection of prehistoric objects and of modern African ones—pottery, sculpture, jewellery, masks, many masks—mostly from West Africa. There is material enough to set our thoughts wander-ing along alluring, but often deceiving, paths. Europe 15,000 years ago. Africa today. The old, and ever elusive theme. When does resemblance mean copy and when does it not? How far will men travel along parallel and similar roads without ever meeting? Sometimes we feel we can be sure and certain, then we get some shattering evidence. For instance, no one with historic sense and some knowledge of archæology and art could visit the astounding and dazzling exhibition of Mexican Art at Paris in 1952 without

"One dancer is veiled white and the other blue-black" *p. 18*

". . . the tunnels, dark alleys of a maze . . ." *p. 21*

finding all sorts of insistent comparisons, figurines like Ægean idols, jewellery that might be Sumerian, statuary archaic Greek, but it is as nearly certain as anything can be that no Ægean, Sumerian or Greek influences ever penetrated into pre-Columbian America. It is, of course, always the early things, what we may call the objects reflecting a generalized spiritual response, which recall others far apart in space and time; when come stylization, conventionalization, when the dogma imposes, the tradition moulds, when art becomes tongue-tied by authority, then we recognize where we are, alas.

Have another glass of Monbazillac with me. It will soon be time to stroll off for luncheon. Félicité, yes, that's her name, 'Happiness' is, truth to tell, just a little backward. She cannot, I think, speak, or it may be that wisely enough she will not, but she does not dribble at the mouth. Just a little backward.

In my pocket I have an invitation to Africa, to parts of it, too, that are not so much blessed with that vague but respectable non-entity, 'Western Civilization'. How right we are to respond to the appeal of most ancient art; we communicate in the art, we can but observe the products of the crafts. The most ancient pictures we have around us in the Vézère Valley can be matched not only in Spain but in Africa, where are more ageless paintings and engravings than elsewhere upon earth.

Spring mists in the Dordogne valleys and the flight of birds. Our short northern summer. The swallows and the house-martins have been here some time. The swifts, the late-coming swifts, are just beginning to arrive from Africa. They migrate in search of climate, they follow the weather, as no doubt did ancient men. In the south we seek warmth and not in east or west. Climate makes us, makes history. Africa is the place. Follow the swallow.

Félicité stares steadily as I get up. Many, if not most female imbeciles tend to be obscene in gesture and act. Félicité is demure. Conditioning or inhibiting? Or just that she is made so? She is hardly human: well, what is human, anyway? I pay in the shop and trip out into the pale, strong sunshine, well, *l'appétit est bon*, the appetite is all right. In this clement climate of France, anyway, there is no joy comparable to that of abstinence until noon and then a distinguished meal. . . .

Not so long ago it was observed that some of the aboriginal Australian children in a remote bush settlement were really

B

remarkable and significant pictorial artists living amid customs and ways of life not, perhaps, so very unlike those of the palæolithic hunters of western Europe 15,000 years ago. So, meddlesome fools, afflicted with the horrid blindness that not seldom strikes pink men, removed some of the children to an Australian town where they were to benefit from 'Western Civilization'. Whatever this may be, one little Australian aborigine felt that it was something very, very nasty indeed. He took an axe and, in protest, hacked to pieces a most expensive automobile.

Good lad.

SAHARAN MASQUE

Here is the comic relief. Scurrying from the shadows, dodging around the solemn mummer's feet, wriggling in and out among the musicians, scamper two creatures on all fours. Little figures, absurd and weird and charming. Toys in German Eastertide confectioners' shops. Paintings in prehistoric caverns.

The twirling Veiled Men were odd and are sinister; shrouded harbingers of foreboding. The mummers emerge from shade and retire into shadows. Neither dance nor music has beginning or end. A masque of life and death.

One dancer is veiled white and the other blue-black. Both are draped in pale-blue copes powdered and spangled dull silver. Each holds in his right hand a long staff tipped with silver. They move as planets round a sun of musicians, dark women in dark blue, women thumping drums, turning their backs towards us, the spectators. At the apex of the mound of bowed women, the flautists fidgeting their flutes while the women sway slowly to the rhythm.

The little boys are blanketed in Italian army greatcoats, grey, donkey-grey. Around the dull-red skull-cap fezes are dishcloths, and a pair of babooshes well imitate ass's ears. Bright, shining eyes; the rounded coffee-brown faces grin. Innocent intelligence, perhaps.

At first the music seems simple, ingenuous, almost silly. Evening warmth, scentless desert air. Then acquiescence not dulling appreciation of subtlety, of delicate variation in theme. A music not wholly White African since, though grave and solemn, it seems ever about to break into daring, mocking, Black African parody though being never bold enough, sinks away in reassuring cadences. A music that does not venture to scoff although hinting that we must have comic relief in our lives' drama.

As the dancers circle they also revolve and, from time to time, abruptly, brutally, stop and stamp and jerk their bodies as though to add force and vehemence to an obvious, unspoken threat.

Round and round and round. Drubbing drums. The fifes' shrill ululation.

The lads play their comic part as actors should and not as larking boys. Subtle capers and clowning never dribbling into petulance or fumbling farce.

Fine, dry sand muffling all footfalls in a square that is a vast hall; the suave air of a spacious palace; above, a ceiling of purple night. White walls reflect as nacreous glow the yellow glare of bulbs.

A highly schematized representation of a world of drama and sound and ritual; nothing tawdry in this simple, humble mime, nothing vulgar in its timeless music. Even the Europeans in the audience—and the French, especially, are much given to conversation against a musical background—do not chatter or guffaw —scarcely move indeed.

The little boys are not, as are the dancers, veiled, and they are not wholly masked, but they are transformed. Their faces changed into animals' faces. A man wearing a mask, what the Romans called a *persona*, a disguise and loud-speaker in one. A person is a mask making noises. A sobering thought that.

Three sides of the square are shallow arcades and stone benches on which once sat the buyers at the *collections*, the fashion-shows of black bodies. The remaining side is in shadows where the indistinct crowd backs up to a towering gateway and a black gate. Opposite us the notables of Ghadames, dignified elders, remote, patrician; the men who have known better days and who know that they are our betters. No over-compensation, nothing of what the ignorant call aristocratic airs. Just self-possession and ease. It takes a generation or two to kill the assurance of a caste ennobled by commerce in men.

Above the row of Europeans, on our left and at the top of a wall, runs a parapet of crenellations clustered with figures, white, black and blue. The Ladies of Ghadames.

This dance must be a prelude. We were warned of Saharan dances, but there is only one. Or are there many in one? Expectancy fades. Delicate variations encourage us to create our own complications. Rumble and throb. The flautists' Swiss wristwatches twinkle. The veiled dancer stamps in our directions. A faceless man.

The mute shrouded forms, topping the walls, sway against the night.

Now more ladies, those of the Ouled-Naïl jangling in and flopping on to the soft sand near us. Six of them, all in white dresses bordered with red braid. Spanish gypsies. Unveiled, of course, they glance about, not brazen but free; they are not Libyans, Tunisians or any subjects at all, but French citizens, though they do not hit the homeward trail when the weather gets hot, as do most of their kind. These Ouled-Naïl are denizens of Ghadames though doubtless they will, sooner or later, find their way back to their home on the uplands round about Djelfa in Algeria.

They are a cheerful lot, not surly or commonplace. A word or two of whispered banter with a hard-bitten, brick-red-faced spruce camel-corps captain. He is evidently a favourite and the Algerians give him tit for tat. The *directrice* of the troupe has the authentic ancient Egyptian appearance not rare among her tribe. Put on her head a ringlet-wig and she would make a very passable image of one of the serpents of Old Nile or of the quite modern women in the market-places of the Sudan. Profile, bone-formation, side-set eyes, an expression of innocence, of unbounded scepticism. Egyptian, yes, Egyptian as on tomb-wall and in coffin, in statue and painting, Egyptian of the time when the men of the Nile Valley had an art other than that of architecture. No, not Egyptian of the all-Arabic talkies.

When this mature Ouled-Naïl woman of Ghadames flings out her bangled arms in gestures of recognition or emphasis, you can glimpse tattoo-marking, antique, prehistoric patterns, the Trees of Life. She is old enough to be a Marked Woman. Her family is, in the flesh, more discreetly ornamented.

The swirling figures, antics of the donkey-boys, the boy-donkeys. Wail and throb of music. We are all having a splendid time for each one of us is witnessing a separate show and hearing his own private music. The dim crowd rustles. A lanky negro pushes to the leading lady and croaks, what we might translate *au boulot* in French or just 'shop' in English. The prima donna sends off two of her charges. They whirl up, smile, fade away graceful, supple white patches in the gloom.

When we have had enough, hours later, we offer to stand drinks to the Ouled-Naïl ladies if they will pilot us back to the false fonduk of Aïn-el-Frass.

Through the crowd, under the gateway and by the corner where until a few years ago sat all day long the ancient water-watcher and with his clypsedra would judge when to open and when to shut off the flow to the different parts of the town that is, indeed, no town as we may understand that word. Ghadames is rather a collection of vast shapeless buildings and blocks of buildings, each section forming a gigantic apartment-house and a social unit. The Ghadamsis are a class-conscious lot and the dominant caste is 'white'. The colour-bar, so rare in the House of Islam, is sharply drawn in this old slave-emporium and the Ghadamsi 'white' women are, it is said, more secluded than any others in Islam. The Ghadamsiyahs indeed pass their lives in their dwellings and on the roofs. If a lady wishes to pay a visit, she does not have to go down into the streets. She walks across the expanse of flat roofs, broken here and there with low parapets from whose corners rise the famed horns, or angle-pieces jutting up to perhaps as much as ten feet and consisting of two sides stepped up to a narrow summit, which seen from below or from afar, appears quite sharp.

The Ouled-Naïl swirl bare-footed on the hardened sand, armlets and anklets clinking, skirts swishing. They laugh and joke as we twist and turn in the tunnels, dark alleys of a maze, a labyrinth lighted here and there by shaft or funnel running right up to what is now a luminous sky, for the moon has risen. The small, low, colourless house-doors are, as often as not, open, but they give on to insidious steps, steep and narrow; another turn, we are out of the maze of moon-shadows; into an opening not far from pool and caravanserai. We know where we are.

What about drinks? It seems that beers can be found though there's none at the Aïn-el-Frass. There the fashionable beverage is grenadine syrup, in itself an inoffensive if sickly preparation, but mixed with Epsom Salts, just formidable.

Up the ladder-like stairs, past low doorways, grey and mortuary.

The central apartment. It is delightful. Two or three storeys high, luminous from moonlight through the triangles piercing the cupola's drum. A masonry staircase runs up the sides of the walls and lends the hall much the appearance of a medieval courtyard in Florence or Siena. A pleasing piece of 'organic architecture' or is it? Perhaps more the indoors-outdoors plan of Mr. Frank Lloyd Wright.

On the whitewashed walls geometrical Sudanese designs, patterns like gigantic masks, malicious, subtle. Mirrors set in the walls and framed in great sweeping gay, irregular pointed frames. The work of slaves from the south. *L'Art Nègre*, a counterpart of the exuberant plastic art revealed to Europe by Picasso, Vlaminck, L-A. Moreau and the dealers. It is at least arguable that the inspiration of Black Africa saved our arts from sinking altogether into the swamp.

And ostrich-eggs, pendant smooth-shelled ostrich-eggs, covered with an open-work nets of lozenges, blue, white and red, and hanging down, like the dangling pendentives of Visigothic crowns, cowrie-shells, sure signs of Black Africa, cowrie-shells prophylactic, a charm, an amulet, a talisman.

Well, we all need something to keep ourselves sobered in passing prosperity and hopeful during bad times. Ritual is good of itself, it is nerve-steadying. Even Islam has plenty of it.

There is not much beer, barely a bottle apiece, but we feel convivial; maybe it is the after-effect of the Saharan dance. The leading lady is epigrammatic. Her last remark was a boost for her profession:

> *c'est fou ce qu'on peut devenir chaste à force de vivre avec une femme.*

Good for you, O Ayesha.

When Balbo and his Italians planned their Aïn-el-Frass they designed it more Sudanese than Saharan. Burnt-sienna walls, cool, windowless halls, tiny enclosed gardens where struggle a few withered fruit-trees; oranges the size of kumquats and the consistency of walnuts. Black ceilings in the bedrooms. It seems flies do not like black ceilings. On an alcove-bed you fall asleep. In your mind's eye that pendant lamp hanging from the middle of the ceiling, a maze of twisted copper rods most Sudanese and

Black African. It is a long figure, first a round, then below it the outline of a snouted mask, then a lozenge with arms, next a tail of smaller lozenges, a reticulated scorpion-tail whose last calipers clutch a naked bulb. *Persona*. A Mask. Magical? ah, if it does not allow us to foretell it does allow us to look ahead.

## THE MARE'S SPRING

The horse is an unknown beast in Ghadames and as fabled as were giraffe and elephant for our medieval ancestors. In olden days there were horses in the Sahara; they were harnessed to war-chariots as prehistoric rock-paintings and rock engravings most conclusively prove. But these pictures cannot be very ancient for there were no horses in Africa until about three thousand five hundred years ago.

There is some legend, how old is hard to say, that the Aïn-el-Frass[1] welled up from the impact of a mare's hoof; the story is, of course, a wide-spread one and Aïn-el-Frass is just Arabic for Hippocrene, the fountain that gushed forth where Pegasus stamped.

All Saharan waters are full of salts, the commonest of which is magnesia. We soon learn to interpret the legends on the map. 'Good and abundant flow' does not signify what we in our pampered ease would call sweet waters. No, Saharan water is 'good' when it just tastes strongly of Epsom Salts. It is 'fair' when the odour and flavour are those of rotten eggs. 'Poor' suggests either that the spring is a mud puddle or that the elusive waters have retired underground.

A French physician, now[2] well over ninety, has devoted much of his life to preaching that people who regularly absorb magnesia will not be afflicted with cancer. The philanthropic practitioner is of venerable age, he does not suffer from cancer and he has for many years, so he avers, swallowed daily doses of his prophylactic. Such is the perversity of mankind, however, that when he does come to die, we may be sure captious critics will declare that had the aged physician abstained from magnesia he would not have died at all.

It is true that there is little cancer in Ghadames, though the

[1] In 1948 the French sank a new well (costing more than 20,000,000 francs) which yields nearly 48 litres (or about 10½ gallons) a second.
[2] 1952.

cheerful military doctor opined that most Ghadamsis die off too
early for cancer, but his was a soured vision, he had had too much
of the desert. Magnesia-laden waters are only distasteful and may
be salutory for there is little cancer among the desert-men and
some of them live long enough. My *médicin-major* being young,
up to date, bored and not often blessed with a willing audience,
favoured me with a disquisition on gamma-rays, cosmic-rays,
ground-radiation and God knows what. Cosmic-rays, he said, are
not constant in quality but some of them are a million times more
powerful than others. There are also, according to him, brief,
sharp chain-reaction showers whose rays are boosted a thousand-
fold in power and effect and these showers rain upon our earth
frequently. He told me that he was sure these rays have carcin-
ogenic properties, but maybe he was showing off. Magnesia-
drinking is deplorably simple and cheap.

I could not get enlightenment as to whether the rays strike
down their victim more readily in one place than another. Does it
matter where we catch our chain-reactions? Are we safer in the
desert or the town? in the heat of the Sahara or in the chilly damp
of Old or New England?

If it is magnesia versus chain-reactions, then proconsul Balbo
missed something; had he boosted his Aïn-el-Frass as a Well of
Immunity, he might have made Ghadames the rival of any spa
or holy well in all the world.

The Kaid was not an imposing figure swathed in ample
robes of white. He handled no amber rosary. In fact he was
attired in up-to-date, atomic-age, business suit. A short shapeless
garment, perhaps a plaid, masked the upper part of his body, the
lower being encased in pepper-and-salt pantaloons. On his feet
were a pair of large-soled slippers attached by thongs round the
ankles and against the big toes. On his head was a fez encircled
by a fairly clean Turkish towel. I did not know who this personage
was, and despite or because of his gold-rimmed spectacles I was
inclined to think of him as the hotel guide. The Kaid had appeared
on the veranda at four o'clock in the afternoon when there was,
it would seem, no one at the Mare's Well but myself slumped in
one of the antelope-hide deck-chairs, relics of Balbo's magnifi-
cence. An hour or two later I awoke from my slumber and there
was the Kaid motionless. When I came back from a ramble

through the streets he was still there. He had been invited to
dinner, and had turned up about five hours too soon, evidently
unwilling to be late for so important an appointment. Perhaps
no time had been mentioned and he, thinking that dinner was a
meal eaten sometimes between noon and midnight calculated that
four o'clock would be a fair hour of compromise. Accidents will
happen when we are shot into a world of new conventions.

The first time I was invited to dinner in a Russian provincial
town was, as may be imagined, well, quite a good time ago. I
was down in the south-west and had got a message from a family,
some of whose members I had known in—I was going to say
Europe. 'Dinner' meant for me, in my innocence, something eaten,
even at Odessa, at some time between seven and nine in the
evening. Like the Kaid of Ghadames I determined to be in time
so I turned up at five, thinking that a little chitchat would not
be amiss. I found that family and friends had been dawdling *à table*
since about half past three and that the hour for dinner was two
o'clock, in fact that dinner was a meal eaten in the middle of the
day as it was in 18th-century England or France. After all, being
an hour late was as nothing in the vile days of capitalist tyranny
before Russia had been set right in the Marxist-Leninist-Stalinian
Line, and my hosts had waited an hour and a half before sitting
down without me.

It was, in fact, past eight before the Congress members got
back from their outing; luckily their every hour was packed with
a full programme of edifying and instructive visitation.

On thinking things over I am inclined to imagine that the
Kaid was a subtle man. He knew well enough that the French
were pulling out of Ghadames, or rather, he was sure that in a
few months his town would be included in the hereditary realms
of His Majesty King Idris of Libya. Possibly the Kaid's future was
not too certain; he had been appointed by the French. In the
first full flush of freedom might not a rival covet his job, a rival
untainted by close contact with the French? The Kaid anyway
must have been in a hedging and non-committal frame of mind
and in these circumstances what is better than to start off by
putting one's hosts in the wrong, by obliging them to protestations
of excuse? Such a thing lands one a definite advantage which,
with but little skill, may be maintained a whole evening.

The dinner was a great success. First of all the Sudanese

steward shouted his piece. This swarthy lad from the south—he was no Saharan negro but a fine shiny blue-black specimen with a face tastefully adorned with raised tribal-mark scars—put on an act each meal-time. He stood at attention, or as nearly at attention as may be when one is balancing a large soup-tureen on the palm of one hand and bellowed out an incantation in exceedingly obscene *petit nègre* or pidgin-French. His pointed references to the pleasures of commerce between the sexes aroused some titters from several elderly ladies who were following the flag around.

The soup, and all the other dishes taste strongly of sorrel; that's the magnesia. The dark slabs of meat are meat, one does not ask what sort.

Despite the difference of the shapes, the colours and the temperature, this Ghadames dining-room somehow does remind me of that long-ago meal near Odessa. The company was not, indeed, so varied and original in its appearance and dress. In old Russian country houses people would come and go, one might be in general's uniform and another have his face tied up in a handkerchief. The vague, anonymous hangers-on, a portly ageing lady with her hair in curling-papers. The servants taking their part in conversation and sleeping in passages and corridors. No servants' bedrooms, of course.

Good old easy-going patriarchal ways.

At Ghadames were a little more provincial and standoffish and bourgeois. But the dinner was a great success, so everyone agreed. We were too far away from the high-table to know what did happen among its distinguished company. We had our modest fun as befitted our station.

The desert is a great place for bringing out a man's best points, or let us say, his main preoccupations. We had made away with the soup before Mahmud es-Said came waddling in. He had nearly cut the dinner, he warned us. He had been with relations. He had them all over the place, "throughout Islam you might say, some in Liverpool and Cincinnati too, I'm what you might call cosmopolitan, thoroughly modern. When I got to my cousin's house there was a large party to meet me and they all kissed my hand . . . well, as a direct descendant of the Prophet, as a *sherif*, one is a personage of consequence down here in the Fezzan. Up in Tunis one forgets these things. So much to fill one's mind, politics, you know, getting our rights, though when I'm a Cabinet Minister I shall not be treated with more deference than I have been here. I must say that I'm pleased, we Moslems are very democratic but after all, families like ours, with an authentic pedigree going back thirteen, fourteen hundred years, that's something you don't get in Europe."

Evidently not, there is no European genealogy which even affects to bridge the gulf of the dark ages. I must say that Mahmud is very decent about his illustrious origin and is smiling and benign and deprecating. However, we have a *gentilhomme* by our side; he does not like such gentle boasting and wants to know if the Moslem pedigrees are really reliable. Mahmud assures him that they are, that the descent has been carefully noted, matter of religion you know and that moreover, owing to the surveillance and seclusion of women every man at least in Mahmud's own line, was his father's son. Sounds all right. What do I think?

Well, I think that what you believe is true, and that although I should not like to comment on the Moslem pedigrees, I do think that if you can believe every child figuring in a pedigree was the offspring of his mother's husband, then you are blessed with salving faith. Then, after all, the chances of anyone having inherited anything from the body of any one forefather even a quarter of fourteen centuries ago are not great. Chromosomes and the like.

The *gentilhomme* finds us frivolous; he is just a little inclined to expatiate upon his mythical descent from a fabulous feudal Burgundian race. Unless he watches himself he is apt to indulge in unaristocratic assertiveness. He has heard somewhere the vulgar nonsense about the aristocratic pleasure of being displeasing. Although Proust in an acute aside has defined the over-compensation in those marked with some special disgrace:

> *ayant pris d'ailleurs l'habitude de la raideur hautaine et compensatice commune à toutes les personnes qu'une disgrâce particulière oblige à faire perpetuellement des avances. . . .*
> "having adopted the habit of haughty stiffness that is a compensation adopted by all those persons whom a characteristic inferiority forces continually to make advances. . . ."

still, such haughty stiffness is a social manner even members of authentically distinguished French families are not seldom tempted to display, so hard is it, despite a pervasive and effective snobbishness, to extort deference in France.

Mahmud and I feel that the conversation is taking a tiresome turn. We switch into anecdote. Has the *gentilhomme* ever heard what Monsieur de Voltaire said to Monsieur de Châtelet? No, not to Madame du Châtelet.

Madame du Châtelet, for long the acknowledged mistress of Voltaire, transferred, if not her affections at least her favours, to a certain Monsieur de Saint-Lambert, for, said the lady, so attached was she to the illustrious man of letters that she would not expose his health to the effects of too frequently repeated proofs of his admiration for her. When Madame de Châtelet, in due course, found that she was with child, recourse was had to a time-honoured stratagem. Monsieur du Châtelet, who did not often visit his wife, was fetched and having been well wined, was thrust into his wife's bed. Appearances were saved. The same classical trick was played on the Lord Yarmouth who was the husband of Maria Fagniani. When Maria discovered she was pregnant by her lover Montrond she got her husband (who was interned at Verdun) brought to Paris, where she entertained him in connubial fashion. The child of Montrond and Maria was afterwards the famous dandy Lord Henry Seymour, founder of the French Jockey Club.

"And, as you know, Monsieur, poor Madame du Châtelet died while her infant daughter did not survive, but what you have, perhaps, not heard is what Monsieur de Voltaire said to Monsieur du Châtelet. About a month after the fair Emilie's death the two men went through the possessions of the *marquise* and each took what he wanted as a keep-sake. When Châtelet made to open a gold watch that Voltaire knew had always contained his portrait he asked Châtelet to desist, but he would not and soon the two men were looking at Saint-Lambert's miniature. 'This,' said Voltaire, 'is something that neither you nor I, Monsieur, will care to boast about.'"

The *gentilhomme* draws a red herring. He wants to know how many noble families there are in Britain. He has heard about twelve thousand. Conversation closes with demand for definition of 'noble'.

On such a journey as mine, one is heralded perforce and so everyone knows one's nationality. One is a butt for every clown who has questions to put concerning *l'Angleterre*. It is not much good stating that even if one is a British subject by birth the England one knew may have been one existing before the British Way of Life was invented.

The best way to take evasive action is to carry on in English. The technique is nearly always effective, but a young reserve-officer at our table was so amusing and disarming that there could be no question of applying this treatment to him. However, I did shy at handing out a succinct sketch of the social, moral, political and economic present and future of Great Britain and associated states.[1] I suggested some required reading. Luckily, the young *capitaine de réserve* is in public life an Inland Revenue man for North Africa. His leading question reflected his professional preoccupations.

"Now, I'm sure you won't mind telling us why the *Anglais* are so law-abiding."

Now we had something, although it may be that the British are not so law-abiding as all that, though, of course, they've now got so many laws to abide that it is easy to make mistakes.

"I can give you an answer and I've got it pat, for I was a month ago asked an identical question at a luncheon in far-off Cabrerets by the leafy banks of the Célé stream in rural Quercy. I won't excite you by mentioning that we were eating very well and drinking the rich purple wine of Cahors. The answer is this. Through most of the 18th century the British were a lawless people, they were almost as adventurous at home as overseas, but between 1800 and 1939 over fifteen millions of men, women and children left Britain for good and these were not the least energetic, truculent, lawless, intelligent, restless and resourceful."

"Thank you so very much, now it's clear why our people won't pay their taxes, we've never had this blood-letting. We Inland Revenue chaps have a devil of a job, things are worse here than in France though taxes are a good deal lighter. You'd be surprised how many people hit the numbers at the lottery or get large money gifts from generous relations."[2]

[1] However inscrutable the British may remain most reasonably honest and sincere Frenchman will echo the words of a friend of mine: "What I admire about the British is their courage."

[2] Income tax in France actually *produces* only 10% of the revenue while in Britain 37% of the revenue come from the taxes on income.

We agree that there is much to be said for having the people of a country rich and its government poor, though if the people won't pay taxes the government prints more and more phoney paper money, so everyone except the very wise boys gets stung.

There are pretty reasonable Frenchmen round about us at the Ghadames feast and the young tax-man is their spokesman. He does not complain so much of the burdens the French have to bear and the drain on the resources.

"We've got to hold on in Indo-China—where the war has been running longer than in Korea—and if Indo-China goes then all south-east Asia goes, including your precious Malaya. We have to furnish large contingents to the 'European Army' or whatever it is and then, most difficult of all, we have to hold North Africa in such a way that Allied—and that means American—bases are secure and at the same time grant Home Rule which would put those bases in peril. Quite a programme."

The complaint is not, generally, that the British shove spokes in the French North African wheel. The reason for this silence is however not very flattering; the French as a whole, especially in Africa, are so bemused by the image of American primacy and mastery that the British take a second place. However:

"I don't know, look at this Fezzan business, you backed Idris as King of Libya. . . ."

"The British were committed to recognizing Idris as Emir of Cyrenaica but it was UNO that made him King of Libya. . . ."

As a matter of fact the 'independent' Libyan sovereign State was forced upon UNO by the joint vote of Latin-American and Arabic-speaking blocks. One State, one Vote. It does not matter whether the State be Honduras or the United States. The UNO delegation which toured Libya in order to ascertain the 'will of her inhabitants', and whose members stayed for a day or two in Ghadames while they interrogated (through interpreters) a number of hand-picked citizens, these delegates came to the conclusion that the Fezzanis would like to remain under French administration. In any case, the French are undoubtedly right when they maintain that no one would have thought of tying the fortunes of the Fezzan to those of Cyrenaica and Tripolitania

had not all three made up the former Italian colony of Libya. For
the Fezzanis, as a whole, know little and care less about the
peoples of Libya's northern fringe, populations from whom the
men of the south are separated by hundreds and hundreds of
miles of pathless desert.

The French have perhaps the right to feel a little aggrieved
that their old enemies the Senussi should have provided the
monarch for the flimsy realm of Libya but such feelings are really
not justified by the turn events have taken. What the French have
every reason to deplore is the creation of an independent sovereign State at the door of their protectorate, Tunisia. The new
Libya will adhere to the Arab League, will provide another vote
in UNO and for the 'Arab' block, while Soviet legation and
consulates shift a good thousand odd miles eastward from the Nile
Valley and right up against French North Africa and its strategic
positions for the whole of the Atlantic Allies. Indeed, the first-
fruits of UNO's creation were to be seen in the convulsed and
troubled Tunisia of 1952.

It is, however, hard to think that the French have not in a
measure themselves to blame for the incorporation of the Fezzan
into Libya. General Leclerc's troops seized the province. The
Italians were run out. It was a prize of war. The French, moreover, had a valid claim to the south-western oases; if these, at
least, had been declared lost property recovered, then there would
never have been any questions of their going to an independent
Libya. The French should have taken Ghadames, Serdeles and
Ghat back into the southern Algerian territories. A handy 'friend
of France' might have been brought forward—there was one in
the person of Ahmed Saif en-Nasr. In fact the French should have
taken a leaf out of the British book. The London government
promised Idris es-Senussi he should be Emir of Cyrenaica and
never again plagued with Italian masters. The British kept their
word, but they did not promise Idris that they would make him
king of a comic-opera kingdom.

The French should have moved before the invention of UNO;
then, later, they could have put forward their own candidate
for the throne of Libya who could have been withdrawn, on
conditions. But, of course, even had some such scheme come off,
the French would still have been left with a Kingdom of Libya,
independent and marching with Tunisia, a kingdom whose mere

existence is enough to make the Tunisians say: 'If the poor and lowly Libyans, why not us?'[1]

However, the French contention that the Fezzan commands all the central and eastern Sahara is a little exaggerated. During the years that the Fezzan was Italian, Mussolini's Fascists certainly did not control the central and eastern Sahara, though the Fezzan in a state of anarchy would be a menace to French positions and the French have bitter recollections of having to reconquer their eastern Sahara after the Italian evacuation of south-western Libya during the First World War.

But, hush, the speeches. . . . The Vice-President of the Congress, the real boss of the show, is on his feet. It is a joy to watch this fussy provincial politician and local big businessman ordering his flock about. The Vice-President's speech was long. It was involved. It was not always grammatical, but it was inspiring. The *Leitmotif* was

*La France et l'Islam main dans la main.*

France and Islam, hand in hand, dawdling down a quiet lane maybe. Splendid abstractions. Can we see the figures of France and Islam? Keep on prodding us, we wouldn't know.

Then the peroration:

"And I salute in you, *Monsieir le Kaid*, the eminent representative of the Civil Power, of your ancient civilization, of friendship for France. . . . Where the French flag has once flown it will fly for ever . . . and now I raise my glass. . . ."

The Kaid did not return the toast. He could not drink wine in public. He did not reply to the rousing periods of the Vice-President. The Kaid said nothing. He did not move. He understood not one word of French. Thus he did not gloat when a few months later he took the salute while the French flag was being hauled down and the green, white and black standard of His Majesty King Idris was broken from the mast.

The next morning the Congress flew away. At dawn we were

[1] Libya covers about 700,000 square miles; has some million inhabitants, 90% of whom are illiterate, 10% totally blind, 20% partially blind; the average income is the lowest recorded, less than $30 or £11 a year; infantile death-rate for first 12 months after birth, 33%; by the time all the government jobs are filled, most of the educated men in the land will be civil servants, there are, indeed, but 16 Libyans with university educations.

"... the expanse of flat roofs ... from whose corners rise
the famed horns ..." *p. 21*

". . . the track over the Hammada-el-Homra—a petrified sea rippled
with murderous lines of stones . . ." *p. 38*

bundled into an Army lorry. By the fort, the Italian fort, half a mile or so outside the town, we tumbled on to the sandy shingle.

A very fine fort, imposing, solid, second only in the Fezzan to the splendid Italian citadel of Sebha. The neo-Romans knew that grandiose edifices impress men more than almost any other work of man.

The Tuareg Guard presents arms. As the tricolor flutters, drums beat, trumpets clarion, the reserve officers salute and we all come to attention.

Dawn splits the sky. Another Saharan day. It is suddenly very warm.

The President, always in uniform with seven rows of mostly civilian decorations, is detached, a little overshadowed by his Vice-President, but a brusque, fine military figure with white handlebar mustachios. He takes me aside. He has spotted my painting-kit, for I am going to do some daubing in the desert.

"You know I'm not a regular officer——"

"No one would ever guess that, why, I thought——"

"I wanted to be, but had to go into the family business, we make *Puro*, biggest bleaching, disinfectant and deodorizing business in France, but I went all through the 1914–1918 war and I've always been a keen territorial. . . . I see you're an artist. . . . I wondered what you could be doing here . . . may interest you to know that I'm a great-nephew of Cézanne . . . yes, if I'd my life to live over again I'd be an artist. . . ."

"Er—perhaps the family would have something to say to that and there's nothing quite so delightful as reliving one's career . . . also, it's never too late to buy a paint-box. . . ."

The plane circles off. In five hours they will be in Tunis. On camel-back the trip takes twenty-one days, if you are lucky. By jeep you can do the run in five days, if you have no trouble.

## YASSAK

You need no guide through the maze of tunnels and corridors; you walk on and on until you come to a dead-end; then you turn back and try another gullet. Eventually you will emerge into a little square bordered with arcades, deep niches and archways set with stone benches where all day long men sit and drowse and dose. Heat and hunger.

No road, no pavement, no sidewalk, a beige carpet of levelled

C

sand that eats all noise. The light intense, diffused, the shadows rich. I was sitting in the shade facing a scene of scenery and I was painting. Despite the two-dimensional appearance, the buildings seem solid enough because it is hard to imagine anything to assail them. Before me a low building with windows, some triangular, some rectangular, a doorless gate, a roof horned, beyond and above this, battened walls, and more slabs of wall, a drooping palm or two, on the left, an unroofed alley breaking away into the wings of this stage-set, dwellings that are cliffs or cliffs that are dwellings, frontages and façades, no sensation of depth, all stained and weathered and baked to a primeval tan. Maybe a prolonged tropical shower would dissolve Ghadames.

To the right, a tunnel, a vaulted passage of contracting gloom. The sitting men do nothing at all; they speak, when they speak, in whispers, and their Arabic sounds less harsh and fierce than that of the north. One of the men rises and comes slowly to me. You cannot guess what he is; maybe he is nothing and does nothing, he may live in modest though not poverty-stricken idleness that lends a man distinction and nobility. This Ghadamsi is grave, courteous, at his ease, one with whom one feels relaxed and benign. There is no provincial tension or anxiety and censoriousness.

He tenders to me a small coin and asks what it is I tell him, that it is Turkish and that it bears the superscription of the Padishah. Is he old enough to remember the Turkish days of forty years ago? Perhaps; he might be of any age but I think that he knows his little treasure is Turkish and desires to use it as an excuse for conversation.

You would think just to look at Ghadames and Ghat and Murzuk that the Turks had held these strong-points for ages. As a matter of fact the Turkish garrisons occupied the Fezzan only onwards from 1841 when the Sublime Porte asserted or reasserted its sovereignty over Libya, but the Turks built forts and barracks and left an impress on the towns and also upon the minds and spirits of the people. The Turkish rule in the Fezzan was of the pattern usual during the decline of the Ottoman Empire. Provided that the local population paid up, things were allowed to ride until there were signs and symptoms of revolt, then the good old Turkish traditions of *yassak*, iron discipline, flared up. The desert men and the oases dwellers got such a lesson as they did not forget in a hurry.

Deep down, or not so deep down, in the memory of all peoples who once were Turkish subjects are traces of the terror the Sultans and their servants inspired. There is a humorous tale told by the Prince de Ligne of what he saw at Jassy a hundred and fifty years ago. A member of the Sturdza family—the most prominent in Moldavia—starting up, sweating and pallid at the sight of a Turkish non-commissioned officer and hurrying forward to wait upon this representative of the ruling people. The Moldavians and Wallachians were, officially anyway, Turkish subjects until 1878. During the Paris Peace Conference of 1919 we could observe how galling are the memories of servitude. One of the Rumanian politicians was almost speechless from indignation when he endeavoured to recount how some tactless fellow had dared to speak of '78.

My Ghadamsi exclaims *ta'arif*, that is our word tariff or notification, 'this is real money such as we had when we were rich and happy.' Things were always better in the past. The humble Turkish coin is now a museum-piece, worth anything or nothing. We exchange conventional confidences. I tell what is my nationality, but he has never heard of it and thinks me one of the new-fashioned Turks.

He does know, however, that of all the many things wrong with our world, the plague of phoney money is one of the most abominable. My Ghadamsi does not know why, or even how, we came to say good-bye to honest currency. He's hardly heard of the 1914-1918 war and, anyway, if he had he would not connect it with the life and economy of Ghadames.

I offer him a shiny nickel 20-franc piece. Possibly this is what he has been expecting all the time. He takes the money without thanks but with a slight smile. He can add the nickel to his coin collection. Soon he will have Libyan currency with the superscription, if not the image, of His Majesty King Idris. Let us hope that the Libyan paper pounds will go farther than those in Britain. I do not point out that the 20-franc piece will now buy less than the Turkish piastre when he was a boy, though despite our phoney money everything is cheaper than it used to be. We do not want to believe this but it us true. For instance, before 1914, twenty-five gold francs a day was an ample allowance for the unpretentious traveller in most European countries or in North Africa; this sum in 1952 made over five thousand francs, possibly nearer six thousand. Of course, in 1912 when the Turks still held Ghadames a man in London or New York who had £2000 or $10,000 a year to spend was, if he had not much overhead, comfortably-off in a modest way. £2000 of 1912 is in purchasing power about £10,000 of 1952 and a man who has this income to spend is so well off that there are few of his kind in impoverished Britain. Living is cheaper than ever; so is money.

Fading Ghadames will not for many a long day know again a happy time when a small coin bearing the image and super-scription of the Padishah would buy a satisfying meal. To the Devil with freedom, independence and the Libyan State, give us back the good old days when the slave-caravans shuffled up from the south and then the men of the city prospered on the gains of honourable commerce.

You walk without sound upon the velvet-soft surface of the alleys. Here and there a stretch with the sky for a roof; little dark boys and girls grin from the street-corners, then the children run off but they do not run far, curiosity conquers and they come creeping up, gay in chintz-like garments, engaging and natural. The men you encounter will salute and sometimes pass the time of day, but the women, of course, make no sign; they are almost all very dusky, negresses in colour and generally in feature; clad in dark-blue and crimson. They are never veiled—and though by general custom Moslem women cover their faces, veiling is nowhere enjoined in the Koran—and do not, as do so often the dusky girls up in the southern fringes of inhabited Tunisia, pull a cloth off breasts or belly to serve as covering for the face.

If you look at the women and children you are in Black Africa, if you look at most of the men you are in White Africa. Maybe the dark men are doing the work of the community.

Ghadames does not stink. It has no Black African odour. Even the closed galleries and passages, though in places rather stuffy, have no perfume but that of mildew or goats. There are a few dozens of them in the town. They hop home in the evenings and, stiffly agile, jump through the house-doors; you would say that they were going to walk upstairs, but they squeeze through narrow posterns and find their rest, together with a few sheep and asses, in dark cellars.

Ghadames is a secret city, secret and secretive; not only is it more phalanastery than town, but there are none of those obvious

"The walls are crowned with teeth, rows and rows of them . . ." *p. 78*

"Here are huts and a line of plaited wattle fencing" *p. 78*

urban features we expect, no vehicles, no shops, no cafés, no
restaurants, no market, no baths, no mosques even which are
visible as such. Just corridors. But after an hour or so of labyrin-
thine wandering you may be out in the open and on a sunken
path between garden walls. Down the middle of it cuts a gutter
deep and corbelled over so that a slit about a foot wide is left.
The running waters are kept in the shade. Watch your step or you
may get your ankles broken. The gardens are above you but here
and there the lanes broaden out and you may see the Ghadamsis
scratching the soil, grey, dead-seeming earth dotted with clusters
of blue women. You can distinguish no plant, just grassy, tan
wisps, but this straggling, struggling straw can be eaten. What
might be called dry farming. Indeed some wheat and barley are
gathered, while under the palm-trees' shade is grown a little
sorghum and millet, useful when food is scarce, that is to say,
nearly always. These palm-trees which, from afar, are fine and
fertile, rich-coloured and thick-set, are from nearby, shabby-
looking, though often tall. Thousands yield fruit and the dates are
small and dry. Perhaps, like the orange trees of Aïn-el-Frass, they
do not like drinking Epsom Salts.

Back into the labyrinth, dark, almost cool, necropolitan.

THE HEAVENS ARE OF BRASS

Light-glare, heat-haze shimmer deform the dunes' contours.
Below, a little to the west, but near is the Sea of Sand with waves
hundreds of feet high, once lake and marsh and mere where
mighty streams spent their waters.

The aerial frontier.

It is a delusion. Where you see the waste stir, it is immobile.
Where you see it still, it is in motion. The light-glare forces you
to see what is not there; what is there is invisible; the eternal
Saharan winds whistling softly and dribbling the thin surface of
the dunes.

Though trackless this *Erg* does bear terrible paths where are
no wells at all and where you may with ease lose yourself and
your life.

We are not much more than five hundred miles south of Tunis,
but it is the real Sahara, that is to say the Sahara created for us
in the old travel-books. The imaginative illustrator produced a
vision more satisfying than does the photographer. The photo-

graph is dead background, or it is figures frozen and paralysed into attitudes you would never seize, so momentary are they. A synthesis enriching our spirit that is what we want. Caravans cowering in the sandstorms' blast, the camels crouching, their necks laid flat and .straight. Simoom and other odd, compelling names. No, of course, the sand-winds never did engulf whole caravans, but yet, they were buried sure enough, for the miserable travellers knew they were being swept into the recesses of the dunes, into the gritty, cold intestines of the earth. How is it possible to discover anything so like what we, in our innocent wisdom, knew that must be?

A view of the Great Eastern Erg from the skies as you fly southwards to Ghadames and beyond. But if you meet the erg you are filled with other sensations. For miles from Ghadames airfield you churn across the soft surface of an ancient lake's bed, poisoned with gypsum and salt. Far off there to the right, a smear; the track over the Hammada-el-Homra—a petrified sea rippled with murderous lines of stones—towards Derdj on the northern edge of the stony waste.[1]

To the left are the fringes of the erg dotted here and there with knolls and outcrops.

The sky high, luminous, friendly, reassuring. To the west the ocean of sands. To the east the rocky wilderness. Under you an arid fossil basin. On this arena the French manœuvred before they engaged the crestfallen Italians and flung them out of Ghadames in January 1943. The Wops swashbuckled up very quickly as a noted message had it.

Fifteen miles of soft sands. Glowing and crumbling, the abandoned fort or *bordj* of Fort-Saint which the French made when they left Ghadames to the Italians before the First World War.[2]

[1] The *Hammada-el-Homra* that is the Red Hammada. A *hammada* is a plateau, a stony waste, sawn flat by the sand-winds; sometimes the expanse will shine like the surface of a lake (where the desert winds have varnished a crystalline outcrop). The usual name in North Africa for the dried or fossil lakes, so common on the northern Sahara's fringes, is *sebkha*.

[2] French domination of the Sahara is not old, the Tuaregs were crushed at Tit (in the Hoggar) in 1903. Ghadames and Ghat and some other points were occupied when the Turkish garrisons withdrew in 1912 but the French handed over their Fezzan to the Italians in 1913 who fled before the Senussi in 1915. The Senussi held the oases until 1924 and the whole Saharan situation was unsettled. The French missionary *père* de Foucauld met his death in the Hoggar in 1916 and after 1918 the French had to reconquer most of the territory from the Hoggar eastwards. The Fascist Italians drove out the Senussi from the Fezzan in 1924.

Round the fort, and north-west amid a chaos of sandstone and boulders, the huge desolation of the dunes is but a mile away westwards. Now the going is not so good as on the cloying sands, but if you have to sleep in the desert lie near the stones for they remain warm all through the darkness whereas an hour after nightfall the sands, that were incandescent under the sun, are as cold as the grave.[1]

To the right there, water, a mirage, no, it is the Lake of Bir-Pastor. Several hundred yards long and fed by wells the French sank years ago, for the water of Fort-Saint is horrid. Water gushed up in abundance at Bir-Pastor but so bitter salt that not even the tiny shrimps can live in it that flourish in the harsh lake of Murzuk oasis much farther east. From time to time stories are set afloat that the Saharan subsoil contains inexhaustible reservoirs of water. There is water, a good deal of water, under the desert's face but we should need a very great deal of proof to conclude that enough water could be siphoned out of the sands to make them blossom like the rose. No, the roses the Sahara bears are, and doubtless will long be, of a very special sort.

The shores of Bir-Pastor sprout a grey scrub fringe stuck with bush and shabby palms among a jumble of decaying shacks. It is a salt-ridden, hungry place, more melancholy than it is because you can just imagine it alive and so shudder at what exile would mean here by the border of a man-made lake.

We swerve to the right and along the age-old camel-track from Ghadames to the Jebel Nefussa and thence to Tripoli by the sea, the ancient slave-route. When we get to Mzezem, yet another fossil lake with an oasis of dusty palms, we circle round and head back over the dazzling waste. We have not done much more than thirty miles but you soon lose sense of distance. Time does not so much stand still as cease to exist, or perhaps it assumes its rightful place as a fourth dimension. It is nearing noon.

The Heavens are of brass.

## ROSES OF THE SANDS

All around the gypsum knolls lie roses of the sands, concretions crystallized into strange shapes, some most beautiful and exciting. There are small, petrified, glittering blossoms; there are much

---

[1] The nights are always cool in the Sahara and you want warm wraps at any time of year. Pneumonia and chills are the curses for the desert men.

larger shapes, animal or vegetable, faceted, glistering, the sole reminders, you would say, that the desert is not dead but asleep. The fossil third of Africa sinks, however, even deeper into slumber.

If we fly across the Sahara today we find it almost impossible to realize that the wastes beneath could ever have been other than as we see them. The sawn-off hills, the pebbles, the stones, the expanses of sand, the tiny dots of oases, all look as though they had existed from the beginning of time. Surely something primeval, everlasting.

Yet the Sahara grew and shrank with the ebb and flow of the Ice Ages' glaciers in Europe.

The one thing which, more than any other, determines our lives and fortunes, is weather, climate. We ourselves, each one of us, we are different men in differing climates. We are not the same in Bergen, where it rains three hundred days a year, as we are by the shores of the southern Tunisian salt-marshes where the temperature is often 120°F. in the shade.

Man's whole story, as far as we can see at present, falls into the last geological period which may have been a millions years long, a period that was gripped by four successive glaciations or Ice Ages separated from one another by long intervals of warmer weather. That these cold periods occurred is undoubted; what caused them is still, despite a number of ingenious and more or less plausible theories, not known. A desert's record is more hard to read than the past of a less stripped, bare and austere region, but it is clear that a remote predecessor of the present Sahara was formed at least as long ago as the second warm period which may have lasted for the prodigiously long space of 150,000 years. This proto-Sahara was much larger than our present desert and extended much farther south, so that West Africa was isolated by the wilderness. The desert shrank during the next glacial period (farther north, the counterpart in Africa was a 'Pluvial' or rainy era), which was a good deal shorter than its predecessor and then spread again in the next warm epoch. After this came still another Pluvial, followed by the beginning of a dry period when the glaciers began to retreat in western Europe, say, about 12,000 or 10,000 years ago.

No doubt climate has oscillated back and forth, but, on the whole, weather has been getting warmer ever since.

Although, in the Sahara, much of the past is obscure, the

desert offers us some of the most precious evidence about ourselves, though it is true that in East Africa the record is easier to read, the dry and wet periods are clear and the remains of men's handiwork more easily interpreted. Man-made stone implements are abundant enough in many areas of the Sahara but those tools tell a somewhat disjointed tale. We can, however, trace the course of great rivers and reconstruct the ravaged face of the wilderness.

Then we have the pictures, the astonishing, mysterious pictures. Right out in the cruel wastes are rock-engravings and paintings of water-loving animals. In areas where no man could or would settle today, the rocks, the caves and the shelters are adorned with men's figures, dancing, running, lively; figures linked on one side with Spain and on the other side with the line of prehistoric pictures that extends down the eastern side of Africa and develop into the paintings, engravings and portraits in South Africa.

All proof of a Sahara much more clement than now.

Yes, the Sahara is spreading and looks as though it will continue to spread. Weather is getting warmer all over the earth, it has, indeed, been getting warmer for the last hundred years and it is, of course, possible that we have not yet emerged completely from the grip of the last ice age. There is certainly still plenty of ice about on the globe. On the other hand the warmer weather of today may be but that of another oscillation. Since the roll-back of the ice in northern Europe, there have been alternating periods of warmer and cooler weather whose exact course we cannot trace since we lack reliable weather-records. But what has happened since about 1850 is quite certain. The great glaciers are everywhere shrinking. Greenland's shores and shore-waters are warmer than they were only a generation ago. At the turn of the century, ice isolated the Spitsbergen archipelago for nine months out of the twelve. Ships can now touch at Spitsbergen for three-quarters of the year—which is so much better for our Soviet 'allies' who exploit the coal-mines there, mines whose very existence shows that countless millenia ago Spitsbergen enjoyed, or suffered, a damp, tropical climate, though there were no men there to check things off just as there were no men to wander over the tropical jungle of Antarctica, for there is coal down there too. This tale of our small earth is so tangled.

Some of the ground hitherto permanently frozen in Canada

and Siberia is thawing out. It is, of course, quite true that small
but cumulative rises work spectacular effects. If, for a century,
the temperature of New York were raised by one-fifth of a degree,
palm-trees, it has been estimated, could be grown out of doors in
the city. As a matter of fact, the mean rise would seem to be about
two-fifths of a degree in the Arctic where sailors agree that there
is less and less ice to be seen.

When it gets warmer in the north, it gets drier in Africa. We
need not expect the Sahara's heart to harden more, but what we
are witnessing is the whole body of the desert battening on its
surroundings.

## The Face of the Waste

We walk slowly. The May sun is brazen. We scramble among
the first static waves, we slither into a sand-dale and then climb
another dune. The Ocean of Sands, terrifying, boundless.

In the troughs are surprising things, no Roses of the Sands, but
things that were once alive, or, let us say, witnesses of things
once living; fragments of ostrich-eggs, clumps and clods of earth
marked with the imprint of plant-roots, relics of the Sahara's last
damp period, the Pluvial of millenia ago. If you scratch about
you will unearth stone-instruments fashioned by men.

It may well be that at no period during the last Pluvial was
the Saharan rainfall very abundant as rainfall is understood in the
Tropics. No doubt much of the Sahara was savanna, but there
would be woods here and there, rich vegetation by the lakes and
along the streams that flowed, often brackish, down from the
flanks of mountains which even today hide a few poor witnesses
of their former state.

None of the Fort-Saint ostrich eggs bears pictures or designs,
though such do exist. There is one bit of shell (from Oued
Mengoub, near Biskra in the Algerian South) engraved with
the figure, in naturalistic style, of some sort of ox. The thing
is ancient, as are also other ostrich egg fragments decorated with
geometrical designs, magic patterns of the Capsian culture maybe
12,000 years ago.

Ostrich eggs have figured in art and magic for a long time;
still the smooth, shiny shells, hang in Moslem African shrines as
well in Ghadames dwellings. Doubtless the nice, even surface of
an ostrich egg is for an artist a tempting object in a world of

rugous, irregular-shaped things. An ostrich egg is a gigantic pebble, a marvellous though fragile one, beautiful and soft to the touch. Small stones were, from remote times, covered with enchanted outlines, figures of beasts, and some of these pebbles were re-engraved time and again, so true is it that what has been tried and found efficacious will not be relinquished but utilized again and again. The virtue is inherent. It may be that ostrich eggs became lucky because easy to decorate, but men would not be long in finding out real, magical reasons for the good luck the big birds' eggs bring.

The ostrich is a barometer—or a hygrometer—he likes being alone, or at least he is not too fond of the company of other creatures. Ostrich is lions' favourite food, a tasty morsel like fine fat capon. The cunning Bushmen hunters disguised themselves in the skin and feathers of the big birds. To this day, there is nothing better to attract big game than an ostrich-decoy.

It is quite possible that animal-masks in the prehistoric paintings, and indeed the mask-complex generally, may owe part of their existence to the age-old habit of disguise and ruse of hunting.

However, the ostriches are such good pointers because we know just what they like and what they will put up with. They must have dry warmth (they get bored if they have to sit on their eggs in the day time) and they must have water not only for drinking but also for an occasional bath. Thus, though it may not be so long since the ostrich disappeared from the northern fringes of the Sahara, it is not probable that ostriches lingered on farther north than, say, the south-central plains of Tunisia. On the other hand, Fort-Saint cannot have been good ostrich ground for millenia. If we may suppose that ostriches left north of the Sahara may have been exterminated by man, the ostriches south of the Sahara go just as far north into the desert as they please and that is not beyond the savanna of the Lake Chad area; very different from the edge of the Sea of Sands and the vision of a land getting drier, a land where life chokes to death.

## MAN AND HIS TOOLS

Among the dunes near Fort-Saint are man-made stone implements. But the desiccated, ever-shifting surface of the desert is one of the most unsatisfactory of archæological grounds; in many parts of the Sahara, indeed, the record is so jumbled that without the evidence from others regions, it would be hard to sort out the different kinds of tools.

As far as we can see today, the earliest undoubtedly man-made tools must include the so-called Kafuan industry of roughly chipped pebbles in Uganda. These pebbles may be about a million years old and are of such importance because they have been found in positions which indicate their great age, whereas pebble industries in other parts of Africa and in the Sahara are not so easy to place.

From very early times (but later than the Kafuan if these really are to be dated right back to the beginning of the last geological epoch) we find one sort of stone-tool, the so-called 'hand-axe' (a pear-shaped chipped instrument) over an immense, area from Java, through India and Asia Minor through Europe to Britain and down through the greater part of Africa. We find another sort of implement—the so-called flake-tool—spread over the more northern part of Asia and into Europe. Of course, we cannot conclude that these two different sorts of tools were made and used by two different sorts of men, but it is at least possible that, in fact, the hand-axe people were one kind of men while the flake-tool men were another kind. Let us see.

On the face of it there is no objection to the theory that Africa was during the glacial epochs in Europe a refuge and a reservoir for men who did not like the great cold. If, from very early times, the hand-axers and the flake-toolers really were two different sorts of men, then it is probable that the former were men more or less like ourselves, or, let us say, recognizable as our direct ancestors. So, also, it is not improbable that the flake-toolers may have been more burly, robust human beings, that is to say the Neanderthaloids and their forerunners.

It used to be the fashion to declare that the Neanderthaloids died out, faded away. Undoubtedly they did as a separate kind of Man, but it is in the highest degree improbable that two sorts of the same mammal, two sorts which are interfertile, could live side by side without interbreeding. We have, moreover, evidence of cross-breeding between the two different kinds of Man. There is Neanderthaloid ancestry in many men of today and especially in the pink men of Eurasia. Extreme racists, or some of them, have even claimed that there is evidence for more Neanderthaloid

"In the real Black African villages . . ." (Moussoro) *p. 78*

". . . the ill-famed Kourizo Pass . . ." *p. 80*

ancestry east than west of the Rhine. Well, such a theory would explain much, or little, as the case may be.

Anyway, 'modern' man, man as you and I, Seretse Khama, Mr. Stalin and Mao Tsetung—for we are all 'modern' men, all *homines sapientes*—came from somewhere or other when he made his appearance in Europe, during the first relatively warm recess in the last Ice Age, about 25,000 or 30,000 years ago. It may be the 'modern' men were fooled by the weather, anyway they could not know that it was sooner or later to get much colder again, though when this unclement spell began our inventive ancestors had learned or devised how to keep warm in the long winters. There was no trek to warmer climes, no return to the old homeland which very well may have been Africa. But what we know now, what we have learned quite recently, is that 'modern' men are not modern at all except insofar as the word means surviving until today. Men more or less like ourselves, or at least not at all like Neanderthaloids, existed in Europe many, many millenia before their 'sudden' appearance, in fact our own sort flourished in the warm spell, a spell, it is true, of several tens of thousands of years in length, before the last Ice Age, and they peopled Europe in other and more ancient warm periods. Our story is a pretty complex one.

Although the identification of the hand-axers and the flake-toolers with two different sorts of men, is a tentative one, we do know that there was one kind of stone-instrument which appears to be associated exclusively with one sort of man. These are the tools of Mousterian technique, the only ones found with Neanderthaloid men's remains. We conclude, therefore, where we find Mousterian artefacts, we have proof that Neanderthaloid men lived there.

The Sahara has no written story to be brought up to date and made conform with a fashionable dogma or doctrine, but the Sahara's record can be read not only in the rock-pictures but also in the stone-tools. From them it is certain that Neanderthaloid men lived in various parts of what is now the desert and especially in the western regions. It is, indeed, fairly clear that the heavy-boned men's remains dug up in North Africa are the bones of hybrids between Neanderthaloids and 'modern' men.

On the other hand, long, long before the appearance of 'modern' men in Europe, the tools used by them—the so-called

Aurignacian artefacts—were being made in East Africa. It looks more than just possible that men such as you and I, Seretse Khama, Mr. Stalin and Mao Tsetung came from an African stock, or let us be more careful and say that some so-called white people came from Africa as so did some not so white. There seems to be a good chance that the 'Mediter-raneans', the most specifically human of the 'white' stocks, the men who invented civilization, were by origin African. And we may reflect, if we are inclined to associate any particular aptitude, ability or intelligence with any particular human type, that the 'Mediterraneans', the certain fashioners of Egyptian and Sumerian civilizations, are represented today by peoples who are not, on the whole, markedly inventive.

No, the Sahara has no written story but it does show what happens to man when he is overwhelmed by climate. It is certain that the Sahara could be traversed on foot for some considerable time after the Pluvial had waned, for a certain sort of stone tools (the Aterian) are found from north to south in the western desert. We know also from excavations undertaken in the Hoggar highlands that caravans were already well established and were making their way right across the Sahara by the 4th century A.D.

Some of us would be inclined to pay more attention to the theorizing of the planners—the planners of the past of course—if they would admit the omnipotence of climate. Climate deter-mines everything, though it is not, of course, an explanation of everything. Art changes with climate, religion changes with climate. We may mark how different were the arts and rites of hunters, pastoralists and agriculturalists.

## BLACK BEAUTY

> *Moins le Blanc est intelligent*
> *Plus le Noir lui paraît bête.*
>
> ANDRÉ GIDE

Jarry, the immortal creator of *Ubu-Roi* and of *Le Super-Mâle*, treasured, together with tame owls, in his garret a large model of a human phallus. A lady, examining this upon his mantelpiece, enquired:
"A cast?"

"No, madam, a copy on a reduced scale."

Abd-el-Kebir—'Just call me Kebir, that's up-to-date'—wears a boiler-suit uniform, it is true, but as he leaves it unzipped his blue-black body is revealed in most of its nakedness. Not only his name proclaims his faith, for in throwing off carelessly that he is a Moslem born and bred, he points in nonchalant fashion to his generously developed male organ. Though circumcision is not enjoined in the Koran, the mutilation is almost universal in Islam; however, in Africa, a man is not proved Moslem by being circumcised. The practice is widespread throughout the continent and looks, indeed, as though it were specifically an African one.

Kebir runs the jerky little motor that generates electricity for the Ain-el-Frass hostelry. He has other occupations too, but is most often to be found sitting in the shade by his hot and bitter pool while he meditates or sings.

He has picked up a good deal of French. He has not forgotten his Italian. He is also quite cheerful about Italians, who even when they were the undoubted and harsh masters of this land managed to get themselves both feared and despised. You have to hand it to the Neo-Romans.

It may be the dusky men of the oases are not in such propitious surroundings for them as they would be in the clammy Sudanese South, still, the negroes of Ghadames are quick-witted and full of a good-humoured slyness belied by their open, innocent countenances. We may, however, reflect that if a man looks innocent, it is possible he is so. But what is revealed is his innocence, his sort of innocence not what we like to think of as innocence—for others. We may be pretty sure that the two sorts of innocence are far apart.

In the tunnel-streets one or two of the old coloured women will put on an act, make the Fascist salute and bawl out:

"*Evviva Mussolini, evviva l'Italia fascists, evviva il duce.*" The few tourists ever to reach Ghadames would be duly impressed: 'Just think, the poor old crone doesn't know the Italians were evicted ten years ago . . . out of this world . . . a bit of history.' But, as she pockets the small change, the wily beldame grins. So is history made. We might have a learned thesis—say one for a Ph.D. degree—on the low I.Q. and ineducability of negroes when transplanted to the Saharan oasis of Ghadames . . . well, that's how history is written; some gossip jots down that the mayor's portrait was not a bit like him, gossip once called upon the great man and found him in bed and with his knees drawn up, his face contorted with the discomfort of acute colic. And so it goes on.

Anyway, in 1951 at Ghadames most of the inhabitants seem to have realized that they soon would be free citizens and subjects of the federal realm of King Idris.

Kebir says he can't speak any Sudanese language. I've an open mind about the subject, he's certainly clever enough to tell what he wants to—no more and no less. As far as can be seen, he bears no tribal marks upon his flesh, but, even if he was born at Ghadames he was born servile, since though for a generation and more there have been no slaves in the oasis, still there are slaves, men and women who for all intents and purposes cannot change their employment or emigrate. They are, indeed, very much in the same position as the bulk of our fellow-citizens after eight years of devastating victory.

## UP THE DESERT OR DOWN THE RIVER

The African maps of two hundred, even of one hundred, years ago are full of phantasy. The coasts had been well surveyed for generations and their outlines were faithfully reproduced. Once, however, you get a few miles from the shores, you are plunged into magic and mysterious ways. Since there were few natural features to be recorded, the charts and maps are covered with enticing inscriptions.

So, in Guillaume Delisle's *Carte de la Barbarie, de la Nigritie et de la Guinée* (1741) down from the Fezzan we engage in the 'Desert of the Lemptunes inhabited by a race both proud and brutal'—our old friends the Tuareg brigands. Farther south, through 'deserts and tracks dangerous and full of robbers', we reach the promised land of Gold and Slaves, most precious of Africa's treasures. There is the Kingdom of Ouangara 'whence come Gold, and Senna and Slaves'—the Sahara and its fringes were, according to Delisle, especially productive of the purgative—and passing through the realms of Temian—'whose Inhabitants are reputed to be Cannibals'—and of Bito 'whose Population is Rich', we arrive in the Kingdom of Gabou *d'où vient du Jaspe et des esclaves*, next to the real and solid country of Benin whose eastern parts were the haunt of the Calbongos, fearsome and familiar:

"... the people of Douirat ... have more houses than families" *p. 120*

"... the fairyland of the Sissé Needles jutting upwards from meadows of saffron sand" *p. 80*

"The hair . . . plaited in rope-like strands . . ." *p. 95*

*Les Calbongos Peuples méchans et trompeurs ennemis des autres Calbongos leurs frères.*

"The Calbongos, a people wicked and treacherous, enemies of the other Calbongos, their brethren."

Slave-raiders? There never were so many raiders on hunting expeditions to kidnap negroes. The professional slave-raiders were rather the desert marauders, the famed Tuareg, who pillaged the peaceful merchants' convoys. Black ivory was sold by rulers and chiefs and in accordance with the ordinary play of demand and supply. The slave-trade was a profitable means of keeping down the population in what is, generally speaking, at least from the agricultural point of view, a thankless and a poor continent. Selling off the surplus population was an alternative to infanticide, starvation and bloody tribal welfare, although, of course, not a few of the slaves were captives seized in war.

Up the Desert or Down the River.

If Kebir's fathers had been sold down the river, he might be a Methodist and not a Moslem, he might speak English instead of Arabic and he would not be warbling beside the springs of Ghadames but be singing Calypsos in Port of Spain; perhaps not very patriotic Calypsos:

"I'm not feeling so loyal today,
They can sell these isles to the U.S.A. . . ."

We can only guess how much British wealth and power was rooted in and around the Caribbean whence came the money to finance the industry whose profits invested overseas enabled the British to live beyond their means for three-quarters of a century.

Hijacking the slave-ships, slave-trading and slave-labour; these were the professions that made us what we are in Britain.

"Slaves on the English plantations were treated by their owners as parents treat their children. . . . The French planters have their slaves baptized and taught some prayers. This has a good effect on the conduct, attaches them to the interests of their masters . . . and is productive of many advantages to the French planters who, despite their being actually more rigid to their negroes, yet have better and more faithful slaves."[1]

[1] Atwood *History of Dominica*, 1783.

D

While writing this story I have been looking over the returns from Dominican estates once owned by our family. The records refer to the latter part of the 18th and the beginning of the 19th century. Slavery was, we may remember, abolished in British possessions during the year 1836.

There were slaves of all sorts. Their occupations: 'field, carpenter, mason, weaver, washer, driver, vines, watchman, domestic, jobber, nurse, sempstress, water-carrier, cook' and the rest. In age they varied from 'Peggy, 80, cook' to the eight-months-old child of Gertrude. They died from a multitude of disorders: 'mal destomach, yaws, consumption, old age, drinking casada water, bad sores, dropsy, lock-jaw, fever, bowel complaints, eating Divs, dysentery, worms, flux and scrofula.' On the whole, considering the fearfully high death-rate among the 'white' masters, the slaves did not appear to have suffered much more in health than did their owners of whom 'few live to acquire affluence or to return to their own countries'.

As late as 1810 most of the slaves seem to have been born in Africa, though the slave-trade was ostensibly suppressed long before emancipation. However, some of them are 'creoles of this island' or of 'Nevis, Barbadoes, Antigua'. The great majority are put down as black though there were mulattoes.

"In the English West Indian islands in general, there prevails a great aversion to forming matrimonial connections and most white settlers content themselves with a mulatto or negro mistress with whom they beget a spurious race of children."

There are 'Cabres' and 'Cabresses', 'Cremontes' and 'Obricums'. A 'Senegal', and 'Ebbo' (that is an Ibo from Guinea), a 'Muceo' (possibly a Mossi from round about Ougadougou in French West Africa) a 'Kissee' ('deformed' this one: the Kissi live in Sierra Leone and Liberia), a 'Mandingo' (from French Senegal) and not a few 'Congos' that would be any slave from the interior sold down the Congo River—and there are others. All the African coasts from Senegal to Angola were slave-coasts, though the slaves themselves might come from far back in the interior where they were purchased by agents who played the same part in Black Africa as did the Jewish and Syrian slave-traders in

Carolingian Europe when English slaves were in brisk demand down by the Mediterranean and such international marts as Verdun did as big a business as Kuka or Timbuktu in their prime.

For the trade up the desert and to the Moslem world, the main collecting-stations were Timbuktu on the Niger, Zinder much farther east, and Kuka in Bornu (what is now Nigeria) a few miles from the shores of Lake Chad. The prices f.o.b. were, during much of the 19th century, about 20 francs gold (say $3 or a little over 16s. gold) for a man, 15 to 20 francs gold for a woman. Of course, the c.i.f. price at Tripoli was many times as high.[1]

From Kuka the caravans took the traditional route followed since Roman times, at least, by the desert-convoys laden with gold-dust, ivory, ostrich-feathers and black men. About ten thousand slaves annually were marched (during the later phases of the traffic) up to and across the Fezzan. Bones of wayfarers marked the track, but it is doubtful if, proportionately, more negroes fell in the Sahara than rotted to death in the hell-holds of the slave-ships.

As the trans-Saharan slave-traffic was stopped as lately as 1910–1912—when the French conquered the Wadai country—not a few of the Ghadamsi negroes of middle age may well have trudged north through the wastes. After martyrdom, life in the oasis was very pleasant indeed.

As the slaves had to trudge the two thousand odd miles across the Sahara, the poor wretches must be rested in the oases, whose masters battened on the caravaneers. Wilting or ailing men, women or children could be purchased at knock-down prices. Moreover, it is not easy to make out what the real connections between the worthy merchants of, say, Ghadames and the robbers of the deserts. On their way south the convoys had little to fear, but the return journeys were slowed down by the mass of shuffling, straggling negroes—a splendid target for the noble Tuareg, Veiled Men of the Sahara.

The trade was financed and organized as were the slave-ships of the British and other European slave-traders. When the

[1] By 1850 when Barth visited Kano, Kuka, Gando and Timbuktu,, the common currency was cowrie-shells, many bought on the eastern coasts of Africa shipped to England, re-exported to West Africa. A profit of 500% was, it is said, not uncommon in such transactions.

caravans got to Tripoli, for instance, the negroes were sold and the profits were divided between the caravaneers and the merchant-venturers who had advanced the funds.

When the slave-trade was killed, places like Ghadames were doomed. It is true that a few camels—about a thousand a year—still pass through the oasis, and as late as 1937 I saw a huge convoy of perhaps five hundred camels swaying and floating through the brown desert round about Nalut, nearly half-way from Tripoli to Ghadames. However, such sights are now unknown, though in 1943 and 1944, when there were no cars and no petrol for trans-Saharan traffic, the caravans began again once more to traverse the Sahara, but it was all a flash in the pan and the Ghadamsis are getting steadily poorer and poorer.

## THE MOST HUMAN OF HUMANS

We are often told that a great mystery hangs over the origin of the negroes. This is true, but the mystery is no deeper than that enshrouding the pedigree of all sorts of men upon this earth.

Of course, what the anthropologists call 'negroes' are not merely human beings with very dark skins; they are a special sort of dark-skinned men whose stronghold is West Africa. However, the very dark-skinned men of Africa are essentially men fitted for living in damp heat such as that of the equatorial rainforest. The main function of the dark pigmentation is to counter the effect of ultra-violet light rays which are injurious to the sweat-glands, for the negro has large pores (so have many pink men and these are they who thrive best in the tropics), perspires a good deal and must, therefore, drink a good deal. A black skin does not render its owner less sensitive to the sun's heat; negroes, like pink men, suffer when the sunlight is too powerful.

It is a fairly reasonable guess that black skins arose as the result of mutations useful to men living in the damp tropics, though it must be confessed that the negroes' genealogy is almost unknown. The only fossil bones of negro type to have been found in the Sahara are those of the so-called Asselar Man dating back, apparently, to the later phases of the last Pluvial—say, ten thousand years ago at least. Moreover the Asselar Man is not what we should call a typical negro but rather one of a 'generalized' sort, something like proto-negro. It is, however, interesting to note that he was drowned; his bones, together with those of crocodile and damp-loving mammals, were found in a region that, today, is arid and dry.

It is possible that during the last Pluvial dark-skinned men inhabited much of the Sahara and they may have been responsible for some, at least, of the naturalistic pictures on the rocks of the desert. But negroes do not like the Sahara today; the nights are too cold and the days are too dry; the sort of men who best support the Saharan climate are the 'white' Tuareg (provided they do not have to engage in much manual labour) and, above all, the apparently indigenous dark men (but not negroes) such as the Tibbu of the Tibesti who are of incredible physical resistance.

One of the striking things about negroes and one of the things most annoying to apostles of *apartheid* is their specifically human character. In their bodies the negroes are the most evolved, that is to say the most 'human', or if we do not like that, the least simian or ape-like of men. One is inclined to say that they are even more 'human' than the 'Mediterraneans', certainly the most *sapiens* of any sort of European.

It is sobering to recall that in slavery's latter days when men were driven to defend their trade and traffic in men—it is always a deplorable sign of weakness when we have to think up justifications—much play was made with the theory that negroes were not human, or, at least, not so fully human as the God-like race of slave-traders, black-ivory merchants and plantation-owners. Negroes were a superior breed of ape. The fact is that the majority of the men in the ruthless slave-racket were more ape-like than their victims. A South African anatomist and anthropologist, greatly daring, has listed a number of features—bones, lips, skin, heart and what not—wherein the negro is more human than the 'white' man, pink man or off-white man.

## La Musique Négre

When we had done discussing life by the swimming-pool where no one ever bathes, Kebir burst into song. What he warbled struck me and my untrained ear as being uncommonly like the sounds we pay a considerable sum of money to endure in Montparnasse now that the old *quartier* is staging a come-back. A rich, throaty voice conveying pathos and mockery, the vocal accompaniment to the music of the Saharan dances, the astringent and moving complement to an instrumental music that never crosses the barrier between White and Black Africa. If the negroes lost their language when they were sold into bondage, they did retain their music. Though the songs of the Maroons in Jamaica are said to be chanted in some strange tongue, it is not any known in Africa, and it is most improbable that African speech long survived the Atlantic crossing. The music of American negroes is, however, clearly derived from that of Black Africa. When, a generation and more ago, we were getting the revelation of *l'Art Nègre* from Africa we were also receiving *la Musique Nègre*—from the United States. Since those days Black African music has been gathered in its native haunts.

The Fezzan is a meeting-place of musical modes and traditions. You may listen to a song so oriental in pitch, intensity and raucous thrust, it will remind you of things Chinese. You may hearken to Kebir and be reminded of Black Africa, but of West not Equatorial. Sudanese music is penetrated with Northern tradition and expression, and how considerable is this influence we may realize if we will hear the variations, the antiphonal chants, the subtle, cheerfully malicious tones of the Congo shielded from Northern fashions which crossed the Sahara.

However, Ghadames, Ghat and the Fezzan lie on the northern slope of song even if their music assumes a rich and southern resonance. It is the negro voice.

What is that now? You look up and expect to see, it may be, a green-topped minaret adorned with a tree of golden balls, but these Saharan oases show no minaret. The mosques are small and hidden. The plangent cry emerges as from loud-speakers. You would say that the earth is sonorous. Some traditions tell that the first of all muezzins, or callers to prayer, was a negro and that the conventional mode of the Call, heard from Senegal to Surabaya, is an echo of Black African song.

Darkness absorbs us very rapidly. The last quaver. For a brief moment before the universe of blazing stars and glory of a Saharan night, for a brief moment, sound and colour and scentless scent, time and dimension, are as one, ineffable.

## THE NIGHT OF MAJESTY

*Et qui donc avant l'aube erre aux confins du monde avec ce cri pour moi? Quelle grande fille répudiée s'en fut au sifflement de l'aile*

*visiter d'autres seuils, quelle grande fille malaimée, à l'heure ou les*
*constellations labiles qui change de vocable pour les hommes d'exil*
*déclinent dans les sables à la recherche d'un lieu pur ?*[1]

On the terrace of the Turkish fort at Ghat and looking towards
rocky ranges beyond the sands that shrink as the mountains
approach, their crests luminous with star-light.

A purple night of such stars as you have never seen. More
brilliance than firmament. The heavens ablaze with cold light. As
you gaze, the sky cannot contain the myriad million suns. The
African stars do not twinkle. They are unblinking and constant.

A hundred million suns in our pancake of a universe? a
universe so small that light takes only a hundred and fifty thousand
years to cross it. How many planets might there be in our little
universe, just our little universe of a thousand million suns? or
is it? Planets fit for life as we understand it, thousands of worlds?
Plurality of worlds? Worlds without end? and what sorts of
creatures—men—on these planets? Anyway, all this means
nothing at all for us.

This is a very ancient fort, more than a hundred years old,
built about 1840 when the Turks, levying tribute on those who
levied tribute, set up their castle to command the road through
the Tassili n'Ajjer heights which bound the horizon swerving in a
gigantic arc from north-west to south-east. The Fezzan's frontier.

We are offered fantastic, hallucinating, incredible, incomprehensible figures—as many galaxies as there are men upon this
tiny earth. It may be so, but perhaps galaxies do not multiply as
fast as does that proliferating mammal Man. There are suns and
worlds and universes, we are told, beyond the dark curtain which
for ever veils our view of uttermost immensity. One is moved to
flippancy and a suggestion that as light takes millions of years to
reach us the universe may have disappeared long ago.

And all this does not have much effect upon the lives of you
and me.

Now, this Tassili n'Ajjer, that's a different story. It is in its
way a Saharan paradise, or semi-paradise if compared with the
Hoggar farther west where it sometimes rains a wetting shower,
but in the Tassili are feeble rills while the fossil Oued Inaleouen
shelters a score of mighty cypresses, ancient and venerable, whose

[1] Saint-John Perse.

trunks four men's joined arms will hardly encircle. Trees that are sturdy survivors of damper days and, it may be, the most antique living things upon this earth.

The Tassili is a sandstone mass of some size, about as large as France, and hiding, it is said, subterranean reservoirs of waters which have percolated through the porous surface of the rocks. The Tassili is, for the Sahara, thickly populated. Over its two hundred thousand, and more, square miles wander some three thousand Tuareg.

It is first agriculture and then machinery which have encouraged men's over-production of their kind. There were, in all probability, not more than a few tens of thousands of human beings in France during the peak of the so-called 'Reindeer Age' when the Magdalenian artists painted the superb frescoes of Altamira and Font-de-Gaume. Hunters' numbers are limited by their quarry.

Look at those flashing heavens, they sparkle and spurt brilliance. It seems there is a gigantic cloud of hydrogen up there merely a thousand light-years away. This deathly cold gas speaks to us and we can listen to its voice on radio-telescopes whence issue rustles, hisses and roars. Maybe our universe is gathering up hydrogen and using it to feed atomic transformation in stars? Or maybe what? Our life, and what enjoyment we may be intelligent and inventive enough to derive from it, all are due to our sun's turning hydrogen into helium.

As the crow flies across the Tassili it is some fifty miles to Djanet from Ghat, Djanet that not so long ago was a Turkish outpost—yes, the Turks held sway at one time from the central Sahara to the Crimea, from Morocco to Persia, from Vienna to Oman—Djanet on the edge of ochreous orange dunes furled against the southern cliffs of the range.[1] The old caravan-route, however, has to pull up over the Asakao Pass and skirt the chasm of Tamrit, the deepest cleft on the face of Africa. The rough path leads through forests of stone columns and walls of Written Rocks, some scrawled with inscriptions in *tifinagh* (that is the ancient

[1] Though so remote, and so strange, the Tassili is by no means inaccessible. The French Touring Club organizes from time to time excursions to this fascinating region. The round trip takes about fourteen days from Algiers to Algiers. You go by car and get back by air—or vice versa. You do about 1400 miles by automobile and also have five days on camel-back while you are exploring Djanet, the Tamrit plateau, the Hagarene Adrar and the other unexpected curiosities.

writing of the Tuareg) but a few centuries old, though there are also looking down upon you from the sides of the crags ochre paintings of chariots, lions, antelopes, elephants, giraffes and other beasts for long unknown in these regions.

The Tassili hides a world of strange rock-pictures, mysterious witnesses of past climates, animals, men, thoughts.

As we stand upon the terrace of the Turkish Fort, far off to the left there where the heights die away in radiance, lies In-Ezzane and a cave lively with images of men and beasts. Over to our right, on the Djanet-Fort-Polignac road that cuts through the Tassili from south-east to north-west, is the Oued Djerat with dog-headed men and other incredible creatures. Maybe confused memories or hearsay of the Written Rocks gave form to legends of beast-faced men and of those whose heads did grow beneath their shoulders.

Even so reliable and respectable a witness as St. Augustine tells that he saw with his own eyes beings we know never had existence. Strange sorts of men. Men we should hardly call men; there have been many such even if their heads did not grow between their shoulders; in fact, looking back along the road behind us it is hard to tell which are the men and which are not.

> Le firmament chante ce que l'on veut . . .
> Astres entre lesquels la lumière s'échange.
> Elle n'est qu'entre vous! Vous n'êtes, pauvres Cieux,
> Qu'un peu d'étonnement des hommes. . . .[1]

Energy into matter. Matter into energy. What's the odds? The great orange disc of the moon is slipping up behind the hilly barrier.

A warm and reassuring glow relieves us from the piercing sparkle of the stars.

While we lean against the parapet of the Turkish fort, a universe has faded away.

Well, what is a man? The query sounds a little odd, a little extravagant, but how can we say what is and what is not a human being? The question thrusts itself upon one here in Africa, for it is, more than anything else, the new evidence from Africa that rocks our self-confidence. Indeed, it not only seems possible that

[1] Paul Valéry.

man became human in Africa but also that the men who made the first civilizations may have had an African origin. After all, the roots of Egypt went deep down into African soil.

## Ex Africa Semper Aliquid Novi

The Romans used to say that 'There's always something new from Africa'. For them the marginal continent, as a French Saharan explorer has called it, was what America was for Europe until a short time ago, that is to say, an incredible region where anything might be seen, experienced and endured.

Africa has provided us with something new, startling and unexpected, during the last few years, and the something is not the boundless wealth and unlimited markets sung by imaginative newcomers to African disappointments; the something relates to each one of us, to our origin, being and race.

Now, it is quite certain that we belong to the same class of animals as the great apes—gorillas, chimpanzees, orang-utans and gibbons—who inhabit the tropics, the first two in Africa and the others in south-eastern Asia.

However, although men and apes are manifestly related, they are very distant cousins indeed. Their common ancestor lived a very long time ago, and this forefather, indeed, may well have been, from some points of view, rather more like a man than an ape, since an ape is a creature more highly specialized than a man. Apes, in fact, look like dead-end products of evolution while men have remained less fitted physically for any one particular mode of life. Apes, for instance, are specialized for swinging about from the branches of trees, though the most ancient apes do not appear to have been very adapted for life in the forest.

For some reason or other—possibly because of the *pithecanthropus* finds in Java and because gibbons and orang-utans are found in south-eastern Asian islands—it was long fashionable to seek man's 'cradle' in Asia, but we do not really know whether man had one or several cradles, so to say. In any case, although until a few years ago, the most promising fossil ape material came from the foothills of the Himalayas, these remains have been overshadowed by evidence from East Africa. In the Kavirondo Gulf area (Kenya shores of Lake Victoria) have been found numerous bones of apes dating back to miocene times—perhaps twenty-five million years ago—and these bones, or some of them, show what look like rather human than ape features, though the creatures were undoubtedly what we must call apes. One of them, 'Proconsul', was certainly not so ape-like as modern apes and although an agile beast, does not seem to have been a tree-dweller, in fact he looks uncommonly like what we might expect a common ancestor of the apes and ourselves to be. But all this does not add up to a pointer that East Africa was the region where men became men; the fact is that nothing we could call in any way human appeared for many millions of years after Proconsul's day.

This Kavirondo material is exciting and interesting enough, but for the human story it is overshadowed by the South African discoveries of the last twenty-five years. Briefly the tale is this:

During the last quarter of a century there has been piling up a mass of fossil bones belonging to several varieties of a very special sort of apes (most clumsily dubbed *australopithecinae*). These creatures were in size comparable to a chimpanzee but they walked more or less upright, that is to say they used their hind-limbs as legs and their fore-limbs as arms. In fact, they had hands. And not only did they walk upright but their teeth and many other features of their bones were unlike those of apes and were like those of men. Their heads were not put on the backbone in quite the same way as are ours and their heads hung a bit, but then so did those of some sorts of men. The brains were small compared with those of any kind of man,[1] though one of the latest of the skulls to be discovered is a good deal larger than any of the others.

The small brains confirm the theory that the upright posture was adopted before the brains got big, but in any case a big brain and a bright intelligence are not much good if we have no hands. We think because we can speak, we speak because we can use our hands.

Unfortunately, we cannot date this South African ape-man or man-ape, but it does not look as though he flourished much more than about a million years ago and this is, we are inclined to say, an impossibly short time for these early South Africans to have turned into a man . . . but we are begging the question. What is a Man?

Some years ago when I was writing a book on early types of

---

[1] Though this doesn't mean much; it is not brain-size but complexity of convolutions which indicate intelligence, and in any case, we do not use most of our brain-mass.

men, my publishers, at my suggestion, submitted the text to a
competent if rather old-fashioned 'expert'. He was, on the whole,
surprisingly indulgent towards my effort, but one thing did set
him off in violent expostulation. I had stated that the Java Man,
the famed *pithecanthropus*, was a sort of man. He could not allow
such nonsense to get into print. Well it did get into print and
today the statement would arouse hardly any dissent. All of which
goes to show how things may change in the short space of a decade.
Today, one of the most eminent of comparative anatomists and
anthropologists,[1] for instance, has not hesitated to declare that
morphological differences (i.e. those in form and bodily shape)
do not justify the separation of the South African ape men
(*australopithecinae*) or, of course, the Java and Peking men
(*pithecanthropi*) from the genus Homo, that is to say the large, very
large family of which our God-like selves are the most glorious
representatives.

The apes may resemble us in their bodily formation and in what
we may call the general balance of their senses, but, owing to our
free fore-limbs, we can do a trick no other animal can do. We are
not only domestic animals, we are performing animals. Other
mammals, indeed, besides ourselves, have some sort of social
organization (apes and baboons, for instance, are pretty fascist
and authoritarian) and bring up their offspring in the way they
should go—generally, of course, to see them go in some quite
other way. Our prize trick is that we can make things with our
hands.

We speak because we can use our hands. Language must have
been conditioned, if not formed, by manual dexterity; it is hardly
possible to imagine stone-instrument making without an accom-
panying chat on how and why the chipping had to be done.
Indeed, the preparation of a tool may be due to a well-thought-
out scheme for using the tool in some special and definite way; on
the other hand, we may make the tool and then think up reasons
for having made it and ends to which it can be put. As a matter
of fact, there is no more deadly pitfall gaping at the historians'
feet than that in which the chroniclers are induced to rationalize
and explain logically the acts of men. Each one of us very often
acts and then rationalizes his act. "Papio's procurer," as Mr.
Aldous Huxley has styled it, is always at our elbow. Of course,

[1] Professor Le Gros Clark, F.R.S., of Oxford.

when we are feeling particularly pleased with ourselves we may rationalize our irrational acts before we commit them. Sustained thought is something men cannot support and it is doing us far too great an honour to discover overmuch logic and reason in our acts.

Creeds, dogmas and doctrines are established first and then justified, arranged and made plausible afterwards. So, as has been so acutely said, "A civilization is acted before it is thought out."

Yes, 'making' helped to form words and phrases and all our lore and legend may be developed from a glorified chat on how to chip stones. It is always salutary to be reminded of our humble origins.

A man is, thus, a mammal which can make objects with its hands and also speak;[1] and not 'speak' as a parrot, but can utter meaningful symbolic sounds—whether repeated or invented, is, of course, no importance at all.

If we try out our definitions upon the South African ape-men or men-apes, we find ourselves up against some serious problems. The creatures seem most certainly to have stood upright, or, let us say, did not use their fore-limbs for walking about; we cannot say, however, that these ape-men spoke or even used the most limited gamut of 'purposeful sounds'.

This South African evidence is so striking, so startling, that in the Union itself museum curators have to be on their guard not to offend susceptibilities voiced (or perhaps excited) by the Dutch Reformed Church and possibly other religious bodies. The explanatory notices had to be changed in one of the South African museums during 1952.

Nevertheless, despite the protests in South Africa, we are on quite sure ground when we say that Man is a member of a large family, one branch of which includes apes (and included other forms of Man now extinct); and when we go on to say that Man is distinguished from apes, first and foremost, by his ability to create his own peculiar, unreal, human world and to make it by means of words and art.

There is nothing unexpected, unique or miraculous about Man's origins, which were certainly not human as we understand that word. However, let us be honest, we cannot at the present

[1] We can speak because our brains are in certain areas more developed than those of apes and also because of the formation of our mouths and throats.

time point to any mammal (whose remains we have) and say, for instance, "This is the *first man*, he made walking-sticks and cudgels, and he could carry on a nice, long chat with his friends and family, probably as significant a conversation as that in which most of us indulge most of the time." But we can say: "This South African ape-man or man-ape, looks very like an ape, but an ape with hands though we cannot say whether he could speak or not." Nevertheless, whether the South African ape-men or men-apes, were, or were not, in a direct line of human ancestry, it cannot be denied that, at one stage or another, our ancestors must have looked, appeared and been, very much like the South African *australopithecinae*.

When we come to the Java and Peking types of men (*pithecanthropi*) we are justified in stating that: "This man could not have denied his cousinship with the apes, but he could fashion stone-tools and it is practically certain that he could and did talk."

It is useful to remind ourselves of these facts and figures, not only because we are always getting new additions to our knowledge of our genealogy but also because the most extraordinary things are still presented to the general public in, for instance, reputable newspapers. In 1952 one British organ published a most curious review of Man's origins. In this article we were informed that no one knows when the first man appeared upon the earth 'but it was not more than 100,000 years ago', whereas if we feel constrained to make any such pronouncement, the figure should be at least ten times as big as that given. In the same bit of popular science a good many million readers were asked to believe that the 'ape-man of South Africa lived about 25,000,000 years ago'. Again, if we feel the urge to guess at the 'ape-men's' age it should be certainly not one-tenth of this estimate. Best of all, Neanderthaloid man, we learn, 'ruled the earth until a new kind of man came and conquered him', a most tendentious statement misleading up to the sapient pronouncement that 'we [i.e. *homines sapientes*] spread over the earth about 70,000 years ago'.

If such rubbish can be offered to interested readers, then it is worth our while to brush up on the ascertained facts.

## INVENTION OF ART

The Mousterian or Neanderthaloid men were skilful stone-knappers, they buried their dead (at least sometimes) with grave-

gear, they practised some sort of religious cults, one of which had
something to do with bears, but there is no trace of Neanderthaloid painting, engraving, sculpture or modelling; anyway no
such has come down to us. Tool-making is, of course, not art but
a craft.

Art is an invention of *homo sapiens* and, as far as we can see now,
he invented it in a region of south-western Europe whose areas
richest in painting and engraving are to be found in the Valley
of the Vézère River and its neighbourhood, in the Pyrenean
foothills and in the Cantabrian mountains of northern Spain.

When, however, we say 'art' we should perhaps rather say
painting, for there was in palaeolithic times a plastic art scattered
over much of the Eurasian continent from the Atlantic to Lake
Baikal. The characteristic product of this sculpture is a statuette
of the female figure, obese and with little or no indication of the
face. It would be flattering to the vague patterns we nearly all of
us carry in our heads, if we could say that the statuettes represent
the art of one sort of men, just as the flake-tools may represent the
industry, whereas the art of painting and engraving is the art of
another sort of men, just as the hand-axes may be the industry of
one particular breed of men. Alas, there is no sort of evidence for
such a nicely balanced view of artistic creation.

We cannot tell what were the first attempts of man to create
art. The earliest art-motifs might be interlacing lines traced in
clay, or they might be imitations of the cave-bear's murderous
claw-marks. The tracing of an outline, an attempt to make the
shadows stay, appears to us a simple thing to do. There is the
well-known case of a captive young gorilla who was observed to
run his fingers around the outline of his shadow on his cage-wall.
But there is no reason to hold that a realistic and naturalistic art
preceded a geometrical, or what nowadays might be called an
abstract one.

Still, in our south-western Europe, our area of invention,
naturalistic art seems the most ancient we have.

When we say 'invented' in this area we really just mean that it
is here we find the earliest examples of representational art. It is
quite certain that men like ourselves, 'modern' men, existed in
Europe long before the time usually set for their appearance and
whether or not during the great cold of the ice-phases 'modern'
men moved off to more clement climes, there are no vestiges of

art dateable to a period before the 'modern' men turn up in our western Europe some, well, let us say thirty thousand years ago, more or less, less or more.

This was the time which used to be set for the 'sudden' appearance of our kind in Europe and for the equally 'sudden' disappearance of the Neanderthaloid men. It is not the sudden appearance of the 'modern' men that is startling, it is the sudden appearance of their art. We cannot help asking ourselves the perhaps vain question: Did the 'modern' men bring the art-traditions with them, or was there something in western Europe that encouraged men to paint and to draw?

In fact, to be precise—at the risk, of course, of being rash—if 'modern' men came from Africa, for instance, was it on African soil that art was 'invented'? Are the prehistoric paintings of Africa the representatives of an immensely ancient African tradition or were they derived from Europe? There is, of course, no sort of reason why techniques and crafts and arts should not be invented by men several times over and in different places. The writing-systems and the arts of pre-Columbian America, as we have noted, owe nothing to any non-American influence, or, let us say, no such influence is traceable, though there are plenty of cranks who spin webs of fancy across the Atlantic Ocean. The hang-over from the deterministic view of man's story is still pretty potent. On the other hand, there is in the European and African prehistoric paintings not only the fact to be noted, the fact of representational painting (or engraving), but also the technique and the subjects. As long as an artist, prehistoric or contemporary, confines himself to the outline picture of a wild ox or a horse or an elephant, although individual idiosyncrasies will be apparent, all the pictures will have a strong family resemblance. When, however, it comes to stylization, suggestion of action and the movement of human figures, then when we find resemblances in Africa and in Europe, we may well ask: What's the story?

To return for a moment to our abstract art. Geometrical designs, points, blobs, checkers, comb-shaped objects, frets and the like accompany the naturalistic prehistoric art of south-western Europe. There was a double tradition running through this art from the first, and it may be, indeed, that the tradition was triple, for there is found in many of the painted caverns (though hardly in the oldest in date) a mass of figures that are

"An Egyptian painting . . . so lively and living . . ." *p. 95*

"... buried cities of the ancient Sao, where are found earthernware
... statuettes ..." *p. 110*

neither man nor beast, but either men masked with beast's heads, or beasts with men's head. The mask is a very ancient thing indeed and partakes of the nature of both helmet and crown.

The naturalistic prehistoric arts of France and Spain, the wonderful paintings, occur, for the most part, in subterranean caverns. It is fairly clear why the paintings were executed. They brought good-luck in the chase; the mysterious art-galleries were theatres of hunting-magic and possibly of initiation ceremonies. We may be sure that the art made to enrich, enhance and sustain the hunting-life, must have influenced the development of language and the word-made world of man.

We cannot tell what were the circumstances which so favoured the development of pictorial art in two relatively small areas of south-western Europe thousands and thousands of years ago. Doubtless a whole complex. We cannot even tell clearly and convincingly what caused the blossoming of pictorial art in medieval Italy, nor can we explain why there have been so many more eminent musical composers in Germany than Britain. We may suppose that the prehistoric artists were wizards in a measure. Anyway, art attracted the good life here and now. Well, it does, of course. Art does not change the universe but it changes us, a much more significant transformation for human beings.

If we cannot say how, why and even in what circumstances the prehistoric pictorial art began, we can say why it ended. It ended because it did not work any more. Art is, in its origin, religious; and religion, in its origin, is a technique for success, here and now. It is only with some phases of human society that we get rewards and punishments shoved off to a future life. We can see now, with the fading of the belief in human survival after death, a demand for a religion that produces results here and now. Well, there are several brands. We can all put a name to them.

The magical art and the artistic magic failed to work because the climate changed. Just that. 'Pattern of History.' The glaciers rolled back. Climate in western Europe got milder. Instead of tundra with Siberian climate, the continent showed dense and impenetrable forest. Man's old herds and game migrated or died out. The men of those days could not fell the trees or tame the forest; art faded with the waning of the cold.

To the Palaeolithic or Old Stone Phase followed the Mesolithic or Middle Stone Phase when, north of the Pyrenees, art

E

dribbled away into symbols and signs, painted pebbles and the like, while the hunting-life was supplanted by a lowly existence of fish-eaters. Doubtless with the change in climate and the change in means of subsistence came a change in cults and religious ideas.

However, European pictorial art did not entirely fade, it survived in Spain where it had a long life in successive variations or manifestations. It is strange how little is known of the later prehistoric art of Spain. An intelligent and well-informed French art critic, when he was reviewing a book about Spanish Painting wrote these curious words:

"The most recent prehistoric paintings discovered in Spain date approximately from 15,000 years before our era . . . the most ancient pictorial evidence in historic Spain hardly goes back farther than the 11th century. . . . What happened during these hundred and fifty centuries? Why do we have to wait for the arrival of Romanesque artists from France or Italy . . . etc."

He might have asked the same questions concerning his native country, France, especially when he goes on to compare the 'clumsy and almost puerile' Catalan paintings of the 10th century and earlier with the 'admirable productions' of the artists of Altamira, La Pileta, Castillo. Well, how does 10th-century French art compare with the masterpieces of Lascaux, Niaux and Font-de-Gaume?[1]

## AFRICA AND SPAIN

In eastern or Levantine Spain there is a mass of prehistoric paintings from some thirty sites stretching from the province of Lérida to that of Almería. Attention was first called to them in 1903—so they come well within our half-century of discovery— the majority of these paintings must be dated to the late Old Stone phase and are therefore contemporary with the northern Spain and southern French prehistoric art.[2]

[1] There are over 34 decorated prehistoric caverns in northern Spain and over 40 in south-western France, and palaeolithic art can be traced in them, and in its main lines, from archaic line-engraving to flat-wash and Magdalenian polychrome.

[2] From 1929 to 1931 the Spanish archaeologist Pericot unearthed in the Parpalló cave, not far from Gandía, and from the very thick filling of a cavern, a considerable number of small stone slabs or slivers, most of them in fragments. The specimens were all palaeolithic and especially Solutrean. The slabs bear either engravings or paintings, some of the pieces are both painted and engraved with representations of animals—horses, goats, some felines, wild boar, ibex, deer, aurochs—all naturalistic and roughly in the same style as the cave-paintings of Aquitaine and Cantabria.

Many, if not most, of these painted rocks are palimpsests and some of the later designs show clear signs of the schematization which was to merge into the harsh designs of Spanish neolithic art.

On the Levantine sites there is evidence of a dual art-tradition. On the one hand are naturalistic animal-forms, and on the other hand are human figures in a style that is unique in Europe but which shows very close resemblances to paintings in the Tassili, in Tibesti, Ennedi, Al-'Uwenat and many sites farther south in Africa. On the Minateda rocks there are no fewer than thirteen layers of paintings, some in the naturalistic style of the north (i.e. of Cantabria and southern France), and some in the specifically Levantine style. What we can see, also, at, for instance, the La Pileta cave[1] may be the naturalistic northern art encountering a hard almost conventionalized native southern art.

The most curious of the Spanish prehistoric paintings are the ones with human figures represented elongated and, as it were, in a shadow-show. It is just possible that the art-tradition of these figures was once, as we have hinted, native to the south. Anyway, it is quite unique in Europe. The human figures are in movement, the men are jumping, leaping, running, dancing, fighting. In no known sites does the remote past come crowding in upon us more insistently than it does from these enigmatic glimpses of life many millenia ago. At Cogul is a round of women clad in cloche-skirts and enclosing a man in the middle of their circle. It looks like a scene of sexual enchantment, some most remote rite of prehistoric Bacchantes. At the Cueva de la Vieja, near Alpera, is a whirl of frantic, possessed female figures, more than seventy of them; it is like a scene at Khargur Meur in the 'Uwenat Hills on the borders of Libya and Egypt; the frenzied women of Spain recall also a Witches' Sabbath on the Maluti Hills of South Africa.

In France and northern Spain the animals are, nearly all of them, static, calm or at least in no fury of movement. If we imagine that these beasts were represented for magic ends, then we feel that the human hunter-wizards were invisible. Remote control. In Levantine Spain, nearly all the beasts are in quick or violent movement and, generally speaking, the hunters are also depicted. Was there some fundamental difference in tradition, in

[1] In the western portion of the Province of Málaga near the small town of Benoaján.

assumption, in belief, a difference reflected in two contrasted art-styles? Many, perhaps most, of the Levantine Spanish prehistoric paintings are anecdotal, or, let us say, historical. They depict incidents; they are, if not news, at least history which, as we know, tells us often what should have occurred, not what did happen. Again, this Spanish Levantine art is one of naturalistic animal-forms and highly conventionalized, stylized human-forms. Anecdote. History. The background, the accompaniments of Man are there faithfully reproduced. Man himself is transformed, he is alone in not suffering a realistic approach, though the scenes are not impossible imaginings.

The beasts are most varied; horses, oxen, felines, elk, chamois, wild ass, wolf, birds, fish, spiders and flies, denizens of an Iberian Peninsular rich in game and poor in men. There is the Los Caballos deer-hunt; the stag chase of the Mas d'en Josep where most strikingly we see a herd of stags, does and fawns running from a scare towards four archers. The hunting-scenes are, of course, not seldom too good to be true, but the pictures were magical and showed what ought to have happened, what would happen next time. Or, again, some may have been memorials to great feats and these are never understated in the inscription. You have sweeping down, in a marvellous semi-aerial perspective, a huntsman leaping after a wounded deer. In the Remigia shelter are boar-hunts and a lively scene of an aurochs turning upon its tormentor.

There is an archers' combat at Morella la Vella, a death-struggle, one group of archers against another, four men ranged on one side and three on the other. It is a close-up; some are mortally wounded. The wire-like figures throb with movement, with energy and agony. Morella la Vella and then Khargur Tahl at the 'Uwenat Hills; the scenes are parallel.

This convention of men's figures drawn out to wires can be glimpsed in the more naturalistic palaeolithic art. In the crypt or lower passage at Lascaux (Dordogne, France) is the now-famed scene of the disembowelled bison, the rhinoceros, the bird on a pole and the dead man, whose figure, all lines, lies ithyphallic and with broken neck and bird's mask or head.

Though, despite the elongation, the human figures of eastern Spain are not caricatural, there seems to reign here also a taboo on the representation of the human face. The men's appearance is

"Near Ghat is such a graveyard, but it is unwalled and slopes
down . . . dotted with cairns . . ." *p. 117*

"From Matmata in the north . . ." *p.* 119

often what we should call African; plumed head-dresses, bangles, anklets, loin-cloths, baggy drawers, garters. A leaping bowman from the Saltadora cave has its counterpart right down at Domoshawa in Southern Rhodesia. Then there is the superb march at the Cingle de la Mola Remigia; a lurching, striding file of five warriors, tense. They wear head-dresses and the chief and leader a helmet, maybe of feathers. The faces, if not masks, are so stylized as to be inhuman, while the leader, though less inhuman, is not wholly of human visage. The scene reminds us of East African things, of Masai on the war-march, and what we will. Africa into Europe? Europe into Africa?

The face is hidden.

To this Levantine art succeeded, over much of Spain, an abundance of mesolithic and neolithic red-ochre paintings; some identifiable with animal-forms and some only recognizable because of a series of modifications. Symbols, dots, circles, combinations of lines, zig-zags, waves, hands, combs, stars, suns, headless creatures, stylized men and women, beasts on their backs and many-legged. The rocks so adorned may have served for ancestor-cults. The schematic paintings and engravings faded away in the Bronze Age though the magic age-old patterns survived in the most unlikely places.

SAHARAN ART

The prehistoric art of North Africa shows almost everywhere traces of what we must call a hunters' art, and this art appears less developed in the extreme west than in other parts. In this west, that is, part of Algeria, Morocco and the regions lying to the south of them, the stone-instruments and tools indicate a considerable lag as compared with those farther east.[1]

However, we can visualize, towards the end of the Pluvial or last damp period in the Sahara (and this period need not have coincided in all its phases with those of the last Ice Age in western Europe), hordes of hunters filling the Sahara[2] with different stone-instrument techniques, one of which, by far the most

[1] The typical stone-industry of this western region is the 'Aterian', which is archaic and presents obvious connections with the Mousterian of Neanderthaloid men who, we know, once occupied much of the Sahara. The Aterian is found as far south as the famed 'Bidon V' post and this fact alone proves that the Sahara was traversable on foot right up to the end of the last Pluvial.

[2] We may not be going so far wrong if we think of the hunting Sahara as flourishing before and after, let us say, 6000 B.C.

important for the art problems of Africa, the Capsian (so named from *Capsa* the Latin name of the modern Gafsa) seems either to have been brought from Spain to Africa or taken from Africa to Spain, since in both countries the stone-tools of this technique are practically identical.

It is curious that the Capsian technique of Africa is divided from the Capsian technique of Spain by an area (what is now western Algeria and Morocco) where there is no Capsian but quite other sorts of tools. Moreover, the art apparently contemporary with this Capsian technique, the strangely conventionalized 'shadow-show' art of Levantine Spain and of the Saharan highlands, is not found in the western African regions of non-Capsian technique.

How did the tools and the pictures travel?

We may remember that the desiccation of the Sahara has proceeded, on the whole, slowly. There are good reasons for holding that during the 4th and even the 3rd millennium before our era, what is now the great desert was still crossable on foot, for, of course, there were no draught- or pack-animals for many centuries later on.

It is possible that the bulk of the western prehistoric hunters' art is not palaeolithic, but the Saharan neolithic may be very old and have arisen during a relatively damp interlude beginning about the middle of the 6th millennium. Anyway, there is evidence of plenty of criss-cross and interplay, and, of course, this is just what we should expect. Today the Sahara appears as the most formidable land barrier in existence, an arid area of scorched earth dividing White Africa from Black. But were the Sahara to be fairly fertile, with wooded uplands, streams and grassy savannas, we should have the solution, it may be, to some of our problems. Here would be the greatest grazing-grounds. Africa is not integrated into our European world because Africa is blighted with its modern climate, but in distant days there was an *Africa Felix* for prehistoric men.

All along the southern hills that rise to form Algeria's bulwark against the Sahara is a number of prehistoric engravings. The animals are elephant (very common), lion, wild ass, antelope, great buffaloes, ostrich, two-horned rhinoceros, panther, that is to say, on the whole, a fauna demanding a good deal more clement and damp a climate than these regions now show, but still a fauna which does not demand that we should set these paintings back in the very remote past.

There are human figures, masked men, a man wearing what looks like a head-dress of the sun, curious half-effaced scenes whose intent and purpose can hardly be guessed at, ithyphallic men, a man whose head is adorned with plumes, wearing a phallic sheath and armed with a boomerang, and many others; while in the Oued Hallail is a masked man, his feet shod with sandals.

Then there are some animal figures concerning which much ado has been made—rams with spherical objects between the horns, the so-called 'divinized' sheep, and comparisons have, of course, been proposed with the Egyptian god Ammon and the whole gamut of animal-headed Egyptian deities.

The best conclusion to hold, for the present, is that this naturalistic 'hunters' art' may have spread over a very considerable space of time.

A comparable art is represented by Written Rocks on either side of the Libyan frontier; these, however, are mostly paintings in red-ochre done on the roofs of rock-shelters. Now, both in Algeria and in the Fezzan are pictures of the big-horned water-buffalo, apparently domesticated in the south of the Algerian Oran province and certainly wild in the Fezzan. The domesticated buffalo suggests a day of neolithic age while the wild buffalo suggests a date of preneolithic hunters. It has been suggested that the very presence of the water-buffalo proves that the pictures must date right back to the last Pluvial, but as we do not know in detail what was the evolution of Saharan climate it is rash to dogmatize. There flourish to this day water-buffaloes in the Lake of Bizerta, northern Tunisia, though these creatures are, of course, descendants of tame buffaloes and are not in any way the descendants of the beasts depicted upon the 'Written Rocks'.

We can visualize possible migrations within Africa itself, and we can think of its land door across the isthmus of Suez, but it is puzzling to imagine communications between Spain and Africa in prehistoric times. We may note that not for many, many millenia have there been land-bridges across the Mediterranean, but we may also reflect that navigation is a much older art than we are always ready to recognize. There were, in the Near East, sea-going sailing-ships a full five thousand years ago. Millenia before that time men could cross fairly wide strips of sea, as well

as drift with the currents over distances which even now appear
considerable. Mesolithic men eight thousand years ago, and
perhaps more, invaded Ireland and came by sea from the Mull
of Cantyre. Southern Spain is, in one place, not more than eight
miles from the Moroccan shores.

The Saharan hunters were doubtless men of varied stocks and
possibly of varied skin-colours, for after all the Sahara covers an
area as large as that of all Europe which even today contains men
as unalike as Lapps, Mediterrean Spaniards, Alpine Germans and
so forth. It is probable that some of the hunters, and indeed
artists, in the north-west were the so-called Mechta-el-Arbi
type of men whose bones show them to have been most probably
of mixed Mousterian and modern man origin, in fact resembling
the later Old Stone Age men of Europe. There may have been
negroes in the more favoured spots but there are no traces of such
men in northern Africa as far back as the Saharan hunters' time.

### THE ART OF THE OASES

When we get to the Art of the Oases, that is of those of the
Fezzan, of the Hoggar, of the Tassili, of Tibesti and of 'Uwenat,
we are on much surer ground. The earliest paintings and engravings were made by hunters whose main prey and quarry was
giraffe. Giraffe, indeed, were for these Saharan hunters what
wild oxen and horses were for the hunter-artists of the Dordogne
in France. Now, giraffe does not need a climate very different
from that of the southern or northern fringes of the Sahara today.
Giraffe is for instance abundant five hundred miles south of the
Tibesti range rising from the sterile sands of the wilderness. On
the other hand, in these same sites, there are engravings of
elephant, rhinoceros, hippopotamus, lion, panther, moufflon,
ibex and other beasts, some of which indicate a climate very
different from that of today while others suggest weather conditions which we have reason to think obtained in the Sahara not
so very long ago, though, of course, several thousands of years.

We can imagine a Sahara much of whose surface was covered
with savanna, but a Sahara where hippopotami and rhinoceroses
were at home would be a very ancient Sahara indeed, twelve
thousand years old perhaps. If we may judge from the Fezzan
and Libyan 'Written Rocks', what has been aptly called a 'Zambesi' fauna extended right up to the Mediterranean's shores at

a time when artist-hunters haunted the game-grounds. Hippopotami wallowed in the mashy swamps that are now the salt *chotts*, rhinoceros, elephant and giraffe roamed over the wild wastes we explore on our way to Bir Pastor.[1]

Lions, we may remember, lingered in Tunisia until about seventy years ago and there were North African elephants in Carthaginian times. It is possible, even probable, that there were both crocodiles and hippopotami in Moroccan rivers up to Roman days and hippopotami were common in the Nile delta until the Middle Ages. We are so used to imagining certain animals in fixed surroundings that we are apt to forget the wide range of adaptability and tolerance many sorts of beasts display. The short-coated Indian tiger and the long-coated Siberian tiger are brothers but they exist in very contrasted surroundings. Hippopotami were found in the rivers of Cape Colony when Europeans first settled there though it frequently freezes at sea-level in that part of Africa. Elephants seem to us to be creatures typical of hot climates, but mammoths (and they are just long-haired elephants) throve in the Siberian frozen tundra.

In the Tassili two of the richest and most enigmatic sites are the Oued Djerat (on the track between Djanet and Fort-Polignac on the north-west fringe of the range) and the shelter of In-Ezzane which, as we have seen, lies on the eastern extension of the range.

In the Oued Djerat the oldest pictures are undoubtedly naturalistic engravings of animals unaccompanied by any human figures or signs or symbols. It is an art, then, which in technique, and perhaps in intention, resembles that of the palaeolithic caverns in south-western France, but there are no 'emblems', 'designs' or 'abstract art'. The engravings are heavily patinated; the incisions in the rock-face are weathered in such a way as to suggest great age. That is to say, in the dry climate we know to have been that of the Tassili for millenia past, such patination is acquired very slowly.

We may remember, however, that the Tassili, and the other central Saharan highlands, were damp, fairly fertile and pleasing long after much of the Sahara had taken on its now familiar face. In fact, for long, the Tassili—as the Hoggar and the Tibesti—was a lost world.

[1] But not, apparently, zebra.

The ancient Tassili animals are giraffes—plenty of giraffes and they do not tell us much—great wild oxen, some rhinoceroses (of the two-horned kind), and at least one hippopotamus. There is also a curious beast which may be a naturalistic version of one of the portentous and menacing and mysterious composite animals not uncommon in the palaeolithic paintings of south-western France; but this Tassili monster is no impossible beast; at first sight you would say it is a rather long-necked ass, but it can be no donkey for it has cloven hooves. Some imaginative observers have recognized an okapi.

The hippopotamus, of course, must have plenty of water and today he is found no nearer the Tassili than the river country of West Africa. The rhinoceros is not quite such a good guide to climate. The Oued Djerat engravings, so life-like and lively, do not, however, clearly indicate of what sort the Tassili rhinoceros was. You would take the engravings for those of the square-mouthed or white rhinoceros which still lingers on, it would appear, in the Upper Nile. This beast lives by browsing and is partial to open prairie country. On the other hand, the common African two-horned black rhinoceros—which has, however, as a prominent feature a prehensile upper lip—lives in bush country and feeds on the leaves of small trees. But all rhinoceroses like water, although the African are as a rule not so marsh-loving as the Asiatic; still neither will tolerate an open, dry savanna habitat.[1]

We can think a good deal about this naturalistic and hunters' art, we may equate it with the naturalistic art of the south-western European palaeolithic hunters, but really we should be justified in claiming direct communication between the two arts if we were sure that pictorial art were a thing which could be invented only once. This we know can hardly be true though we shall see what sort of connection we can trace between the later Saharan art and that of Egypt. Of course in thinking of these things we are back and floundering about in one of the fundamental human problems. Do men, in similar circumstances, tend to do the same or similar things?

---

[1] In late Palaeolithic times, rhinoceroses were fairly common in western Europe, but the beast is now everywhere much diminished in numbers. I have spent weeks in the south-eastern jungles of Asia and in areas where rhinoceroses are reputed to live, but have never sighted trace of any. In fact the rhinoceros is a stupid beast and is on the way to extinction. To find the nearest rhinoceros to the Tassili we must go to French Equatorial Africa a good fifteen hundred miles away.

Of course, the catch lies in the word 'in similar circumstances'. We know what some of these are in what we may call everyday life. To escape a lion all sorts of men may try, if they are unarmed, to climb up a tree, but when we come to communities of men we cannot visualize all the 'certain circumstances'. An American anthropologist has declared that if it can be proved that certain inventions were made all over again in the Americas then:

> "We must assume that if you leave human beings alone long enough their inherited biological equipment is such that they will go through the same successive stages in building their ways of life."

Perhaps all that we can reasonably conclude is that the Sahara was once inhabited by hunters who painted and engraved pictures of the beasts they hunted and of those they hoped to hunt. There is no evidence in the desert of those ceremonies of magic and initiation whose image so moves us when we visit such places as Lascaux or Les Trois-Frères in France.

There is, however, a thought that must occur to most of us who see these Saharan rock-paintings. Could they not have been executed from memory by men who had known these beasts farther south and may not the pictures be comparatively modern? Well, if, for instance, the Tassili rhinoceroses, giraffes and elephants were drawn from memory then the artists must all have had remarkably retentive mental vision; again, in many places the naturalistic pictures are in part covered by others of other epochs and to these epochs we can assign if not a date, at least a sequence; finally, there is no doubt that during the last Saharan Pluvial water-loving beasts did subsist in what is now arid desert.

When we leave the naturalistic animal pictures and get into those with human figures we are transposed, transported and find ourselves in a different and more comprehensible world, though one in which the great Africa-Europe puzzle is displayed in all its complexity. It is a fascinating story and perhaps not the least exciting because not all told and finished.

The animals shown with the human figures are almost entirely of cattle (although there are goats figured in the Tibesti); there are no water-buffaloes and no pachyderms. We have an art of ox-herds, pastoralists who, doubtless, were in contact, and not always peaceful contact, with the hunters. The cattle are, in many cases, piebald or dappled—that is to say of long domesticated stock—and there is clear proof of these pastoralists' settlement on the rocks of the Saharan highlands from the Hoggar to 'Uwenat.

On our Tassili rocks is a multitude of human figures, many of them, in a strange convention, represented as 'diabolos', that is with broad, pointed shoulders, wasp-waists and skirts or kilts of triangular shape recalling those worn in Egypt of dynastic times. Some of these diabolo-men wear plumed head-dresses of ostrich feathers. There is a whole series of giant engravings representing animal-headed men, their bodies girt with sashes, a jackal's tail pendant behind and wearing a penis-sheath or *karmata*. Astonishingly Egyptian. Similar figures exist upon predynastic Egyptian objects.

There is one mastiff-headed man most imposing and menacing. Masks of Black Africa, animal-headed Gods of Egypt, masks and animal-headed men of a remote and age-old Sahara. In the time of the pastoralists the population of the Tassili was a mixed one of Libyans, tall negroes, men like pygmies and persons of Mediterranean type which, in this connection, Breuil calls 'aristocratic'. It is a curious medley. Of course the pastoralist period may have lasted very long; for instance, the succession of rock-paintings in the Hoggar, farther west, and especially in the Oued Mertoutek, suggests a complicated evolution of art-styles.

In the Ido cave of the Tassili are beasts and men in a technique recalling that of the Spanish Levant. In the Oued Tiratimine of the Tassili is a painted scene that is an image of Black Africa.

Towards the end of the cattle-breeders' Sahara we have a horse-breeders' Sahara; the pastoralists indeed copied the horse-chariots, or, at least, we find pictures of chariots drawn by oxen. But we also have bulls with discs or spheres between their horns, just as we have in Algerian *Oranais* rams bearing radiant discs. Are such symbolical, and we can say religious or cult-animals, to be regarded as borrowings from Egypt or as ancestors of things Egyptian?

In-Ezzane is one of the most complicated sites. Here are a spring, a well and a solitary palm-tree, the only living thing to be seen for a hundred miles. By the well is a grotto whose walls are covered with a mass of paintings.

We may take it as a general rule, applicable to any part of the

"*Méharistes*, the Camel Corps, Tuareg far from their homes . . ." *p. 120*

"Below . . . is an arid dale of crumbling arches and dilapidated masonry . . ." *p. 120*

world, that paintings, scribblings, inscriptions and the like attract others; moreover, if a place has acquired a reputation for sanctity its holiness will be preserved through a succession of ages and of cults. It is not rare to find in western Europe, Christian churches on prehistoric sites. The most ancient paintings and engravings were placed one upon another. At In-Ezzane there are, at one end of the scale, inscriptions in Arabic and Tuareg *tifinagh* writing, and at the other end naturalistic pictures of animals long vanished from this arid spot. There are things to remind us of Levantine Spain and of South Africa, there are diabolo-men with their sex very clearly marked, there are dogs of Asiatic type, there are men mounted; there is a white horse prancing.

In the Oued Djerat picture-galleries are war-chariots drawn by horses painted in red-ochre. On one chariot is a man crouched along the yoke-pole and urging on the steeds, while around are posturing figures.

Another chariot-scene, an engraving. The charioteers are in full sweep of pursuit. Their quarry is a man, a fleeing man, but no ordinary one. He's a Minotaur, he has a bull's head and holds in his hand what seems to be a tall mace. The half-bent, harried figure is not a little like some of the earliest Egyptian statuettes and predynastic pictures. Can these be scenes from the life of the shadowy Garamantes? It would seem so. Did they import with horses from Crete also Minotaur legends? Masked men. There is a bull-headed man upon the rock-walls of the Gasulla Gorge in Eastern Spain. There is a bison-headed man in the Trois-Frères cavern (of Pyrenean France), where also may be seen the prancing wizard masked with stag's head and antlers. Masked men of Africa. Some at Oued Djerat have little stumps for heads. This strange convention can be found in 'Bushman' paintings on the rocks of Cape Colony and upon the prehistoric pictures of Levantine Spain, as at Minateda where there are headless figures, figures with stumps instead of heads, headless figures ithyphallic and steatopygous. Dead men. Symbols of death.

Saharan Economy

A short while ago a man bicycled from Switzerland to Cape Town. When he got to the end of his journey he said that he found the Sahara the most expensive region he had struck. He was, indeed, uncommonly lucky to find anything to buy. In this Ghat, for instance, everything imported costs more than at Ghadames. The price of petrol rises steeply as you push out into the desert. Liquid fuel at Ghat airfield is from 20% to 25% more than at Ghadames port. No one visits Ghat and the place has, it would seem, no part to play in cross-Saharan traffic. The automobile routes lie, or will lie, much farther east where the water-holes are not so far apart as on the Ghadames-Ghat-Zinder tracks which are most difficult. The Ghat airfield may serve for military planes as long as the French keep troops in this part of the Fezzan, but few commercial and no passenger planes are going to touch down at Ghat which is, for all the world, a minor Ghadames.

A minor Ghadames with some special features of its own. There is less water at Ghat and the town is not horned but serrated. The walls are crowned with teeth, rows and rows of them, rather small and very pointed as you look up from below, but here and there are taller, sturdier points, eye-teeth, you might say. Ghat is, in fact, a little more Sudanese than Ghadames. The last outpost of a White Africa. To the South stretches the oases of blue-black men.

You turn out from the shade of toothed walls and tread a sandy roadway scored down the middle by a sunk conduit, a roadway bordered with palms, almost an avenue. You bear to your right and you are in an open space, shapeless. Here are huts and a line of plaited wattle fencing against which stand out figures of naked black boys and girls, of dark-blue men and women robed in indigo. You see little of the chintzes and multicoloured dresses of Ghadames, but the negroes dominate; there are few 'white' men at all. In this straggling market-place you might be in Black Africa, but no, the air is too resigned and even sad.

In the real Black African villages of the southern savannas you may think for a moment that you are among the Ghat men and women in summer outfit; the same impermanent walls, the huts of Black Africa, but in the South the people are often gay, or seem so; their silky skins show a fine sheen. The air is damper. The black men do not really flourish in the sharp variations of temperature and the dry air of the Sahara. The negro keeps to the oases and even then he greys a little and loses much of his pristine cheerfulness.[1]

[1] Still, the Tropic of Cancer divides the Black Africa from the White, though there are, it seems, still the queerest ideas entertained about what is and what is not 'black'. A noted classical scholar recently lumped, for instance, the Egyptians and Tunisians together as 'coloured people'.

In the Sudan the great pestles thump the millet-mortars as at Ghat but the men of Black Africa sing and grin as they work. There is not only Saharan climate. Islam subdues even negro exuberance.

Still, here is the junction of Africa; well did the medieval Arabic writers divide the Continent into three, nay four parts, *Misr*, that is Egypt, the only area of African civilization, *Maghreb*, all westward of Egypt and north of the *Sahra* or Great Desert beyond which is the *Sudan*, the Land of the Blacks.

> *Ah! qu'on brûle, ah! qu'on brûle, à la pointe des sables, tout ce débris de plume, d'ongle, de chevelures peintes et de toiles impures.*
>
> *Et les poèmes nées d'hier, ah! les poèmes nées un soir à la fourche de l'éclair, il en est comme de la cendre au lait des femmes, trace infime.* . . .
>
> *Et de toute chose ailée dont vous n'avez usage, me composant un pur langage sans office.*
>
> *Voici que j'ai dessein encore d'un grand poème délébile.* . . .
>
> SAINT-JOHN PERSE

The remote Tibesti is, in my mind, linked with the wild marches of south-western Chinese Kwang-hsi, since it was on an exploring expedition in those unknown valleys that François d'Alverny excited me with his story of the Tibesti pictures of a vanished world. With one Thô rifleman and an old Ford car we pushed through the lavish jungle where you flush golden pheasant as you do partridge at home. We forced our way among mountains as fantastic as you may see in Sung paintings. We talked of Africa and painted rocks. d'Alverny was a man naturally African and hardly at home in the reptilian damp and inhumanity of the Chinese fringes.[1]

There is nothing adventurous in a Saharan crossing now. You just find a plane going the way you wish. There are, it is true, regular airlines linking Tunis with Fort-Lamy.[2] It is, however, much more exhilarating to get adopted by the pilot of a French

[1] Some of this journey I described in *Little China*. On 1st April, 1945, Captain d'Alverny was killed while covering the retreat of a small French force combating the Japanese in the Tongking mountains. His Tibesti documents—drawings, paintings, photographs and notes—were deposited in the Museum of Man, Paris.

[2] Once a week in either direction you leave Tunis at half past four in the morning and are at Fort-Lamy at one o'clock p.m. non-stop. The plane goes on to Bangui and Brazzaville.

military plane and then from Ghat eastwards skirt the Tibesti highlands—that are really a continuation of the Tassili; farther south you mark the gradual reluctant shift from desert to savanna and from savanna to desert where the slow spread of the Sahara is stifling the land.

Not long after Ghat and stretching off leftwards is the full splendour of the Tibesti peaks through which drives the long valley beginning on the north with the ill-famed Kourizo Pass, leading past the Toussidé's peak over ten thousand feet high; then revealing, rose in the sunlight and indigo in the shade, the fairy-land of the Sissé Needles jutting upwards from meadows of saffron sand.[1] It is not difficult to imagine the Tibesti green and a fount of waters.

You can make out Zouar, in the southern lee of the hills. A little farther on the whole mighty mass of the Tibesti swells and broadens, northwards and southwards, a gigantic triangle of ridges straddling the Libyan frontier. It is this eastern Tibesti which is so rich in prehistoric paintings.[2]

There are prehistoric paintings on rocks in many parts of the Tibesti range and there are also pictures on the hills of the Ennedi highlands to the south-east.

Although there are details of the Tassili and Tibesti series which can be compared with things farther north in the Fezzan and north-western Africa, still what we have here in the central Sahara is an art-complex which is richer and more exciting than that of anywhere else in the desert.

The Tibesti pictures, for instance, can be sorted out into three main groups. The first, and doubtless the oldest, comprises animal figures of which those of the giraffe are the most common (giraffe, by the way, is to be found today about five hundred miles south of the Tibesti) : this is undoubtedly a hunters' art. There are,

---

[1] There is as yet (1952) no regular service of cars from Tunis to Fort-Lamy (though there is one from Benghazi to Kufra) but in 1950–51 two automobiles were driven from Tunis via Fort-Lamy to Cape Town and back. The track was, of course, and to a certain extent, conditioned, but the exploit was a noteworthy one. MM. Lapalu bought their Land Rover, so to speak, off the peg in Tunis while MM. Desparmet and Aubert used a jeep. The route was Tunis, Bir Zar, Point Biondo, Sinaouen, Derdj, Bir Ghazeli (in the middle of the Hammada-el-Homra), Brak, Sebha (the main Italian fort in the Fezzan), Gatroun, the Kourizo Pass (where fresh human skeletons were found), Zouar (that was Leclerc's advanced position in 1942), Largeau and Fort-Lamy.

[2] Visited in 1934 to 1937 by d'Alverny, then a camel corps subaltern commanding a flying column.

". . . we stand at the arched gateway and survey the dunes . . . a
Door on Dreams" *p. 138*

"Men slumped in the miserly shade. A hungry land" *p. 140*

however, very many paintings of cattle and of dog-headed men armed with bows, the same sort of fearsome beings we meet at Oued Djerat in the Tassili. It is not clear whether we have here the portraits of a society that was half-hunting, half-pastoral, or of two different societies which met here in the wooded and watered Tibesti highlands.

The second main group of paintings represents herds of cattle and goats, men armed with spears, plumed 'medicine-men', masked and beast-headed men.

The last set of pictures is quite evidently much more modern. In them are camels and figures of desert-nomads wearing surcoats and crossed bandoliers like the Tuareg.

It is impossible to examine these paintings without being struck by their resemblance to the Levantine Spanish on the one hand and to early Egyptian things on the other.

Among the more outstanding of the Tibesti frescoes are those at the Fofoda rock-shelter (piebald cows, men brandishing bows or stick, a man wearing a tail) with a mutilated scene which might be either a dance or perhaps a burial. There are men with plumes on their heads, there is a man sitting with another upon his knee. All the men as masked or have animal's heads. On a wall of sandstone at Tiézy are dog-headed men and dancers while at Karnasahi are six men dancing a ballet. The very faded paintings at Tiéréoké include a skirted woman with an elephant's head and several queer designs that might be boats or well-heads. At Mossei is another ballet scene not unlike that at Tiézy but the men have cymbals tied to their feet and their heads are horned. In a grotto at Bodoa are speckled cows and engravings of giraffe, while an aged Tibbu who once scratched a bare living from a little plot near the well related that he had rifled mysterious tombs nearby.[1]

Dappled or piebald oxen, very like those we can see today on the Sahara's southern fringes and round about Fort-Lamy, are

[1] Other sites are Gonéké (nearly 4,500 feet up), Faraouanama, Kozen-Michidin, Fofoda-Kiri, Gaorlé-Ouania and Tadogra. The paintings all fall into the same general classes as we have mentioned. New rock-paintings are being found all the time in the Tassili and Tibesti areas, but these new pictures do not disturb the general picture as we see it of two sorts of art: one of hunters and another of pastoralists. As far as the Tibesti is concerned, the paintings are most numerous in the eastern portion. In the Ennedi uplands, the south-western region appears to be the most rich. There is a nice little summary of the latest prospections in an article by Colonel Huart in the periodical *Tropiques* for October, 1952.

common on the Written Rocks of the Hoggar, the Tassili, the Tibesti, of the 'Uwenat Hills and of oases nearer the Nile Valley. We can say therefore, that pastoral herdsmen were flourishing in what is now the Sahara a certain number of millenia ago. It is clear that these pastoralists were in contact with hunters and, moreover, it is by no means certain that when we see domesticated cattle on the same frieze or fresco with hunters, we behold proof of a semi-hunting, semi-pastoral way of life. The South African rock-paintings not seldom show conflict between the little Bushmen and the intrusive Bantu 'Kaffir' herdsmen. The object of the Bushmen (themselves hunters and food-gatherers) was, of course, to capture and drive off the Kaffirs' flocks. Maybe we have in the Sahara evidence for much the same sort of activities, inevitable when two such contrasted ways of life as those of herdsman and hunter come into contact.

Cattle-raising is a distinctively African occupation; the Black Africans are, whenever the nature of the land admits of it, devoted to pastoralism. They will never consent to be parted from their cattle, as is all too well known to the planners whose task it is to rid the African countryside of such insect pests as the tsetse fly. The ancestral stock of domesticated African cattle seems to be indigenous to East Africa, and, at a guess, one is inclined to say that the pastoral herdsmen's home may have been in this region also. The dispersal-centre of the Bantu-speaking cattle-breeders looks as though it had been in the region of the Upper Nile—in the widest sense of the term—and there is, for instance, at Genda Biftu (as well as at other sites) in the Harrar province of Abyssinia, a number of paintings representing herds of long-horned black cattle peacefully grazing together with female buffaloes which, like the cows, have their calves beside them. These beasts, then, are, it would seem, domesticated, but are not in appearance far removed from the wild stock. The Saharan pastoralists (whom we find with dappled, that is, long domesticated cattle) probably derived their way of life from east-central Africa. As the hunters waned with the weather, so the pastoralists spread.

THE FOSSIL ISLAND

We now come to what well may be the crucial area for African prehistoric art, that is to say, to the 'Uwenat Hills. Al-'Uwenat is a mass of high ground, in part crystalline, and of a total area about the same as that of the Island of Majorca. The fossil island is so situated that it is in three different countries: about half is Libyan, most of the remainder in the Anglo-Egyptian Sudan, while there is a relatively small portion in Egypt, though the hills—the culminating point of which the Jebel-al-'Uwenat rises to nearly 6,500 feet—may be regarded as the most westerly of the Egyptian oases; if we remember that 'Uwenat is more a small-scale Tassili or Tibesti than an oasis in our sense of the word. As the camel saunters it is less than four hundred miles from 'Uwenat across the sands of the Libyan desert to the Nile at Wadi Halfa, the Second Cataract and the Egyptian-Sudanese frontier.

At 'Uwenat is a number of painted sites with pictures falling into two sharply contrasted classes, those of ancient hunters and those of pastoral herdsmen.

What makes the 'Uwenat story so fascinating is its connection with things to the east and to the west. At 'Uwenat and at the Egyptian oases of Dakhla and Kharga (both to the north of 'Uwenat and also about half as near again to the Nile) the animals of the hunting art are the same—lions, giraffes, ostriches—some of them amazingly well executed. At 'Uwenat the pictures (both paintings and engravings) are mostly of giraffe and ostrich, which do not necessarily indicate a climate very different from that of the Sahara's fringes nowadays.

In any case, though there are also antelope and moufflon at 'Uwenat there is no elephant, and this is significant because there are at Dakhla oasis two prehistoric elephants, their bodies decorated with an arrangement of what may be called tesselated triangles, the same as is found on the palettes and pots of the third Egyptian predynastic culture-phase (Nagada I) some time in the fifth millennium B.C. However, it may be that elephants were not common in the eastern Sahara in later 'hunting' times; anyway the beasts must have early disappeared from Egypt since they do not figure either in the mythology or in the folklore of Egyptian civilization.

At Khargur Tahl in 'Uwenat is what looks like a fight for the possession of a bull, possibly a domesticated bull, so the picture may commemorate a tussle between pastoralists and hunters. The scene is oddly reminiscent of the Levantine Spanish frescoes. The warriors are armed with reflex-bows as on the Minateda rocks in Spain. The reflex-bow may be of Asiatic origin, but, in any case, it is difficult not to conclude that there was some contact between the Iberians and the pastoralists of the Sahara.

In the 'Uwenat rock-shelters of both Khargur Tahl and Khargur Meur, the women are often very fat and with projecting buttocks (steatopygy), suggesting the figures of Hottentot women of South Africa. These 'Uwenat beauties wear kilts or short skirts and sometimes their breasts are depicted. The 'Uwenat men have, for the most part, broad shoulders, wasp-waists and often 'diabolo' shapes. These stalwarts sport phallus-sheaths, garters adorned with thongs and are often masked, especially in a Khargur Meur scene where the runners are as frenzied as in the famed witchcraft scene depicted on the Maluti Hills in South Africa. The weapons are, in addition to bows and arrows, straight or curved cudgels.

The cattle are mostly piebald and display very full udders.

Of course, the obvious conclusion is that the 'Uwenat things are closely akin to those in the Tassili and the Tibesti; in fact, we may say that they are of the same art-style and reflect similar ways of life, though there are some things at 'Uwenat that are more like Levantine Spanish paintings than any at Tassili or Tibesti. For instance, there is a lively little frieze of men armed with spears and wearing pointed caps; they are sprinting along like a company of imps. Again, the plumed 'medicine-men' may be almost identical with those in the Tibesti but some of the 'Uwenat warriors remind one of the lurching, ominous file of braves in the Cingle de la Mola Remigia.

Of course, when we talk of 'Uwenat being a crucial area for African prehistoric art, we are using what in some way is a metaphor or a conventional term, still; here we are: westwards and then north-west is the long road to the Iberian peninsula; eastward is the Nile Valley; east and then south lies the long sweep of southern African prehistoric painting that leads from Tanganyika through the Rhodesias, the Union of South Africa and to the rupestral marvels of South-West Africa.

Did this shepherds' art we see in the central Sahara cross the vast spaces down to Tanganyika where the southern painted rocks begin and where also there is represented a naturalistic art of hunters? Or did the Saharan pastoralists' art arise in some region farther south, or south-east and spread into what is now the desert where it received some art-influence from Iberia? We

may be sure that the pre- and protohistorical Sahara was traversed by a criss-cross of influences and of traditions, back and
forth, and in many directions.

## The Southern Painted Rocks Leading To The Brandberg Ballet

The painted rocks of Tanganyika, at the earliest levels, show
line-drawings resembling those of the French mid-Aurignacian.
Such a style is either quite absent or most rare south of Rhodesia.
In the Tanganyika cave-paintings it is only in the sixth level that
human figures in what may be called the 'Rhodesian' style are
discernible. Some of this Tanganyika-Rhodesian art may be as old
as some of the Levantine Spanish and of the diagrammatic art
which followed it.[1]

Tanganyika sites show naturalistic animal figures and human
ones in elongated shadow-show, but they are, on the whole, rather
static and not in such frenzied movement as the South African or
the Levantine Spanish. Kisese, however, resembles both 'Uwenat
and sites farther south.

There are schematized human figures at Bwanja near Bukoba
in the Victoria Nyanza region which are very comparable with
those of mesolithic or neolithic date from the Sierra Morena in
southern Spain. And then there are the Harrar pastoralist paintings. From Tanganyika down to the southern regions of Cape
Province there are stencils and imprints of human hands.

It certainly looks as though, for a great mass of the southern
African prehistoric paintings and engravings, we must imagine
art-traditions borne southwards and the distribution of the
prehistoric pictures points to the route of the east. The least
difficult way to reach southern Africa, by land, is to cross the
Zambesi and keep on through what are now Southern Rhodesia
and Mozambique (in the latter colony are rock-paintings, though
they have not been exhaustively examined or described) into
the modern Union of South Africa.

It is obvious that some of the southern African rock-pictures
(some of which are possibly fairly late in date) are closely related,
in style, to the Spanish Levantine art. It is difficult to hazard even

[1] The dating of the African rock-paintings is an even more arduous task than that
of similar pictures in south-western Europe, but stone-instruments are found apparently contemporary and these are dated by the beaches; hence the African Middle
Stone Age began at the beginning of the last interglacial.

a guess as to what people inaugurated the prehistoric arts of southern Africa. It is certain that many of the existing paintings were the work of the little yellow Bushmen who look as though they had been in southern Africa for many millenia (some of the fossil human remains look very like those of the Bushman type); did the Bushmen learn from others, or did the Bushmen, at one time, extend much farther north than they have done in any historical times?

Anyway, it seems as though the region we call roughly the Sudan was a mighty *vagina gentium* whence issued peoples and their arts. Of course, we might do well to reflect that what we may call a 'hunters' art' suits well a hunting way of life (and the beliefs which may depend upon it), so that hunters without art might be eager to pick up a 'hunting art' from hunters who had an art, either original or borrowed. It is not safe, then, to conclude that similarities of technique indicate similarities of the artists' physical types. After all, in the iconography and imagery of a religion, we find the figures much alike over a wide area. Christian artists in colonial Mexico, in Spain and in medieval Germany produced representations which we—if devoid of means of comparison and historical knowledge—would perhaps confound.

Some of the invaders coming south from east-central Africa down into the blind alley of South Africa may have been pastoralists who, seeking fresh pastures, lost their herds through the poison of the tsetse and had to adopt a hunting mode of life. There have been movements from side to side—one does not like to say backwards and forwards—all through man's later story, as we see it.

Then again, we must not overlook the great probability of seaborne invasions. Men have been navigators for a very long time; the Egyptians seem to have had sea-going ships at least five thousand years ago, and the second phase of the so-called Nagadan culture-area was brought from across the Red Sea and certainly not by swimmers. Though the channel looks so narrow upon the maps, it is a good fifty miles between the port of Qusair and the coast of Arabian Hejaz. However, for six months out of the year sea-currents alone will, without the aid of sail, carry a boat from the Persian Gulf to the shores of eastern Africa. The Sumerians (and also the early 'Indians' of the Indus Valley) were merchant-adventurers whose ships sailed far and wide in search of exotic produce.

There is a considerable number of southern African prehistoric pictures (of course, prehistoric in this part of Africa has a very different connotation from 'prehistoric' used in connection with our western Europe) which depict the most un-African and alien-seeming figures. For instance, in the Impey Cave (discovered in 1927) in the Ndanga native reserve just north of Zimbabwe, there are images of light-coloured people, 'white' people, with red hair and long noses. In the same region there is a site (Chibi) with comparable figures, one of which has been compared with a Cretan girl bull-fighter, a sort of most ancient Conchita Cintrón, carrying a large white flower.

In Southern Rhodesia, South-West and South-East Africa are many thousands of human figures, not a few in 'Capsian' Levantine Spanish style. There is, also, of course, a most abundant naturalistic art depicting animals of all kinds.

Among the human figures is a number of non-African ones which are, on the Drakensberg and Basutoland rocks, for instance, shown clad in robes and cloaks. African ivory and gold must long ago have attracted prospectors from the earliest civilizations of the Near East.

The southern African paintings and rock-engravings sweep right round and extend up well into South-West Africa where their culminating point is the great ceremonial ballet of the Brandberg, a most astonishing scene comprising twenty-seven or eight figures painted on the walls of a rock-recess never struck by the rays of the sun. There are no less than eleven superimposed layers of paintings; paint and repaint, carve and recarve the sacred site.

The ballet is the topmost and latest of these layers.[1]

Here they march and dance and posture, sinister and strange: a man wearing a crocodile-mask, musicians, steatopygous women, a dark man with a horned head, a human-legged oryx antelope, a hermaphrodite, two infibulated men. Then the famous White Lady clad in pink-and-white tights and a close-fitting jerkin, a figure from Knossos and carrying a white cup or flower. Behind her, a figure clad in dusky raiment, his face a skull; he is infibulated and his hat is adorned with a spotted bird's wing, his gauntlets have black studs, his right hand holds a staff set with

[1] The frescoes are in the Maack Shelter in the Tsisab or Leopard Ravine, about seventy miles from Cape Cross (where the Portuguese navigator, Diogo Cam, anchored in 1485) and about on the same parallel as the sites of the most southern part of Southern Rhodesia.

teeth and his left hand two daggers and two heart-shaped objects.[1] Behind him run two red-haired youths; and there are others, some African, some spectral and phantastic, some alien, possibly even European in appearance. This charade is hidden in the arid recesses of waterless hills rising from a sun-baked desert.

Mysteries of Africa. Whatever may be the date of this astounding climax, many of the southern African rock-paintings must be prehistoric in our European sense of the term, that is to say contemporary with some of our Western rock-paintings.

Of course, the insistent question which buzzes in our heads when we look on the complexity of the African scene is the query that goes to the root of the whole subject of man's art: Did 'modern' men, the men who produced the first representational art of the world and produced it in Europe, did these men come eventually from Africa and did they bring with them from Africa a tradition of representational art? Which comes first, the African egg or the European chicken?

## THE SUM OF EGYPT

When, from 'Uwenat, we turn our eyes eastwards to the Nile Valley we can see, if not much clearer, at least a connected route with no breaks. Both at Dakhla and at Kharga oases are traces of a hunters' and a pastoralists' art and at Dakhla especially some of the drawings are remarkably like those of early Egypt. There is quite clearly a connection, and a close one, between the art of early Egypt and that of the Sahara. The question is this: are the Egyptians things derived from, or, let us say, of common origin with, those of the Sahara, or was it Egyptian influence which percolated into the desert?

Those who maintain that the Sahara owed everything to Egypt seem to have overlooked the changes in Saharan climate and also not to have read aright the story of historical Egypt's peopling and settlement. Moreover there have been, of course, plenty of anachronistic comparisons. After all, Egyptian civilization lasted three thousand years and features we often look on as common to the whole thirty centuries are peculiar to certain periods only.

One thing is quite certain, the roots of historical Egypt were

[1] Infibulation is the fixing of a ring, clasp or buckle on the penis; it is a very widespread African custom in the past and survives in some regions today.

deep in Africa. The earliest (predynastic) 'Egyptian' things we possess are specifically and entirely African: men wearing beasts' tails (the practice lasted long in historical Egypt), curly hair and beards pointed, men with feathered and plumed head-dresses, penis-sheaths, kilts, men carrying spears and maces and bows; then there are the 'standards' (which became so important in later time) or bird-headed sticks. Na'rmer, a king of the first dynasty, looks with his kilt and his animal's tail like a figure from the Tassili or Tibesti.

Another thing quite certain is that the ancestors of the historical Egyptians were not 'roving bands of hunters' (as some would have it) chased by the increasing desiccation of their hunting-grounds and invading the Nile Valley from the west. During the last Pluvial in the Sahara, the Nile Valley was a pathless swamp and much of the river's bed remained marsh until comparatively late times, for it is obvious that it dried up slowly from south to north and not from any other direction. We may take it that during the Pluvial men with old Stone Age instruments hunted the Eastern Sahara, the home of savanna-loving beasts.

As far as the immediate neighbourhood of the Nile is concerned, traces of men get rather scarce towards the end of the Pluvial while mesolithic tools are so scarce as to suggest a very sparse population moving about in perhaps wetter conditions than those of the Pluvial itself. In fact, Egypt went through a humid phase corresponding to the damp Atlantic weather which covered western Europe with dense forests. This Egyptian Mesolithic may well have lasted for a long time from after about 8000 B.C. On Saharan prairies northwards grew grasses ancestral to wheat and an agriculture took its rise with progressive desiccation, but Saharan hunters, Saharan pastoralists and even Saharan agriculturalists may have been, for long, in contact.

The first 'Egyptians' we can identify, the so-called 'Tasians', moved northwards along the high ground to the west of the Nile's trough, then a broad swamp full of water-fowl and water-loving animals.

The earliest Egyptian dynastic dates have now been checked off, and fairly accurately (that is to say to within a hundred years or so); we may take it that the first dynasty began approximately in 3000 B.C., which, we know, was the peak period of the 'optimum' or most favourable climate that prevailed when the first civilizations were appearing. The first settled village cultures (possibly on the Caspian highlands and in Syria) are about two thousand years earlier than the beginning of the first dynasty. We may not be going so far wrong if we think of the Tasians as having flourished round about 5500 B.C. The Tasian flint-implements were quite different from those of their shadowy predecessors and the whole culture of the Tasians was entirely African.

Their home was, unquestionably, somewhere to the south, somewhere in the Sudan let us say.

These Tasians had flocks and herds, they made a poor sort of pottery and they appear to have grown cereals, they were, in fact, a people in a fairly advanced neolithic culture. The Badarians who followed the Tasians seem also to have come from the south and either Badarian culture was richer than Tasian or we have more evidences of it. We have statuettes and worked copper articles from the Badarian cemeteries where beasts were buried with men. These Badarians were semi-nomads but they had permanent huts, and they knew how to weave and to grow plants. Though there may have been some contacts with Asia, the Badarian 'complex' is still quite African, as is also the culture of the Nagada (I) people who were the next immigrants into the Nile Valley. The variety of objects left behind them by the first Nagadans is astonishing but the painted pottery is the most revealing of the relics.

On this earthenware we have pictures of elephants and hippopotami, of horned deer, of antelopes, of *slughis* (the African hunting-dog still common on the northern Sahara's fringes), of men with plumed head-dresses and with *karmata* or penis-sheaths as we see shown on the prehistoric pictures in many parts of the Sahara.

There are on Nagadan (I) pottery scenes of what look like ritual dances, there are scratches and scrawls which may have served as potters' marks and thus as a vague sort of script. We find also some of the gods who were to rise to great stature in later Egypt. There is the emblem of Min (or what serves as his emblem afterwards), there is more than just a possibility that the Nagadans (I) may have venerated a jackal-headed divinity (the later Set?), and trees may have been sacred. There is a fertility-goddess shown with her hands supporting her breasts in an attitude familiar from statuettes in many lands and especially

Minoan Crete. This Nagadan Mother of the Gods wears cow's horns.

Now we may conclude. These first three prehistoric and predynastic cultures of Egypt were unquestionably quite African and owed, as far as we can see, nothing to any other continent. The three cultures were related to each other. They all came from the south, that is to say from somewhere beyond the present Sudan frontier.

There was a well-established Egyptian legend (in, of course, much later dynastic times) that the ancestors of the Egyptians had migrated from somewhere in the south. Somewhere whence came, as from the legendary land of Punt or Puenet, the tribute of the Aethiopians' lands—incense, ebony, ivory, odoriferous woods, eyepaste, spices, baboons, leopard skins, green gold—in fact, the merchandise you may see today represented in a humble form and spread out for your custom in the market-place of Fort-Lamy. We may take it as proved that the Nile Valley colonizers came from the Sudan; as this is an indefinite name, it will serve.

We may assume also that these Tasians, Badarians and first Nagadans probably spoke a Hamitic speech, that is to say akin to the present-day Berber (Libyan of the Ancients) of the Sahara and of the Maghreb, and also to the languages of some of the peoples of East Africa right down into Kenya. At a guess, we should say that the Saharan pastoralists, creators of the characteristic pictorial art of the oases, were also Hamitic speakers, as were perhaps in neolithic times most of the Saharan dwellers who were not, of course, necessarily all of the same physical type.

We may also think that the earliest predynastic Egyptians took with them into the Nile Valley cultures and arts similar to those prevailing over wide spaces in the Sahara's southern regions and in today's Sudan. The main argument against those who would hold that Egypt civilized the Sahara is that when Egypt became recognizably Egyptian, that is to say a few centuries before 3000 B.C., there was not much Sahara to civilize. The protagonists of the Egypt-into-Sahara theory do not seem to take into full account the progress of desiccation in the Nile Valley, nor do they trouble to sort out, in order of antiquity, certain Egyptian art-motifs and symbols. After all, the Egyptian civilization lasted a full three thousand years, that is to say as long as from now back to before 1000 B.C.; before Greece and while the Ramesids were ruling in the Nile Valley. There is only one existing civilization which was living in 1000 B.C.—the Chinese. We can see at once how foolish it would be to take customs and images which belong to the Sung dynasty and transfer them forcibly to early Chou times, or to take manners and pictures of the T'ang and saddle them on Mao Tsetung, and so on. The old, old crimes of anachronism. The local legend, the Romans' Camp on the hill just outside the village, always been called then from time immemorial, yet on a 17th-century map it's marked as Gallows' Hill, if you like.

In the Dakhla oasis in the Libyan desert of Egypt is the prehistoric picture of a hunter armed with a bow and wearing what looks like the classical Egyptian point-fronted kilt. At Wadi Barqa, only six miles from the predynastic site of Nagada, is an outline drawing which if really dateable to dynastic times shows a clear link between the prehistoric Saharan rock-art and that of the highly accomplished Egyptian dynastic art of the Third Dynasty.

Of course, these Saharan and African things were not enough, of themselves, to lead up to the astounding civilization of historic Egypt. It was the culture of the Nagadans (II) (of Asiatic type and brought into Egypt through the Red Sea port of Kosseir and thence down the Wadi Hammamet to the Nile) which—most probably—carried Semitic speech into Egypt and the impulses which vivified the old African complex and swept the people of the Nile Valley along to their glorious destiny.

A FABLED LAKE

The scene shifts back and forth over a hundred miles; these are fringes where the dead fingers of the desert poke through the grass tassels. This must be the savanna. No, you are over the sands. You lose distance, you lose height. The specks are agile, discreet-coloured beasts, all sorts of horned creatures, bucks and antelopes and gracious gazelles, the fauna of the African plains.

We skirt the northern edges of Chad bounded by tall sand-dunes. The area of the lake is not much more than half what it was in 1822 when Clapperton, the first European to reach its shores, gazed on the expanse dotted with islands and girt with vast papyrus-beds.

Chad may be the Sigismis of the old maps but possibly that is but a fabled sea born of vague legends of the Niger's breadth.

What Delisle in 1741 dubbed 'Lac de Bournu' may be our Chad for both are bordered by the lands of old Bornu now in Nigeria. Anyway, the fading lake is fed only by the Shari and one lesser stream, the Waube. All others have vanished, including the fossil Bahr-el-Ghazal that once flowed down from the Tibesti heights. Chad is drying and may soon become a *chott*, a salt-marsh like those of southern Tunisia far away to the north. Kuka, the old marshalling-yard of the slave-traders, was once on the lake's edge. It is now a good thirty miles from it.

## BLACK AFRICA

This Black Africa is red. The airfield is swept out of the ruddy dust of a desert. The Shari river rolls red waves that mingle with those of the Logone and often flood the five-mile length of straggling Fort-Lamy town, a featureless place, though here and there intriguing as broad streets are when bordered with dumb, white façades.

The settlement was once but a minor mart for slaves. It has spread its nondescript mass in quite recent years since it has been the administrative capital of the vast Chad territory, more than four hundred and fifty thousand square miles—nine times the area of England—and less than two million inhabitants.

Black men on red soil, though the people are not all negroes in the sense that the inhabitants of West Africa or of Equatorial rain-forest are negroes; still Fort-Lamy is black and barbarous, smiling and strong-scented.

Apart from the proud representatives of Western Civilization and their often shrewish as well as presumptuous female counterparts, the population of Fort-Lamy is made up of what are commonly called Arabs and Saras. There is not much to choose between their skin-colours, both are decidedly dusky. The 'Arabs', who are for the most part camel-breeders, are only 'Arabs' in the sense that Alabama coloured men are 'English', that is to say the Chadian 'Arabs' speak Arabic. They are also Moslems while the Saras are not True Believers.

Religions, whatever may be their other benefits, do not change the colour of one's skin, though some religions make men less colour conscious. The Chadian Moslems, moreover, have not been for long inmates in the House of Islam. The Faith did not sweep over this land until the latter part of the 16th century.

We may take it that 'Arabs' and 'Saras' are pretty close relations, though in mien and comportment there are differences between the two groups. It is difficult to read character in faces, but it is not so hard to note fashions in faces as we may see if we glance at the magazines and then look around us in the subway or bus. The pleasing thing is that we all get to believe we are what others think our faces show us to be.

Fort-Lamy market-place. Shacks and huts and one-storeyed houses once washed white. A black man's town. A market of nearly naked men and women. No one dresses up to come to town and, truth to tell, the Chadians generally look better nude than clothed; what dress there is will be a white cotton robe and a skull-cap or turban for men and a sari-like robe for the women, but those so adorned are 'Arabs'. If you jolt off in a jeep to explore the surrounding savanna of dried grasses, trees like bundles of barbed wire, not the least attractive features of a grey plain eaten by the sun are the silky, polished, tattooed skins adorned with heavy baubles and bangles of copper and silver. Strangely enough it seems that people wear more and more clothes as you head for the heart of Equatorial Africa. Piece-goods drummers at work? Nakedness is offensive to God, buy our cotton.

The sellers sit under a bit of stuff propped up against the heat—this is a market and not a bazaar with built-up shops, as in White Africa. Over the whole place hangs a southern perfume compounded of odoriferous grains and woods, meat, and the scent of the people themselves, not sour or stinking but supplying a rich basis for the varied odours of dust and merchandise. Here are the smiths, a strange people, still regarded almost as men apart, as they were in early times when iron was a magic sort of stone. The Chadian smiths have closed faces as they hammer out tools and spear-heads. The rope-makers are even more remote, for they are blind—about 90% of the population of Fort-Lamy suffers from trachoma—and the rope-making, they say, is, like piano-tuning, a craft more skilfully practised by the sad blind than by those who can see and so rarely understand what they behold.

Little mounds of aids to beauty, *kohl* or antimony for the eyes, not only embellishing but protective; smear some on your eyelids. The older European explorers knew what they were doing when they daubed on the *kohl* and walked untroubled in blazing glare. The Sara women crouch over their heaps of rubbish neatly heaped on cotton squares, they point to the merchandise, 'everything a *pata*'—it's an African *Uniprix*, and a *pata* is five francs, and that is, well, so little that it takes some time to work out, let's say about a 1½*d*. in British money. After all, meat here is maybe 1*s*. a lb. and a woman is traded for ten bullocks, that is a lot of avoirdupois weight. How much is a woman worth in money? One of these delightful Sara girls chewing tobacco and squirting the juice on to the dust. The hair is not frizzy, as that of negresses, or curled; it is plaited in rope-like strands, giving many of the women a most ancient Egyptian appearance. In fact some of the Saras with their straight open-eyed gaze and their sharp features recall 4th-dynasty statues. The more you see of Black Africa the more you realize how solid and thick was the African substratum of ancient Egypt. Here is one of the sellers, her eyes set on side-ways; she can gaze at you without turning her head as you pass by. She is most uncommonly like an Egyptian painting I saw sometime ago.[1]

## L'HONNEUR DES HOMMES, SAINT-LANGAGE

In the French Black African possessions there is clash and tension as between two groups of Frenchmen. On the one hand are some civil servants, including the school-teachers, and on the other hand an odd confederate front compounded of army officers, missionaries and the mass of the *colons*—very few of whom intend to stay in the 'colonies' for longer than they can help. They mean to make their pile and clear out. Some of the *colons* are tough, even brutal adventurers, some are very decent fellows who have a shrewd idea of what can and cannot be done nowadays even in Black Africa. What this heterogeneous collection of crooks and honest men, or rough illiterates and reasonably educated Frenchmen, has in common with army officers, priests, nuns and some civil servants, is a dislike of the government education policy.

The *colons* would gladly foot the bill for shipping back to France every teacher and *professeur* in the province. Schooling

---

[1] In the small Egyptian collection in Périgueux Museum; the painting was originally the bottom of a wooden coffin. The thing is late but so lively and living that I got a photograph of it through the kindness of Monsieur Secret, the curator.

makes the natives hard to handle. Where are the good old days when the negroes were kept in their proper places? The French officials have imported a ready-made education-system into this country. It is the end of everything.

The army officers—most of whom, in the overseas possessions at any rate, tend to be favourable to the Church—and the missionaries also have their grudge against the schoolmasters. The missionaries do not of course make any headway with the Moslems at all—Moslems are impervious to attempts to lure them to another faith—but among the non-Moslems, the so-called 'fetishists', there are far more converts among the young people who have not been to school than among those who have. It is take it or leave it in Black Africa where the inhabitants have absolutely none of the subconscious respect for and tolerance of something which even if not believed in, is still regarded as part and parcel of civilization, art and manners.

The Moslems, as a whole, resist the proffered education and stick to their Koranic schools where little is taught but reading and writing in Arabic and in Arabic script and the recitation of the Koran. As everywhere, the social effects of Islam are such that the black Moslems of Chad are intimately convinced of their essential superiority over their non-Moslem neighbours.

The result of all this is that the non-Moslems are now better versed in the white man's lore than are the Moslems.

The non-Moslems clamour for schools and show a most commendable ardour for learning. Although but a fraction of the children can go to school, it will not be so very long before some of the men—and even the women—we may see sitting and crouching over their mounds of merchandise in Fort-Lamy market will be able to read and write *in French*.

Yes, here in the Chad province—as elsewhere in French Black Africa—the little black boys and girls, for there is no attempt at adult education, are transported abruptly from a world of reed-huts, tom-toms, medicine-men, masks and magic into what are to all intents and purposes French village schools.[1]

---

[1] Although native monitors are being trained most of the schoolmasters are still. French and the curriculum is only slightly different from that in metropolitan France Each pupil costs the government about 15,000 francs (some £15 or $42) a year, for the children have to be fed and lodged. In 1952 it was estimated that out of 440,000 children of school-age less than 8000 were at school, but the education budget absorbs one-tenth of the colony's revenue.

". . . the *Limes*, the Outpost of Empire . . ." (*p. 140*)

"... the forepart of a stupendous saurian, a dragon of the wastes" *p. 143*

"Ksar Lemsa is an unrecorded treasure . . ." *p. 193*

The boys and girls of this Black Africa are learning French, to think in French, to speak in French, to argue, to reason in French. Ours is a word-made world, speech by means of its symbols induces our own peculiar 'reality'. When men learned to speak, they learned at the same time to create the world in which they lived and which we ever since have lived. Conception was added to perception. Not for nothing did the ancient Egyptians (together with other peoples) believe that by pronouncing a Name they did not only control but create. As the late Edward Sapir put it, "the 'real world' is . . . unconsciously built up on the language habits of the group".

The meaning of meaning. Our special human world made of words depends of course for its shape and form upon the sort of words used. It is grammar—syntax, accidence, prosody and the rest—that moulds our faiths. To convince ourselves of this we have only, perhaps you will agree, to regard such things as Indian and Chinese Buddhism. The Chinese words will never spin the same cocoon of refuge as will the Indo-European phrases of Indian Pali. It is just like that.

Any language, indeed, by its interpretation of the word-made world, does impose a peculiar view of life, a philosophy of living and a way of regarding human affairs—those of the past as well as those of the present. But a language works its magic according to the nature of the theatre in which it is performed. Words do not perform just the same enchantment in Paris as they do in Fort-Lamy, language operates in one way with little French (and Polish, Jewish and Senegalese and Annamese) children in a primary school in the neighbourhood of the *rue Mouffetard* in Paris and language operates in another way with little Saras near Lake Chad.

Words are wayward things and not always possessed of meaning. New 'ideas' produce new words and new words induce new 'ideas' and, as we can all see if we look around us today, there is a special, asphyxiating web spun for the benefit of those who allow the word to dominate them. We are all of us far too inclined to think or to hope, that what is written and what is spoken must mean something. But languages have a way of dissolving into thin air when we try to make them do something which we do not understand. Even the glorious Greek classical tongue, we may remember, broke down into hollow and

G

resounding blather under the blows of barbarians, casuists and purveyors of Asiatic mysteries.

The heady wine of words plunges us into strange deliriums, and there are not wanting signs in French Black Africa of the sway of verbal monstrosities and the vague shapes of fantastic new religions. The new words are making the new world. Will it be just the sort of world 'white' men would like to see in Africa?

Step into school in Fort-Lamy or, indeed, at any other of the large towns in French Equatorial Africa, Fort-Archambault, Brazzaville or Douala. There will be a class of little black boys with a sprinkling of little pink boys, they will be wrestling with the subtleties of Racine and be proffering comments on *Britannicus*:

> *Non, non Britannicus est mort empoisonné :*
> *Narcisse a fait le coup, vous l'avez ordonné.*

And it may be that the juvenile class will at any rate learn more about Racine than is retained by some Parisians, for I heard a young lady, while M. Jean Marais was being starred at the *Théâtre Français* in this same play, remark "Another bit of British propaganda, I suppose." Quite so.

You may find a schoolmaster discoursing on the Punic Wars; well, after all Carthage was an African town and if the little boys and girls of Chad are going to learn to think in French, why, then, they will just have to know something about the Mediterranean. The French are right, one cannot learn a language without learning what to say as well as how to say it.

It is not true, or it is no longer true, that little Africans are taught to recite: "Our ancestors the Gauls were tall and fair", but you can hear a Fort-Lamy usher explaining Voltaire's *Prière à Dieu* and furthering 'racial' tolerance by observing that 'our ancestors the Gauls' Caesar regarded in much the same way as misguided 'colonials' used once—but of course now never do regard—native Africans.

The first language, the mother-tongue as we say, affects in different ways the acquired language, but much depends on the status of the two tongues. It is one thing being bilingual in Arabic and French and another thing being bilingual in French and Peul. In the latter case there can be no difficulty in deciding which is the *Kultursprache*, the language of culture. The more I see and the longer I live the more I come to regard French (when commanded by an intelligent and cultivated man) as the most explicit of human tongues. In fact so lively, so epigrammatic, so allusive and so subtle is French that it tends to make a dull man appear much less obtuse than he is, while English—rich in terms not so much explicit as implicit—not seldom causes its speaker to seem more stupid than he is. English, to achieve precision and lucidity, must often become graceless, while I am inclined to hold that certain essential vices both in grammar and syntax are more numerous in English than in French.[1]

In fact, one may wonder if French is not altogether too clear and too explicit a language for the purpose of civilizing black African tribesmen. A phrase in French must mean something. Grave and portentous statement. Manifest superiority of English, particularly of the English which is being forged and fabricated by our illiterate and muddle-witted masters. No phrase or sentence must mean anything clear and definite at all.

It is not certain that the little Chadians will think like any sort of little French children, not quite in the same way, but the little Chadians are using a language whose words and phrases will influence them as they use it. We make our language but it makes us much more.

It is not certain that the little Chadians are all going to grow up into loyal—well, loyal what shall we say?—loyal subjects of the French government. Sometimes the indoctrination acts as an emetic especially when the victim is required to accept a complex in which he takes an inferior position. There's many a true word spoken in jest and the French journalist had something who opined that such and such an American Press magnate having been at school in England was naturally very anti-British.

Still, there will be no turning back. What is going on, on a small scale if you will, is something without any real parallel in any other part of Africa outside the French dominions. The change of a culture, the implanting of a civilization.

CIVILIZATION

Of course, that sounds quite impressive until we come to ask ourselves just what a civilization is. 'Civilization' is what the

---

[1] I write more in English than in French, but I am bilingual and not infrequently I am tempted to treat certain subjects in French and not in English.

psychologists call a 'trigger-word' setting off any number of unreasoning and often unreasonable reactions. In fact, 'civilization' is a propaganda-term to which no definition can be attached. We can, however, tell what *a* civilization is. It is a fairly complicated complex and elaborate culture whose bearers (or some of them) know how to read and write. In fact a culture marked, as the saying goes, by the presence of script—doubtless in all senses of the word. A writing does not, of course, have to be practised by all the persons who live in the civilization's area.

The more elaborate a civilization the more layers it contains. It is the fashion in some quarters to lump together, irrespective of education, breeding, training, tradition, aptitudes and brains, all the men and women who share the same sort of passport. Maybe we are moving towards the classless society but we have not got to it yet though we are hardly so far removed from it as are the inhabitants of the blessed lands behind the Iron Curtain.

A civilization, then, is a special form of a culture. What is a culture? We do not in Britain or in America hear so much about culture as civilization. For we are always assailed by phrases shouted or written: 'Civilization is in Danger', 'Western Civilization is at Stake'. We do hear much about *culture* in France (though in the Frenchman's mouth the word may as often mean growing turnips as participating in the feasts of the soul), *Kultur* is often a nonsense-word, while *kulturniy* will, by Soviet Russians and in exact compliance with the Party Line, be applied to a house with that fabulous fitment, an indoors water-closet. In Britain we do have 'cultured pearls', and the other day I was ingenuous enough to imagine that 'cultural hints' might be interesting, but the article was devoted to the cultivation of strawberries in a barrel. As a matter of fact, a 'culture' is any form or pattern of human life as lived in a community.[1]

Still, we must ask where this education programme of the French is likely to lead. The Black Africans are being given something to interest them, something to feed their immense vanity and self-respect. In some parts of Africa there is a real danger that the native Africans may just fade away, for they are bored to death

---

[1] No doubt we shall best steer clear of taking abstractions for concrete things if we drop the words 'civilization' and 'culture' in favour of 'civilization-area' and 'culture-area'.

and their own fabric of life has been rent and torn to tatters. Gone
are the comfort of ceremony, the purge of ritual and the magic
essential for man's existence. The appalling vacuity of so many
pink men's culture lies like a cloak of lead upon its victims. So we
find that the Africans are accessible mostly to the calls of Communism or Nationalism, and this latter even means reaction
against the pink man and revenge for the generations of contempt
the African has had to shoulder. If the West African Nigerians
are today bursting with energy it is because they like to feel that
they are getting rid of the British.

The native Africans are by no means grateful to the French for
schools and schooling. In fact the typical African reaction is to
regard the pink man as so afflicted with uneasy conscience that
he must do something to justify his presence in the black men's
land. The reasonable, spontaneous and entirely human reaction is
not that we fancy, in our muffled masks, is ours. If you save a man
from drowning, then you owe him a present.

Of course, schooling will not for a considerable time touch
more than the fringe of the population, and indeed it is not
desirable that too many should know how to read and write, for
almost anything is preferable to a glut of semi-educated and pretentious proletariat in a poverty-stricken country. As it is, the
literates already tend to display a ludicrous vanity and even
fatuity. With a real desire to learn goes the more potent urge to
acquire accomplishments with a cash value, perhaps, but certainly
with a snob value. A hundred and fifty years ago most men and
women in Britain were quite illiterate. I can remember the time
when the majority of the middle-aged villagers in Devon could
neither read nor write while those who could read were a little
self-conscious in their superiority to their fellows. Then came a
time when mere ability to read was no longer a sign of superiority
though the novelty of the art had hardly worn off. People read
because there were no movies, radio or T.V. The time when vast
fortunes were made out of publishing newspapers. Why trouble to
read nowadays except just as much as is necessary to obtain and
hold down a government job?

For some time to come the educated Chadians will, for the most
part, become school-teachers and therefore members of a privileged
caste rivalling the sons of chiefs. Then will come political ambitions. As we can so often see in France itself there is only one

step from the blackboard to the Cabinet. Already the blessings of parliamentary democracy are being felt in the Chad where in April 1952 the people who had backed (and therefore lost money on) certain defeated candidates at the local elections, accused the government of rigging the returns and then raised an ugly riot. Just democratic growing pains maybe.[1]

There cannot be any turning back in the sense that the French in the Chad cannot listen to the *colons*. They are dead against all schemes for educating the natives and they are full of foreboding, holding, perhaps rightly, that the French government is digging the grave of its own empire.

There are two schools of thought regarding the future, and the two reflect not only, in a measure, political and social prejudices, but also 'racial' ones. It needs an exceptionally subtle and acute observer and one moreover skilled in some anthropological learning, to appreciate the intelligence of, say, a little Chadian. Those qualities of observation, curiosity and imagination which, if we are wise, we shall seize upon in an appraisal of a pink child's possibilities, are qualities we may find difficulty in appreciating in the black child. His language may lead us to believe him more or less observant, curious and imaginative than he is. In fact, in devising an intelligence test we may perhaps come to put to ourselves the salutary question, 'What is intelligence?' Well, the answer is luckily ready by our sides. Intelligence does not exist, any more than whiteness or evil or any of the other abstract terms. We coin or we adopt the word expressing we think, or we hope, a feature common to a number of objects and then we use the word as though it defined an object and we are merrily set upon our way to play the fascinating game of False Premises. No, not 'what is intelligence?' but 'what is an intelligent child?'; the planners and the products of the managerial revolution and the indoctrinators and the handers-out of guidance, direction and information, hate this bump down to earth. 'Intelligence' as inexistent can be cut up and tucked in and made to fit a lovely pattern. Intelligent children are individuals, that is, highly suspect in our world of today. The old, old problem, how to get them bright and obedient.

[1] The Belgians keep their Congo native in a condition of strict subordination, the French have made a certain number of what are not perhaps always very wise political concessions, but nowhere have they taken such a leap in the dark as have the British in West Africa.

Well, in the Chad the search for the intelligent children is rather eased and in this way. The Moslems seem rather less intelligent than the so-called 'fetishist' children. Is this so because of 'race'? Well, most of the so-called 'Arabs' are indistinguishable from the 'fetishists'. Is this because of language? Well, Arabic is a world-language of culture, and Peul, for instance (one of the vernaculars of the Chad), is, let us say, not such. No one could hold, I should think, that because a child spoke Arabic as his native language he was stupider than a child speaking Peul. What can be the reason? Well, not improbably, religion. The religion of the fetishists, all-powerful and magic in the bush, fades in a town and its forms and shapes are so peculiar, so inexpressible in our languages that the sense of witchery and wizardry drops from the children. Not so with little Moslems; they have been moulded to a certain extent by one of the world's great religions, they have acquired a mass of prejudices and prepossessions which are proof against change of scene. Some wise men urge that children should be brought up strictly in the religious and social conventions of the society in which they are born, for thus bright boys will be able to sharpen their wits in discarding the traditions, while the stupider members of the community will continue to give that lip-service and obedience which are essential to all ordered society, more or less. All this may be true, but little Chadians from the bush, as they have few prejudices, may seem more intelligent than they are.

But there are incredible advantages to be gained from a French education. If the darkness of mind be not too crass, if a child be educable, its expression at least will be lucid and coherent when formed by the innate rigour of French judgement.

The two schools of thought about Chadian education are these. Some would set up a bush school in every village, more or less. Others would spend all the money on creating a really first-class secondary school at Fort-Lamy where the sons of chiefs and notables would receive a privileged education. Old school-tie spirit.

Men—and boys—with personal status stand better, so it is urged, the heady wine of learning than do lesser mortals whose sole title to consideration is derived from their education, their achievement and their acts. Most sapient and wise.

There is a sage saying of the Chinese:

"Wealth and birth give everything and take the place of
nothing.

Beauty and ability lead to everything and accomplish
nothing.

Wisdom and virtue deserve everything and aspire to
nothing."

The tiresome bores who endeavour to extort everywhere the
deference they hope is due to them in special conditions, such
fellows are a curse to the harmony of human intercourse, and
that whether they be big business bosses, vice-consuls or politicians. Let us have the people, and especially the women, of
status, self-assured, at ease, well-bred, men and women of the
world; and nothing, as we see so often in the ingenuous imaginings
of historians and commentators, nothing can make up for not
having been *mêlés à de grandes affaires*, for not having taken part in
great business. All deplorably undemocratic and only applicable
of course to Africa.

By the way, I was dining not so long ago with one of the
most famous of French advocates, who is also a notable man of
letters. He was consumed with indignation at a judgement just
handed down by a Parisian court. It was, I think, one of his
juniors who had defended the vendor of a talisman he styled the
*Brahma Porte-Bonheur*, or some such name, and which he did a
thriving trade in Black Africa. No single one of the wizard's
customers complained of the inefficacy of the scapular. The
case had been brought at the instance of missionaries and
military men who were shocked at Africans purchasing
magic.

We may guess what were the real reasons for the suit but its
result was astonishing for France where the law is generally
administered with good sense and human understanding. The
sorcerer got twelve months' imprisonment. As our host remarked,
"The Wars of Religion over again." Well, this sort of thing goes
only for Africa, though the case was brought in Paris. It is difficult
to imagine any wizard getting a year inside for selling amulets in
France. If he were so much as prosecuted, defending counsel
would let fall faintly sacrilegious remarks concerning scapulars,
holy medals of all sorts and kinds.

By the way. In French Equatorial Africa there is a White

Mass and a Black Mass. No, this last is no blasphemous travesty. Just a Mass for Black men only.

"An admirable evasion of whore-master man, to lay his goatish disposition to the charge of a star."

Yes, Fort-Lamy is a jerk-town. Dusty ruts for roads. No water-mains, no gas, nothing approaching the palaces of the Belgian Congo. Here you've two hotels and the Mickey-Bar. However, the Air Hotel is a paradise after the desert. You dine in a large, twilighted room that is almost cool. It is strangely, nostalgically, fitted out to resemble one of those 'regional' restaurants which are factitious enough in Paris but which here is rather moving. Bagpipes hung on the walls, plaster hams dangling from the rafters and a huge fireplace where nothing ever burns save, they say, a Yule-log at Christmas-tide. You are waited on by clean black boys in white. The whole hotel is in working order.

For dinner you will, of course, get *capitaines*, the succulent fish from the Shari. Maybe you become a little tired of them in the long run but even if you are from Britain and have sworn never to look a fish in the eye for the whole time you were abroad, any fresh food after the Sahara is appetizing.

You get *croissants* with your breakfast coffee. All your dirty linen—and you'll have plenty of it—is washed daily. You will be served watercress salad for there is a bed in the garden and it is watered by the only fountain, so it is said, in all the Chad province. You have a view over the pelicans and marabout storks flapping and flopping over the dark-red Shari's banks. Maybe, you will not feel much inclined to do anything else but just sit and doze most of the time. It will be 118° or 120° in the shade; in that shade you are sitting in. . . . It is not surprising that most hotel-keepers out here are, like a good many other unsettled settlers, possessed with one dominating desire—to make a pile as quickly as may be and to get out from an inhospitable and unfavoured land.

You will creep carefully under your mosquito-net, the female anopheles, poor dear, must have nice, warm blood in order to ripen her eggs. All so natural but we swat her mercilessly. Kindness to animals? Kindness to mammals and not to all of them, no not at all. Through the window the gurgle of Black Africa in the unfinished streets that never will be finished.

Men familiar to me from my childhood and my father's black South African servants; yes, I know they are really two distinct sorts of Africans, Kaffirs and these Saras and 'Arabs' of the Chad, but the colour and the look are much the same.

In my early years I was accustomed to seeing negroes around me, men I thought much more beautiful than the people I saw in the streets, no blotches, no red noses, no dirty shaves, no rotten teeth. My Africans were kind and understanding, they held, for me at any rate, secrets of good-humoured wisdom. A legendary and incredible England before the British Way of Life had been invented.

Whenever I am in Africa I realize that I have a private Africa of my own. *L'Afrique*, as a popular writer has put it, *n'existe pas*. Quite so. My Africa is a legacy from childhood and it is a legacy from a part of Africa I have never visited, at least in days that I can remember. Much talk of Africa filled my childhood's abodes from which an earlier Caribbean legend had almost faded. There was one of our forbears in the early 18th century who did quite well for himself in privateering, slave-trading and other activities usually veiled in discreet euphemisms.

One of my great-grandmothers had been about the last to bring direct news from the good old days of plantations and sugar-wealth. She was born in the Isles and spoke French as her first language but she died young and her story came to me, of course, at second- or third-hand.

There was also an Indian tent, rather that than a habitation. The old British-Indian legend is impossible to explain to those whose contacts with India and Indian fable go back only to two generations ago. India was never of course a *colonie de peuplement*, a land where Europeans settled and became acclimatized. You might have plenty of soldiers and administrators among your kindred, you might have heard of East India Company collectors who left large dusky families fairly well provided for, but India in my infancy was resolved into old men's pipe-dreams, secret codes and vocabularies, affected regrets, real longings after prestige and deference. All set against a background of violent colour, movement and lavish, easy-going independence. A few wild tales would stick in one's memory. Old Fred who was out one or two lakhs of rupees in his accounts and when called upon for an explanation, just let fall, 'I wasn't bred to be a damned bookkeeper'. He was allowed to send in his papers and no more questions asked. How different from today when any poor devil of a temporary-commission officer is court-martialled if he has sent a £10 cheque bouncing. Stories of harems . . . all very improbable and exciting, and still more improbable it struck me when, later on, I visited the depressing India of this century. But India was no one's home, only a scene, a theatre.

As the faint, far-off echoes of West and East Indies receded, anchorages in the West Country, in Scotland and in our Ireland were loosened; out of a world of soldiers, sailors and squires in the middle years of the last century some of our family took the route to South Africa where, later on, blazed up the fabulous adventure of the gold-mines. It was in a haze of revolutionary discovery that my own particular Africa floated.

It seems that two men bearing the names of Pigg and Button[1] were the first to find gold in South Africa; I have, indeed, seen a photograph of their improvised crushing-machine. It was a large boulder balanced upon a rock. However, the first discoveries of the Witwatersrand, were made by connections of ours. They were the men who, all unwittingly, set in motion the vast machine that flooded the world with new gold and changed the economy of the earth as effectively as did the Spaniards with the wealth of the Americas.

In a complex which I know now to have been one of boundless ambitions and hopes, my Africa took shape and it marked my early years; though, later on, all was changed and I was brought under the clarifying influence of France, it may be true that *on ne se guérit jamais de son enfance.*

But I am sure that all the talk, descriptions and the strange, vague figures of adventurers would never alone have sufficed to make anything as vivid and real as my own special Africa. Without a dominating visual image that a child can subconsciously weld into a mythical world, the verbal memories would have faded as do the commonplace reminiscences of stables, paddocks, horses, pets, grooms, governess-carts, young friends whose dim figures we need to peer very hard indeed to discern.

[1] As a matter of fact, the first mining company in the Transvaal was one started in August 1866, and although Button formed a company late in 1874 it would seem that the first real gold-mining concern was a modest one named the 'Nil Desperandum Co-operative Quartz Company' of which my grandfather (who had also formed the 1866 company) was the chairman.

My visual image was formed in my father's smoking-room, of vast proportions it seemed to me though doubtless it was not very large. However, it was spacious enough for me who could with difficulty manage to dab and touch strange shapes upon the walls. It is hard for visitors to imagine now what the veld was like only two or three generations ago; it swarmed with game of all sorts and their spoils hung heavy around me. On occasion I was lifted up to scratch the rhinoceros's head and to caress the elephant's tusks. Elephants, I learned somehow or other, will pick you up in their trunks and bash you against a tree-trunk until you scream no more. For the rest the room was filled with what then were dubbed 'curios' but which nowadays would be named pompously enough 'ethnographical specimens', but no one in those days, at least in the traditional circle of my relations, had ever heard so pretentious a phrase. The things were 'native curios' or 'hunting trophies' and that was that; the former were quaint and the latter were interesting, and that was that.

Some of these things I can see quite clearly now—assegais, shields long and oval plastered with dark strips like hyphen-marks, wooden utensils with designs, karosses of furs, hide and skin rugs on the floor; things from the southern parts, then some objects from farther north, masks and the like. For me, all these were living in a strange world which I knew quite well. The alien and familiar quality of dreams.

An encaustic bowl adorned with dancing figures, tall, elon-gated men so like those on the images of eastern Spain or on Saharan and southern African rock-faces, men striding, running and jumping in lithe ease. I have the bowl still. It just holds an ostrich egg, it is not a prehistoric ostrich egg, it has the rugous, pitted surface of the south and not the smooth shell of the north, but to this day if I look at this egg and bowl, I have before my eyes the childish vision of a gigantic black man sitting down to his breakfast of boiled ostrich egg and cracking the shell with the bowl's ladle.

This assemblage was called Fidafote—by me, that is Feed Yourself. Such things make the real fabric of our lives.

But there is something more. It may be significant, I do not know. Astrologers, horoscopists, wise men and candid friends agree to find in this story evidence and proof, were any needed, of anarchistic temperament and of inability to distinguish between

right and wrong. I was conceived in winter and born also in
winter, a few days after my mother landed in Europe from Africa.
Most unpropitious, so I am told.

## THE CRUEL HARMATTAN'S LASH

Chad lies at the line where the palm-tree fades away and also
a little above the yellow-fever belt, though you have your choice
of almost all other diseases. There is malaria everywhere and a
host of other ills awaits the traveller; they range from amoebic
dysentery to cerebro-spinal meningitis. Also, wandering about
on foot is to be deprecated. Between nine in the morning and
six at night you have always a chance of being laid out with
sunstroke. Cars are not so easy to come by in the Chad but if
by truck, command-car or any other vehicle with strong springs
and axles we range the savanna there is a vision of the Sahara that
has rolled back, the Sahara of hunters and pastoral herdsmen.

Utterly African and unimaginable elsewhere. The tan plain,
retted and dry, the scattered trees, all spiky branches, insignificant
leaves, stumps. At a well-head naked men and animals waiting
patiently, speckled oxen, tough and muscular, dark wide-horned
cows as on the Written Rocks, small, scraggy camels, heavy-eyed
and resigned, no margin, no surplus, nothing to spare. Africa;
no luxury. Black buffaloes under the scanty shade of barbed
twigs. Rather like a circus. It must be the tan underfoot.

Farther afield, the ceremonious ostriches, gazelles that spy
you from afar. Scent and sharp perfume in the air; your car may
slice the wild peppermint.

Turn round and head towards the city. Clumps of smiling
black men proffering ostrich eggs, some adorned and talismanic,
calabashes, plates and platters of spiced meats. Food. There is
always something moving about food hawked by the roadside.
One is reminded of the more pathetic appeals of half-starved
Spanish children in hard times, or the queer comestibles pushed
upon one in the Balkans. And when the women sit and hold out
food it is as though they were reduced to selling the family's meal
—but no, no one is starving here, there is even modest plenty, in
the sense that it is cheap to eat, cheap even for those who earn a
living in this black man's Africa.

That is to say some food is cheap. Meat—zebu meat—pretty
tough but quite edible; butter, milk and cream are abundant.

But vegetables are priceless, a cabbage is worth five or six shillings, maybe more. The commonest things from our northern cottage gardens—carrots, leeks or potatoes—are, in the Chad, luxury articles for rich men only.

The full fauna of the old Sahara, the fauna pictured upon the Tassili rocks, lies farther to the south-east, round about Fort-Archambault where the climate is damper—you are moving towards the tropical rain forest and the Congo. It is near Fort-Archambault that live the *négresses à plateau* who insert plates into upper and lower lips so that their appearance recalls that of a hippopotamus, the story says. There are matter-of-fact explanations that the hideous custom was adopted in order to scare off slave-traders, but this is too rational, we have here something of totems and a hippopotamus cult maybe.

It seems that to the south-east of Lake Chad are buried cities of the ancient Sao where are found earthenware statues and statuettes. The Black Art of Africa. But these things lie in a land hard to face. In the rains, plagued with vile insects. In the dry season the cruel Harmattan east wind laden with sand blows incessantly for weeks on end, desiccating the earth and draining all the liquids of one's body.

## The Sum of Africa

A sky hot turquoise. A lambent firmament of azure streaked yellow. A whole universe darkening into amber. The lustre slips off. In black night you are heading northwards. We must fly high; still the plane starts and shudders. No sleep.

The Sum of Africa. This is the fossil third, the Sahara, for ever closed to pink men and their females and offspring, the great desert where no man can move about in the sunshine for half the daylight hours in half the year. The Sum of Africa? What of the rest? An uneasy feeling that nearly everything we hear about it is false or at least misleading. How many inhabitants are there? No one knows. In 1939 we were told 'about 151,000,000'; now it's 'just under 200,000,000'. One or the other or both untrue.

Mr. Pirow, a former Cabinet Minister of the Union, says that two-thirds of Africa is "climatically unfit for white men though Africans can live there". He is certainly not far from the mark. One third of the continent arid, waterless desert that is rather spreading than shrinking. Indeed, it is hardly too much to say that the whole

Continent is drying up. The soil is fertile only in rather rare patches; the African earth generally needs much put into it before it will yield bountiful crops; moreover, when all is said and done, it is doubtful if 10% of the surface is arable, though it is thought that the upper reaches of the two Niles are among the most fertile areas on this earth. Stock-raising could, doubtless, be much increased, but where is the labour to come from? As has been well noted "Leisure occupies a high place in the African scale of preference." Africa is certainly a store-house of immensely valuable minerals whose exploitation and export will be for long, it would seem, the main sources of African riches. The dazzling boom in the Belgian Congo, however, is due, first and foremost to uranium, the demand for which may not keep up always at present rates. Though the untapped hydraulic resources appear to be immense there is little fuel in Africa and, of course, a crippling shortage of labour for any large-scale 'development' in the industrial sense. Africa is not going to be, for a very long time, a source of cheap food or an exciting and expanding market for manufactured goods on the heroic scale.

There are few signs that Africa is getting more friendly and Africans more open-hearted towards pink men who, anyway, if they would settle in, must keep more or less to the eastern zone from Abyssinia to the Union. Not only cannot the pink men thrive in the tropics but even in temperate Africa many 'white' men tend to sink in the social and economic scales. It is estimated that 30% of the non-Africans in the Union of South Africa fall into the category contemptuously spurned by the Afrikaners as *wit Kaffirs*.

The African scene, as a whole, whether in the harsh savanna of, say, the Chad province, or in the lush, grey tropics, is somehow hostile. Africa is ominous; man an intruder. Strangely enough, it is—leaving out of consideration the un-African North-West—rather in the Sahara than elsewhere that the traveller feels at home—or such is my own sensation. No, the magic of Africa is certainly Black Magic.

And so on through the night. . . . It would be edifying if we could get a cool, factual survey of African resources as they now appear, and not woolly references to 'boundless wealth' and 'vast potential markets'. Let us beware of muddled musings leading to the conviction that because we are being squeezed out of Asia, because German and Japanese competition are alarming, because American and dollar markets are tough, therefore Africa must offer all we want and then some. . . .

A sweep through the cold blue-grey twilight of dawn, but before we have time to bump over the sands to Ghadames, the whole world is glowing and blazing.


## THE MEMNON OF GHADAMES

*Où vont les sables à leur chant s'en vont les Princes de l'exil*
*Où furent les voiles haut tendues s'en va l'épave plus soyeuse qu'un songe de luthier.*
*Où furent les grandes actions de guerre déjà blanchit la mâchoire d'âne.*
*Et la mer à la ronde roule son bruit de crâne sur les grèves,*
*Et que toutes choses au monde lui soient vaines, c'est ce qu'un soir, au bord du monde nous contèrent*
*Les milices du vent dans les sables d'exil.*

*Saint-John Perse.*


In the Greek legend Memnon, King of the Aethiopians, was the son of Eos, the Dawn, and of Tithonus whom Zeus made immortal. Memnon was as beautiful as his father had been and he was black; black and beautiful. Our Memnon at Ghadames gazes out over his domains of the Scorched Faces, the Black Ones, and like his fabled counterpart at Thebes he is a column but one on which he rather stands than sits.

It is quite early. The sun is very warm and, as so often in the desert, one has the impression of being high up, and this perhaps because elsewhere such limpid air is met with only on mountains. Here we are not more than eleven hundred feet above sea-level. The air is so dry that even when you get 110° in the shade you hardly feel so exhausted as in the clammy heat of the coast or the tropics where your thermometer may not register more than 90° or so.[1]

We are walking on tracks from the gates of Ghadames—or are there any tracks? A fairly level expanse of colourless grit sprinkled

---

[1] The highest shade temperature ever recorded anywhere on earth was in Aziziyah (not more than an hour by car south of Tripoli) on 13th September, 1922. The thermometer marked 136° Fahr. in the shade.

"The effect is that of an edifice set upon an artificial hill" *p. 143*

"The camels stroll and nibble as they please."    p. 152

with myriads of murderous pebbles. No growth at all. The palms stop dead at the walls, or the walls enclose the last palms.

## THE LORDS OF THE DESERT

Here and there are the dry beehive huts thatched with palm. The homes of the Ghadames Tuareg. It is a sure sign of dire poverty when nomads accept the constraint of sedentary ways. Sitting near their huts are a few Targuis—Tuareg women—clad in dark indigo.

All over the Sahara the Tuareg are changing fast, the old Lords of the Desert have seen better days. The fact is that the Tuareg have been absurdly romanticized. It is true that the fine, open-air, gentlemanly life of rapine, plunder, murder and robbery did form an aristocracy. The Tuareg bred themselves into a lazy, stupid, elegant, distinguished, presumptuous lot, often handsome, but they were specialized and find it hard to adapt themselves to a humdrum, middle-class existence of servitude. The Veiled Marauders of the Sahara must either fade away or breed themselves into something different from what they were. Unfortunately it is always more agreeable to fit ourselves for luxury than for penury, and likewise, it seems that human groups, once they have bred themselves into a special physique for a certain way of life, find it difficult, sometimes impossible, to turn round and trudge back.

The social and political system of the Tuareg is everywhere in decay though by no means all the tribes are as crestfallen as the dwellers on the way to the Memnon of Ghadames.

It is little wonder that their dances are solemn and baleful. There is always hope, maybe under the beneficent rule of His Majesty King Idris of Libya, a more easy-going administration may spread over these wastes and opportunities for adventurous fellows will become apparent, but then, alas, probably the wretched Tuareg will have adapted themselves to whatever 'pattern of life' or 'way of living' is fashionable, for the Veiled Men are now soldiers, cameleers and improvised agriculturalists. Their character is changing with their circumstances.[1]

---

[1] The *moudir touareg* or chief of the Ghadames Tuaregs lives in a stone house outside the town and on the way to the Statues. These sedentary Tuareg are mostly of the Iforha tribe and rather markedly different from the inhabitants of the Hoggar far to the south-west. Among the Tuareg there are, or were, noble tribes, plebeian tribes and slaves. Fables have been woven around the figure of the Hoggar *amenokal* or 'king', but in reality the political system of the Tuareg was a pleasing anarchy.

H

There is hardly any wind; there is always some wind in the desert but this morning there is nothing more than a breeze, a warm breeze, one raising no sand. In the distance, how far off it would be difficult to say since the desert air fools even experienced wayfarers, rise two columns, startling monuments in the desert. From afar the pillars, blotched with shadow and therefore obviously corrugated, may remind you of Egyptian Memnons seen reflected in an elongating mirror.

In a vast region where you come across no sculpture but that fashioned by the gritty winds and the weather, such man-made monuments are bemusing. The Ghadames Memnons are of the colour of the desert, that is to say, they change with every shift of light and even from a distance they are for ever altering their contours.

Perhaps you are three miles from the oasis, far enough, in any case, to be seized with the sublime indifference of the desert. You are stripped of frills and trappings, you feel that nothing is important but survival. Just a twist, a quirk and the silly complexity of our lives is pushed away. The whole end of Man? Why, just to find some shade, some water, even some food and to go on living at least until the night falls.

The columns get no nearer, the going is hard, maybe you have exaggerated a full three miles? Well, you have been walking for an hour but the walls, colour of clotted blood, and the dull palms do not seem to be far off.

At last you get to the pillars; they rise up it maybe thirty feet or more and their upper parts were certainly once carved into the semblance of human figures, or so it seems, but the sand-laden blasts, the weatherings of countless centuries, have removed all style and the carvings belong to that undefinable category of dream-objects that are several things at once. In fact, they are four-dimensional, your time-factor here is what you will. Are these monuments Roman, or even Byzantine, or a legacy from the vague Garamantes?

We shall probably not go far wrong if we think of the Sahara as untraversed and almost uninhabited during the millenia that elapsed between the establishment of the present desert conditions and the introduction of the camel. Doubtless the Sahara had been, in part, colonized by negroes; we can see them on the painted rocks, and it is possible that they, like the game and beasts, split into two parts one moving ever farther north and the other ever farther south, but there does not seem to be much evidence for negroes in the north until after the camel-caravans began to cross the wastes. It is true that Herodotus tells a tale of the Libyan Nasamones, youths who fared over the sands to the Land of the Aethiopians, that is of Black Men and river-horses.

Camels became common in North Africa in the reign of Septimius Severus (that is from A.D. 193 to 211), the Emperor who was born in Libya, died in York and ruled an empire stretching from Scotland to the Fezzan. It was only after the introduction of the camel that the Sahara was invaded by 'whites' from the north; the Roman Sahara was 'Aethiopian', the Berber-speaking camel-nomads were the real *barbari* who enlarged if they did not create most of the famed oases. The great rush to the desert was, no doubt, caused by Sidi Oqba's 'Conquest of Africa' in the 7th century, but even more marked was the flight to the south before the devastating onrush of the savage Beni Hilal Arab tribes who laid waste north-west Africa in the 11th century.

We know that in 19 B.C. Cornelius Balbus Minor[1] subjugated the realm of the Garamantes, that is, roughly, the south-western Fezzan. The imperial troops came southwards from the Tripolitan coast. There is mention in the Roman chronicles of an *Agisamba Regio* possibly the Air, uplands that are a continuation eastward of the Hoggar central Saharan highlands, but there is no reason to think that the Romans explored or even reached the *Agisamba Regio*. It may be that detachments from the forces of Septimius Flaccus (in A.D. 70) or from those of Iulius Maternus (in A.D. 86) may have pushed farther south than the limits of the Garamantes realm, but there is no evidence for such venturesome excursions, and, then again, we do not know what are the limits of the Garamantes domain, if, indeed, it had any and was not, for the most part, a vague overlordship.

The Garamantes were, it seems, a people of Berber speech, and either the direct ancestors of or closely related to the Tuareg. The Garamantes' name is preserved in the oasis town of Jerma or Garama in the Fezzan on the track from Ghat and Serdeles to Sebha. 'Garama' figures on Behaim's marvellously inaccurate Nuremberg Globe of 1492. The desert realm may have been

[1] His home-town was Cadiz and he was of a family of 'new Romans' from the 'colonies'. It is possible that the Gaditan Balbi were of Punic descent.

constituted before the 5th century B.C., and it was a military one
as we have seen from the war-chariots adorning the Tassili rocks.
We may conclude that the Sahara was less desiccated than
today for there were no camels in Africa as early as two thousand
five hundred years ago.

Roman dominion was held from north to south, and so, indeed,
is that of the French, but they have to contend with more formidable opposition than faced the Latins. Cutting right across the
north-south lines runs the west-east line of Islam intersecting all
the routes from Europe to Black Africa.

Ghadames and Ghat and other strong-points in the Fezzan
were for centuries held by Roman garrisons, but the Vandal
invasions disrupted the imperial organization and the Byzantine
hold upon the oases of the Fezzan must have been slight, though
it is probable that many, if not most, of the desert men were
nominal Christians for we read that in A.D. 666—fateful number—
when the Moslem conquerors swept down, they quickly effaced
all traces of the Levantine-Roman religion which had been so
profoundly influenced by Africans.

We are sometimes told that the Romans left an indelible
impress wherever they established themselves, that Germany is
barbarous because never Roman, and many other fond fancies.
Well, Ghadames was a Roman town much longer than London
was and the Fezzan was a Roman province for long years after
the imperial administration quit the shores of Britain. The
Romanized Gauls imposed their Low Latin upon their Germanic
conquerors, the Britons accepted the Germanic tongue of their
victors. You may search in Ghadames for evidence of Roman
rule and civilization. Even the Memnon is not clearly Latin.
There is one Christian Roman or Byzantine lamp found at
Ghadames and now in a French museum.

After the veil of the Faith falls upon the Fezzan and its drying
earth, the history of these wastes is obscure. They were country
over which the caravans fared; so effective did the cross-Saharan
traffic become that in the 13th century the Fezzan was more or
less subject to the sovereigns of Kanem in Bornu south near Lake
Chad. The Saharan oases were taking on a black tinge and the
political history of the desert had become the economic history
of its slave-trade.

There was always movement from east to west and from west

to east as well as from the Mediterranean to the Sudan. The
founders of the short-lived but mighty Almoravide dynasty of
Moroccan and Spanish sovereigns emerged from the Sahara, and
in the 16th century a Moroccan sheikh, founded in the Fezzan the
Beni Mohammed dynasty, styled himself Sultan and established
his capital at Murzuk where the Blue Sultans held sway for long,
lords of a mercantile realm battening on rapine and pillage. In
those days Ghadames was a flourishing commercial free-town.

The Beni Mohammed lasted until 1811 when the last of them
was killed during a punitive expedition sent out by the last
sovereign of the autonomous Caramanli dynasty of Tripoli. There
was getting to be too much wastage by the way, the exaction of
the Beni Mohammed increased with time and habit, profits
showed a falling-off in the merchant-venturers' counting-houses
of northern Libya. The treacherous natives of the Fezzan must
be punished and good faith re-established. A story faintly familiar.

And then, naturally, the biter bit, no sooner had the Caramanli
murdered off the Beni Mohammed than the Turks came back to
Libya and claimed their rights, or at least, took over the country.

Any pattern in history? Garamantes, Romans, Byzantines,
Bornu, Beni Mohammed, Turks? Yes, maybe the pattern of
climate and means of transport. Tell me what the climate and the
gadgets will be and I will look ahead; let us call it that but we
mean prophesy, though it is so much better form to use a metaphor, turn space into time, and equate staring down a road—
that is a feasible if boring occupation—with foretelling what will
happen—that is to say putting over an irrational concept.

The dark, colourless walls of Ghadames are there as a land-
mark. What may be a straight line to them leads past a graveyard,
low-walled with dry-courses of masonry and enclosing some
plastered monuments, some tombs with Arabic inscriptions. Most
of the sepultures, however, are of antique Saharan type; just a
raised border of sharp pebbles, at the head a jagged rock. Near
Ghat is such a graveyard, but it is unwalled and slopes down a
declivity dotted with cairns.

The Tombs of the Garamantes, they say.

It may be nearly noon, the silence is absolute, it is not merely
there is no sound perceptible, but noise is inconceivable. The air,
you felt, would not transmit sound. Supersonic, infrasonic.

No living thing is visible, not even any of the pale-coloured, jumping, running beasts proper to the wilderness. The ground heat burns through your sandals. But this is not the summer when gazelles cannot bear their hoofs upon the Saharan sands at mid-day.

## THE MOTHER OF JACKALS

While we were on the other side of the desert the Eve of Doubt had passed. When the slim sickle of the moon is sought in the sky and not always found, that is the Eve of Doubt; it may be that the Great Fast does not begin until the morrow. This year Ramadan[1] fell in June and the weather, even far in the Tunisian South, was not as hot as it gets later on in the summer. It is when the fasting month is in July or August that the precepts of the Faith become irksome to obey; still it is marvellous to observe how much outward compliance is general. Even in lands outside the House of Islam there will be acceptance of the fast. A year or two ago I saw two very smart and modern-style North Africans in the great saloon of the Mosque's bath in Paris. One of them made to scoop up the bowl from the central fountain—and indeed the temptation to drink when you come out of a Turkish Bath is overwhelming—but the other young Moslem remonstrated 'Abstain', and the venturesome fellow let fall the cool and refreshing draught.

A neat landing on the pebbly strip at Foum Tatahouine and there is a car driven by Hilali and containing Monsieur Macrosène.

Foum Tatahouine is just a modern village around a military post, the airfield is a secondary military base, but the local café seemed inviting after a sleepless night; hot bread and coffee and the radio blaring away to relaxed and self-possessed Tunisians more easy in their attitudes than peoples farther west.

We could drive from Foum Tatahouine over the Djebel Ksour—the Mountain of the Castles—and reach Kebili that way, but the going is hard. Though the track ends at Goumerassen this side, there is a road through *Ksar-el-Hallouf*—The Castle of the

[1] Ramadan means 'excess of heat', i.e. more or less *Thermidor*, for when the Arabs' months were renamed Ramadan fell in mid-summer. Of course, as the Moslem calendar is lunar the months slip right round the year. The Ramadan fast is prescribed in the Koran itself and is one of the main acts of Islam. By the way, the oft-repeated story that the nights of Ramadan begin when a white thread cannot be distinguished from a black one is not true. The word (*khait*) used in the Koran means not a 'thread' but a streak of light.

Wild Boar—on the eastern slopes of the range and on through
Bir Soltane and Bordj Zoumit, but the last twenty miles or so
before you get to Kebili are just sandy track. In March 1952, when
the exiled Tunisian ministers were at Kebili, the American
reporters announced that there are only two roads linking it with
the outer world; as a matter of fact there are no less than five paths
leading away from that dying oasis, but the mistake was pardon-
able; you cannot see the roads until you are on them and by no
means always then.[1]

The Mountain of the Castles has no fortresses made by human
hands; they are strongholds cut through countless ages by wind
and weather. They stretch from Matmata in the north, through a
wide arc and right down to the Djebel Oum-ed-Diab (that is the
Mount of the Mother of Jackals) past which you fly on your way
north from Ghadames to Foum Tatahouine or Djerba. Just
south of the Mother of Jackals are the ruins known as Briga
Kriba where the Romans had an outpost on the desert way to
the Fezzan.

The Ksour range deploys strange summits, castellated heights,
bewildering panoramas of natural buildings for ever changing
form with shifting light.

## The Other Side of the Mountain

> *Même si vous ne*
> *le voyez d'un*
> *bon œil*
> *le pays n'est*
> *pas laid*
> *c'est votre œil*
> *qui*
> *peut-être est mauvais.*[2]

Ahead, the strange rock-village, Douirat, in a prohibited area but
not infested with brigands or the home of secret weapons. We
must get special passes. Splendid. No other visitors whatsoever.

The road is a band scraped free of the grey grass tussocks
blotching the plain up to the line of curious hills, stripped and

---

[1] It was on the western side of the Ksour Mountains that Leclerc's men swung
round on their way to Gabès and northern Tunisia in 1943.
[2] Jacques Prévert.

ribbed with strata-lines. Gigantic saws showing blunted teeth. Two colour schemes. From the yellow ochre of the soil to the pale buff of the sky and from the sage of the grass to the dark green of a palm-clump. Incredibly arid. The sky veiled and reflecting a changing luminosity. The desert has bones, a skeleton, but no flesh, no life save that lent by play of light.

Maybe one is either developed by the desert or it fills one with horror; maybe, also, one is first developed and then filled with horror. A subjective place.

Here they come. Flap, flip, flop, swaying easily. The closely-veiled figures upright, faceless, dead bodies in some fabled funeral procession and jolting now to the left, now to the right as the camels plod, flip, flap, flop. *Méharistes*, the Camel Corps, Tuareg far from their homes in Air, or Hoggar, or Tassili.[1]

We begin to move upwards as the hills close in upon us, we are in a huge cleft, a blunt valley on one side and ahead of us the Rock of Douirat pitted with holes. We halt where the track ends. Below us is an arid dale of crumbling arches and dilapidated masonry. The general appearance, so common hereabouts, that either it has got much drier fairly recently or that men have become discouraged and no longer make the efforts they once did.

Beside is the beginning, or the end, of the village street. The path leads on, rises, sweeps round the head of the valley and the mass of the village which is the tall hill. A small blue girl struggles with her donkey, the beast is cunning and runs in circles; out from the rocks strides the child's mother and takes the girl under one arm and the ass under the other. Hurrying down from the peak is the honorary gendarme. His position, he says, is one of trust and he has nothing to do, the people of Douirat are law-abiding; they are also hospitable and as they have more houses than families they gladly put you up for the night or for as many nights as you will, though it is best to bring one's food with one; things are so nicely calculated in these parts that even one extra mouth to feed may upset all the economy of the village. After

[1] The camel's normal speed is not more than two miles an hour, and though the finest *méharis* (riding camels) can jog along at about three miles an hour they cannot keep this up for more than a day or two. Trotting fatigues camels very much indeed and though they can be forced into a trot, they may drop dead if worked too hard. Much rubbish is written on camels and their exploits. The credulous Kinglake thought that a 'dromedary' (i.e. swift riding-camel) could do from 10 to 12 miles an hour and keep up this pace for three days and three nights without rest.

supper with the gendarme, but at which we were hosts, each of us turned into his cave. When I staggered up from my hard couch and looked out there was the amphitheatre of hills more rose than yellow standing against a sky faint mauve.

Hilali is already about, an elegant figure in blue uniform and low, soft Tunisian fez with full blue-black tassel flopping on his back. He wears his *chéchia* pushed well back so as to reveal a white lock barring his wavy black hair.

"This seems a bad country."

"Depends what you mean by bad; the people manage just to get by, the population's not growing . . ."

"I mean I don't think Douirat is the place for me, would not be so good for my health as Salammbô, but they tell me there are groves and olives and many good things on the other side of the mountain."

On the Other Side of the Mountain. I would say that when you get there you find yourself in heartless rock and rubble stretching to the waste of sands.[1] Monsieur Macrosène gives us good morning and we tell him the tale. He seems pensive and then blurts out:

"Europe doesn't interest me."

We express no wonder at this fine, independent judgement.

"When I retire I shall settle in Africa."

"In Tunisia, of course, though Morocco's the real place if you want to have some excitement and possibly pick up some spare change."

His eyes became a little filmy; talking himself into a dream:

"No, no, not Tunisia, it's expendable, wouldn't be defended in case of war. . . . I'm thinking of Algeria, somewhere in the South, perhaps . . . no, I've never been in Algeria, but I've heard. . . . The Other Side of the Mountain."


DJERBA OF THE LOTOS-EATERS

Monsieur Macrosène and I have been on a visit, we walked out into the country, through sandy highways bordered with

[1] There are camel-tracks only from Douirat through Ksar Rhilane to Bir el Hadj Brahim though thence, across the Nefzaoua country, to Douz and Djemma and Kebili there is a road but it is getting yearly worse and worse. Fifteen years ago I drove south as far as Douz but they told me at Kebili in 1951 that it was hardly possible to push and coax a car along through to Douz nowadays. The sands are creeping and choking the land.

hedges of sand, past ancient trees, olives and carobs, and tilled fields brown under the early summer sun. We had passed an hour with a portly Tunisian in a strange house; it was large, isolated and imposing, a country mansion in fact, white and luminous, deserted halls, a large courtyard of elegant arcades, a tower from whose roof you can see all over the expanse of shallow seas dotted with figures of the ground-fishers pushing through the water a mile and more from the shore. A dead palace which you may, if you will, hire; since the master resides not here but a thousand yards away in a house of cupolas that he says has been in his family for five hundred years.

As it was Ramadan we did not even get a cup of coffee. Monsieur Macrosène was non-committal in the face of the portly Tunisians' protestations of friendship for France and we strolled out into the dusk before I had troubled to guess why we had come to see him, though his park, his courts and his roof-walks were pleasing enough.

We ramble back towards Houmt Souk in the cool mauve twilight and the listless frustration of eve in Ramadan.

"Just wanted to show you one of the Djerban country-places. Of course, the old chap was angling for a recommendation, he's out for some government job, he'll not get it, at least as long as we're in Tunisia. Maybe he was not like some others who couldn't collaborate in Djerba as the enemy didn't occupy the island, but moved to the mainland and operated there. After all, were they working for the enemy? For their country's enemies? Perhaps not. . . . In any case you couldn't call our friend for or against us, he's just indifferent, and that is more than can be said of most of them. Maybe he'll have trouble as pro-French if we ever have to get out of Tunisia."

Monsieur Macrosène thinks I have let him down. He asked me in Tunis to see if I could not pick up one of these small Berettas, a very nice, handy little rod they sell for about £E1 down in Kufra,[1] but I did not get to Kufra, neither did I find any Berettas for £E1 or more, anywhere that I stopped at in the Sahara. Certainly one pound Egyptian is not much to pay for such a useful and ladylike weapon.

[1] Kufra in south-eastern Libya is a centre of clandestine arms traffic, one can still pick up German, British, American and Italian stuff there and at knock-down prices. One of King Idris's brothers is the governor of the oasis. The Berettas, Italian made, are much sought after.

Only the Djerban Jews are lively. We meet a few shuffling back to their villages of Hara Kbira or Hara Srira, but not a few live in Houmt Souk, the capital of the island. Twenty years ago these Djerban Jews, although keeping up fairly close contacts with their co-religionists in Tripolitania, had hardly changed for centuries.

Things are different now; the Jews of Djerba are packing up. Many have already emigrated, soon there may be none left, in fact they are following the example of the Jews in Libya and in other Moslem countries.[1] We may read the signs thus. Libya is not going to be a good place for Jews, moreover that the Tunisian Jews consider that autonomy, or independence, is more likely to come to Tunisia before it does to Morocco or Algeria. The fact is that the Jews, always well informed of the news before it exists, realize that the nationalistic wind blowing through the House of Islam bodes them no good at all. Unquestionably the reasoning is sound. Libya, a sovereign State, more or less under foreign surveillance, will not be able to indulge in Jew-baiting for some time, but there are many ways of making people feel that they are not wanted. Determined as the French may be to keep their foothold in Tunisia, a large measure of Home Rule would appear to be inevitable; moreover, Tunisia has not quite the same strategic importance for the Western Allies as has, say, Morocco.

As large-scale emigration to the United States is not possible, the Chosen People of the Moslem lands around the Mediterranean and the Red Sea are flocking to Israel. Yemen and Iraq, for instance, will soon have no more Jews. The Djerban Jews, artificers, artizans and in some cases peasants, who get to Palestine will want to stay there, but for the more sophisticated an Israeli passport is a precious possession enabling a man to travel where he will. Not all the prosperous Israelis one runs across in smart Paris hotels spend much time in Palestine. Quick change is the order of the day and that young man over there crouching on his jeweller's bench in Houmt Souk may possibly, not so many years hence, be roaring his Cadillac down the Champs-Elysées; if you crane your neck you may be just in time to spot the Manhattan number-plate.

But though the Djerban Jews have had no trouble for many

[1] Most of the Libyan Jews have got out, although there remain several hundred thousand Jews in Morocco and Algeria.

centuries with their Moslem neighbours (who are for the most part members of an unorthodox sect and so rather dwellers in glass houses), there is always an undercurrent in Islam and it is one of uncompromising hostility to the Jews; this is not a prejudice excited only by social and economic causes; Holy Writ itself confirms the attitude and is full of denunciations of Jews' errors and faults.

## BLUE CATS

There are one or two villas set back from the soft, sandy streets lined with tall trees:

"That's a remarkable house, just a touch of gay fantasy here and there. Not so long ago it was an ordinary Djerban villa, it's now owned by one of your fellow-countrymen. He's got exquisite taste; notice the turquoise-blue porcelain cats he's put on the roofs? Just a few bits of glazed pottery but it makes all the difference. The place has distinction . . . you've got to hand it to the British, they always strike an original note, at least the British we see in Tunisia . . ."

Probably they are an élite. Monsieur Macrosène might be a little disappointed were he ever to visit our hospitable shores.

Tomorrow we shall head for Gabès on the mainland. It is strange that after the fierce furnace of the Sahara one feels the heat so much here. You do not have the soothing nights, and the damp is more fatiguing than the dry air.

We will spruce up in Gabès. I need a hair-cut. Hilali opines that the desert is death for one's hair and that don't I notice that the Saharans have their hair shaved off; yes I do, but hesitate to follow their example.

"I wonder, Monsieur, that you don't have your hair dyed with henna, it's true that the reddish shade is a little spectacular at first, but henna makes the hair wonderfully supple and soft. Moreover, dyed hair grows slower than natural-coloured hair, so the use of henna saves money. . . ."

Hilali is always sensible, no romantic fog. What did he tell me the other day when Monsieur Macrosène wasn't listening? "We Moslems generally divide foreigners into two classes, those who think they understand us, and those who think we like them. If you will excuse me, I should like to say that you don't seem to me to fit into either group."

Gabès is no tourist resort; the hotels are not luxurious and the town mean and almost rowdy. It is a garrison town and like all garrisons exudes of air of, well, let's say acceptance of the facts of life as our magistrates declare while indulging maybe in the national pastime of gratuitous and censorious comment. And then there is the peculiar intellectual atmosphere of the army. As the flippant French say, "We know why all generals are fools; it's because they've been colonels."

Monsieur Macrosène and I set forth to find the barber's shop.

"Now Hilali's out of the way, I'll tell you what our cook said to Madame Macrosène the other day . . . she'd heard we're not only much poorer and weaker now than we were but that we've rich and powerful masters who sympathize with the Moslems and that, moreover, there are the *Russi*, very good people who frighten everybody . . . only repeating what her husband tells her, of course, but it just goes to show you what's being said nowadays."

"Pretty well hits the nail on the head too. The President of the United States has said publicly that 'the peoples of Asia and Africa are determined to share, as equals, in the benefits of modern progress. They are determined that their resources should no longer be developed in the interests of foreigners on the pattern of the old imperialism. They are determined to establish their own political and economic institutions. This I believe is the mood and tempo that have come to Africa and Asia in my lifetime. It is real. It is good. It holds tremendous promise.'[1] This same Mr. Truman urged all the world to benefit by the secret of American success, the secret of the American Revolution. In any case, we may be sure that nearly all Americans are fundamentally anti-imperialist and that if the Washington Government seems to support the British and French in their so-called 'empires', then such aid is given largely for strategic and political reasons. As for the *Russi*, well they are still a long way off and they're a good stick to beat the French and British with. Do you know, I think that there's one rather important point we're all apt to overlook when we're discussing political and social matters, we're always trying to find some explanation, some line of conduct, some reason, some valid and logical reason and so forth, words . . . for hostility displayed towards us. The most potent reason for enmity is that these 'colonial' and 'subject' people—call them what you

[1] Declaration of 8th April, 1952.

will—just loath the look of us, our colour, expression, the sound
of our voices, our manners or lack of them, the insolence of our
women, the impudence of our men, and above all our deference
to success and power and our obsequiousness once we think we're
on the way out."

This Gabès restaurant is not luxurious. Gabès is a straggling
and formless town that I for one do not find very attractive. The
guide-books invariably boost the place as a most beautiful oasis
full of tall trees, shade and fruits, but the oasis is not apparent in
the town. The palm-groves and the springs and rills have to be
found; you must drive out to them. What is most visible in the
town itself is a number of curiously impermanent streets of houses
rather like a movie-set of a Mexican Far West.

But Gabès is lively, especially during the nights of Ramadan
when the blare of the radios mingles with the raucous voices of
the crowds. Strange, but each radio seems to be bellowing a
different tune from the others, yet there cannot be so many
stations giving forth Andalus music. Records maybe.

In our restaurant, whose walls are daubed a peculiarly
indecent shade of blood-red, are two American soldiers, quite
the quietest people in the place. We do not bother them so I do
not know where they came from—possibly from Wheelus Field—
but they have chosen a queer place for leave. The endlessly
attractive oases of Tozeur and Nefta out to the west, or the
delights of Tunis city, would offer more amusement one would
think.

Hilali was the first to spot the discreet visitors; for him the
chief difference between British and Americans lies not only in
the obvious wealth of the latter but also in conventions of personal
adornment. He knows what he is talking about for he was a
volunteer in the late war and fought through the later phases of
the campaign in Western Europe. There is nothing very martial
about our Hilali's appearance or manner and the Tunisians,
despite their many amiable qualities, are not usually reckoned
as naturally inclined towards the profession of arms, but Hilali's
record was an exceptionally honourable one. He must be on our
side, a man of right feeling and good sense who would risk his
life for Liberty. On the other hand, it may be that his experience
of Europe confirmed him in political and social leanings which,
despite his reticence, are, I suspect, rather to the Left.

"You may behold that all American soldiers, or nearly all, wear finger-rings and that they wear them also, as do we, upon our third or ring-fingers. The British cannot afford rings as a rule but those who do display them have them on the little finger. Now, there must be a reason for this? Is it religion?"

In Oriental societies it is as well to make a little display. When I am travelling in the more out-of-the-way parts of such a country as Tunisia, I generally assume, temporarily, some of what the French tax-collectors dub 'external signs of wealth'—an imposing ring or two, for instance. Such things serve, on occasion, as a useful starting-point of conversation as well as a possible stand-by in time of financial stringency. Reilly, our adventurous agent in Russia during the First World War, told me that he always wore a couple of platinum rings on his travels; sometimes they came in very useful.

You can slip a ring from your finger and hand it round for inspection. This should be done with a careless air. I have a large topaz set in gold. The credulous are free to think that it is a a yellow diamond; indeed, the right and proper thing to do is to admit that it is a diamond. Few believe one, still fewer think that one believes the story oneself, but a convention of understanding is established.

"Perhaps I can suggest an explanation, Hilali; men used, once upon a time, to wear signet-rings upon their third fingers even in Britain, and I know a number of old-fashioned, or let's say traditionally-minded, men of quite secure social position who so wear such rings even today. I think that the shift of the ring to the little finger came about when men gave up wearing other rings on their little fingers—it's become a habit maybe. The Americans have got ring-conscious quite recently and few of them, except professional gamblers or prospectors who struck it rich, ever had rings on their little fingers, so the traditional, ancient custom of sporting a ring on the ring-finger is today in the American tradition."

Now I come to think of it, that must be the explanation. You remember in that amusing play *His Excellency*, some censorious mem-sahib damns a man—it is true that he is only one of the native islanders of Salvia—in the Mediterranean, though, it seems —because he wears a diamond ring? Such a remark appears natural today and to a British audience perhaps. Yet in my youth

men of the world and men of fashion—men, it is true, rather of
the generation of my grandfather than of my father—often
displayed rings of precious stones and wore them, as I recollect
it, on their little fingers. Look at old portraits of King Edward VII
and you will see on his carefully manicured hands (with the nails
a good deal longer than present British conventions would allow)
several rings of precious stones. The tradition of wearing such
baubles must have faded with the progressive *embourgeoisement* of
the British privileged classes and with the adoption of standards
established by people who had neither the money nor the occasion
to display jewellery. When, in middle life, Mr. Gladstone was
once at Oxford he was shocked and amazed to notice how shabby
and unadorned the undergraduates were. "Why," he exclaimed,
"in my day none of us would have been seen without at least £100
worth of jewellery on him"—gold chains, rings and suchlike trinkets.

Hilali is sharp in a way. He is sharper than Monsieur
Macrosène, or is that Hilali is younger and has seen the world
of war in Italy, France and Germany, has watched British and
Americans and French when they were all soldiers together but
when Hilali was always the odd man out? Not odd because of
colour or feature, but African and Moslem and indifferent to
many things we hold so dear when we can remember them.

Monsieur Macrosène puts bookish questions, he knows his
Tunisia, as a foreigner, but he has forgotten or never seen our
new millennium in Europe. He is concerned with things that were
of importance in the good old days when it was accessories and
incidentals that were important and not essentials in commerce
with North Africans. He does not really know what a knock we've
taken. He, quite pardonably, thinks like the old ladies who
believe what solicitors, politicians and some journalists tell them.

"Monsieur, one should never employ grey- or blue-eyed men
in contact with the men of Africa, light-eyes mean duplicity, or
better, cruelty. . . . I suppose they're vetting pretty closely the
people you are sending to Libya."

I suggest that these boys are not chosen because they're
pretty, not all of them, anyway. Monsieur Macrosène is out of
date. There is not much we can do to make ourselves popular
except get rich and powerful again.

'Colonies' exist, first and foremost, because as such they bring
in fatter profits to the dominating Power than they would as

"I . . . prepare to daub a little . . ." *p. 153*

". . . the Capitoline Temples, luminous and majestic" *p. 153*

independent States. The rest is literature. Moreover, all colonial empires are splitting at the seams, are coming to bits. Finally, our masters, the Americans, are traditionally anti-colonial. Their country was born of a revolution and of a defeat of a colonial Power. They reflect, moreover, that had they remained British subjects they would hardly be where they are today. Not only are Americans anti-colonial by tradition, but they are anti-colonial for economic reasons. Moreover, the Americans are realists and as they see the empires foundering, they are disinclined to bolster them up.

On the other hand, there are the most cogent reasons for the Americans swallowing their traditions, economic interests and realization that the day of the empires is over.

There is a tussle on between policy and prejudice. Still further losses by the British and French would still more weaken the parlous economies of Britain and France, which must be kept afloat since the Americans must use British- and French-controlled territory in order to defend the United States.

The struggle between policy and prejudice can be seen all along the line.

"The legalistic-moralistic approach to international problems runs like a red skein through our foreign policy of the last fifty years," wrote Mr. George Kennan.

We often have to listen to a deal of nonsense about the Americans not being fit to handle such and such business, not being able to carry this or that 'new responsibility'. If this were true there would be no point in wailing about it since neither British nor French are in a position to bargain upon equal terms with the Americans; and, as far as Asia is concerned, and especially the House of Islam, we may remember that British power and prestige in Asia and in Moslem countries was based, in large measure, upon the Indian Army.

The fact, however, is that the Americans and their government are taking surprisingly skilfully to their new role, although American policy has been, on occasion, vacillating since the end of the late war. After all, we should do well to remember in North Africa that it is only since 1918 that foreign policy has become of prime importance for the United States. The Fathers of the Republic so ordered matters that their country should not have what in Europe would have been called a foreign policy.

I

In 1914 the United States was a debtor country. In 1918 it was a creditor country. World War No. I smashed temporarily one commercial rival, Germany, and permanently weakened another commercial rival, Britain. World War II made the United States far the most powerful, wealthy and dominating Power in the world.

The new role, then, has been assumed only for seven years. Anyway, we cannot do anything about it.

## THE DYING OASIS

Here on the desert's fringes it is not enough to consult the map and pick out your road, you must discover whether the road is still there or if it has taken a dip under the sands. The quicker of the two ways from Gabès to Kebili seems to run along the northern slopes of the Djebel Tabaga, but the road on the south side of the mountains is in much better shape. In fact, until you get to a dump called Bordj-es-Senan the road is a real road, that is to say it has a sort of artificial surface. Thenceforward the road dribbles off into the usual track that is just a path swept in the sands.

You cannot tell very well from a skeleton whether the human being it supported was fat or lean. However, big, coarse bones will reveal that the man or woman was ugly.[1] I am inclined to think that the Djebel Tabaga was an unattractive and commonplace range even when it was clothed with vegetation and trees. It lacks distinction. Just that.

Early afternoon, yet the nearer we get to Kebili the darker it becomes; the air is laden with grit, the whole landscape is a camaieu of yellows. . . . A clump of palms, gigantic palms, half shadow and half substance and beside them a herd of camels sitting and coughing. We are running in a trough with ever heightening walls; the car moves slower and slower, churns to a stop while the wheels revolve in whirls of sand. We are thrust right in the dunes, we are stuck in the drifts. We cannot move. There is no storm, no violence, nothing spectacular or dramatic, there is hardly any wind though the androgynous hacking of the camels reaches us in gusts.

[1] An examination of the famous and edifying object labelled *squelette d'Anglaise* in the Museum of Man, Paris, will illustrate what I mean.

Out of the haze stumble figures in old Army jackets and with mouths veiled by odd kerchiefs. The relief-gang. The son of the house. We can walk fairly easily over the drifts. Broad steps lead up to a square as large as that in a minor capital. There is sand here too, but it forms only a shallow carpet over a hard foundation. The square is bounded on two sides by a fairly high whitewashed wall and on the other sides by low buildings, domed here and there, interrupted by a great horse-shoe gate and enlivened by a minaret. Through the gritty yellow mist the buildings loom like those shown in gaudy colours on boxes of dates.

The Bordj Philibert, the Hotel of Kebili and a House of Exile where in the spring of 1952 the arrested Tunisian Cabinet Ministers spent a fortnight or so. Tough methods to straighten out the Tunisian imbroglio.

That minaret does not serve a Call to Prayer. It is a water-tower. The domes cover no saints' tombs but bedrooms and halls. This extravagant palace was once an ostrich-farm, but nowadays no one wants ostrich-feathers except the ladies in the Paris nudist shows. Not enough demand.

This *bordj* or fortress is splendidly isolated. No electric light, no telephone. Some water though not much. Kebili is a dying oasis. The sands pile up, the sand-winds blow often for a fortnight on end. If we want to get an idea, some sort of an idea of what the Sahara ought to be like, then we should make for Kebili. The journey is not too long nor too fatiguing. But Kebili is not a typical Saharan oasis. In the desert you cannot waste time and money in trying to save the life of dying oases. Either you are out in the perilous adventure of the wilderness, or you are somewhere where the sands are kept at bay; Kebili, they say, is shifting; soon there will be another oasis nearby to which the men of Kebili will repair. To the dispassionate onlooker the sands are just rushing instead of creeping forward. If Kebili is shifting at all it is shifting downwards and not along.

The Europeans of Kebili have a markedly African look in the eye, the sort of look one does get after a bout of Africa, or some parts of Africa. The appearance is compounded of expressions far-away, a little haggard and resigned. It is not a look of unhappiness or dissatisfaction. It is the look of one who has grown wise on disappointment.

The people who run the *bordj* make you welcome and feed

you as well as you have any right to expect in such a place. Eggs with surprisingly little sand, some resistant, sturdy grey-green vegetable. In comes a group of young men. Oil-prospectors? No, well-sinkers. The wells cut down all right, but no water seeps into them at all.

*Presque tout ce qui arrive est inexprimable et s'accomplit dans une région que jamais parole n'a foulée.*[1]

My bedroom had once been that of the chief ostrich-master. In size and shape it was a small Orthodox chapel. A low red, four-poster bed, Portuguese, or Italo-Turkish, on a raised platform. Here should be the ikonostasis, but at head and foot of the bed are doors leading to a mysterious passage. For furniture two benches of masonry, covered, like half the walls, with multicoloured tiles. Carpets supplying a dull red answering that of the ceiling and contrasting with the dead-white walls from above the tiles. Neither rugs nor carpets of the really criminal colours now so common in North Africa. Maybe the sands have ennobled the hues. It is most oddly difficult to reproduce, in other lands, either the framework or the suggestion of North African life. We can, with some taste and a few objects, create the atmosphere of a Chinese assemblage, we can much the same for those of Persia, colonial Spain or Italy. But if we try evocation of North Africa, either we make a shop-window display of bric-à-brac such as adorn the tourist agencies, or we produce something spiritually akin to a palmist's consulting-room.

Can it be that the content of the civilization is poor? Is it that there is an essential triviality in the trappings of life? Hardly. We cannot take small objects and dispose them for the re-creation of a dream, for the setting of a poem or for the consolidation of a refuge. The fact is that the furnishings are adventitious, whether they be the tiresome adjuncts of the Moroccan tea-party or whether they be the often ill-designed and flimsy objects that clutter up the so-called 'Islamic' sections of museums. In Islamic lands, those of the West, at any rate, the only art is architecture. The rest is crafts.

This is the royal suite of Kebili. A few months after I was there the room served as the cell, or at any rate abode of the

[1] Rainer Maria Rilke.

Tunisian Prime Minister, whom the French arrested together with some of his Ministers.

It seems he had been disloyal.

"Such is the frailty of human reason . . . that even . . . deliberate doubt would scarce be upheld did we not enlarge our view and, opposing one species of superstition to another, set them quarrelling while we ourselves, during the fury and contention, happily make our escape."[1]

It would be such a bore if we were all obliged to define our terms before we began to write or to engage in discussion on the radio; it would be such a bore because we should, in nine cases out of ten, discover that we had nothing to talk about. Since the cold war started there has been much ado about treason in the lands to the west of the Demarcation Line. In the United States excitement has shrieked into hysteria, even among the sluggish Britons there has been heart-searching. The French seem to be less perturbed; maybe their experiences in 1940–45 have made them wise.

The first and perhaps the most important thing about treason is that it does not exist; the word is properly meaningless and therefore powerful, persuasive and indispensable. There are, nevertheless, such men as traitors, or we must suppose that there are, although the appellation appears to be getting just a trifle old-fashioned. Let us see. First of all, we have no word to express the opposite of a traitor—a man who is loyal. We can say 'loyalist' but that is not the same as a man who is loyal. Immediately we seek for the contrary of a traitor we find ourselves confronted with a problem. In Europe five hundred years ago, and that is far enough back for us, a traitor was a man who had betrayed his sovereign, who was disloyal in act to his overlord. People who remained loyal needed no special name. They were just the true-hearted and decent simpletons who form the backbone of society.

Disloyal to one's overlord. In 1452 there were still parts of western Europe where a man was not quite sure where his loyalty should lie. A few generations earlier the problem was more urgent. Must a man be loyal to immediate overlord or to his

[1] Hume.

remote sovereign? The Captal de Buch, K.G., in the time of the Hundred Years' War, was a subject of the King of England as feudal lord of south-western France, but the King of England was, for his French dominions, the subject of the French King. Where should the Captal's loyalty lie? Well, he took the money and he made the choice.

The fact is that in this matter of traitors counsel has been confused for generations past. We can define and understand who are loyal and who are treacherous to the person of the sovereign; it is more difficult to define who are loyal and who are treacherous to a 'flag', a 'patrie' or to 'society'. In this business as in so many others we expect to maintain and to find fine old loyalties in bad new causes. We expect that men should be as truly loyal to God knows what code as they would be to the person of king or emperor. It just will not work.

It is becoming the fashion to dub traitors all those who do not share our ideas or our sentiments. Indeed, one of the simplest explanations of 'treachery' is that the 'traitor' just hates the whole look and being of those whom he 'betrays'. Such explosions of most imprudent antagonism are not infrequent among naturalized persons and those whose sojourn in a foreign land has brought not acquiescence but a daily exacerbated resentment and perhaps contempt.

The list is long of illustrious traitors from the Cid to Condé, from those who forsook Napoleon, much to their own good, to some living patriots whose frequent changes of nationality would have been suspect had they been undertaken by less successful politicians.

No doubt it is not what we do but how we do it. Throughout history many have prospered as traitors while not a few have rotted in their loyalties.

With an excess of ordinances, laws and prohibitions; with an excess of new fabricated crimes and misdemeanours, comes a general contempt of law. The faint echoes of an older morality fade fast; 'wicked', 'sinful'; the forces of organized religion brought up to reinforce the administration of law. Not only criminal but sinful. Then there were relatively so few classes of crime that no one dared ask, 'Are there cases where an act is criminal but not sinful?' and if the reply was 'No', then might come the embarrassing query, 'Then anything our masters tell us is a crime is therefore and at once endorsed as such by Lord God Almighty?'

We are wiser, more reasonable today; what is a crime is anything a pack of politicians decide is such, what is sinful is anything some government clerk deigns to inform you is such . . . we may get as long a prison sentence for doing something that was encouraged fifteen years ago as we get for highway robbery, yet highway robbery has been frowned upon in respectable circles for quite a long time. So it is with our poor traitors. There are really so many treacherous acts nowadays that one feels like the nervous passenger when the printed list of prohibited or dutiable articles is shoved under his nose in the Customs shed.

The communication of scientific data was for long considered a duty, the concealment of such information is now imperative. Half our traitors would not have been traitors twenty years ago; don't let's get worried; with the progress being made in garbled neology nothing will soon have any meaning. All our problems will be solved.

In Tunisia there is an urgent and pressing problem. It is that of how to know who is a traitor. The Tunisian Prime Minister was disloyal, so the French said. Disloyal to whom or to what? Who is a traitor, or disloyal, in that ludicrously old-fashioned arrangement called a 'protectorate'? Unfortunately the silly inhabitants of protectorates persist in complaining that not only are they treated as children but that injury is added to insult. The Dutch in Indonesia, the British in Burma, the French in Tunisia did not have time to do so much protecting during the late war.

Who is a traitor in a protectorate, a protectorate such as Tunisia with a sovereign ruler? Is he the man who betrays his sovereign or the man who betrays the sovereign's protectors? We may say the dilemma should not arise, there should be identity of view between the sovereign and his protectors, there should . . . why of course, but the dilemma does arise and there is no identity of view in Tunisia as between His Highness the Bey and the mass of his people on the one hand and the French Government on the other hand.

The dilemma should not arise. It did not in the olden days when the French ran Tunisia with no regard at all for the nominal and titular monarch. The Tunisians knew where they got off and how to behave themselves so as not to attract unpleasant consequences.

But we have a changed North Africa. Why? Because we live in a changed Europe.

## THE LITTLE WORLD OF THE BEYS

Not so long ago, in Tunis City, an eminent Tunisian politician—after a surly start so different from his suave address of the days before the late war—thought fit to remind me that Tunisia is as large as was Elizabeth's England and that there are about twice as many Tunisians as there were English in the Spacious Days. I was moved to murmur that while what he said might well be true, the soil and climate of the Regency are most unEnglish and one does not come across many Tunisian Shakespeares, Drakes, Walsinghams and so forth.

It is, of course, undeniable that Tunisia has had a long history of what might be dubbed national identity. We need not look back to Punic and Roman times but only to about 600 years ago, when the Tunisian satrap representing the Moroccan overlords rebelled and declared himself independent; with independence comes, very generally, either decline or a spurt of prosperity. In Tunisia there was a little golden age lasting until the 16th century when under the attacks of both Turks and Spaniards the Hafsid realm disintegrated.

The Turks remained as masters. Order reigned. In 1704 the Bey, or military governor, one Hussein ibn 'Ali, the son of a Cretan convert to Islam, proclaimed himself sovereign though under the suzerainty of the Turkish Sultan. The present ruling Bey, Sidi Mohammed el-Amin, is the head of this Greek Moslem dynasty.

Piracy and slave-trading were the principal sources of national revenue; when, however, in the early years of the 19th century the profession of piracy was outlawed by the European Powers and soon effectively suppressed, the income of Tunisia was cut off; the Tunisians were like the slave-owners after emancipation. The slump struck Tunisia though the Beys not only wanted to keep up appearances but also to live altogether beyond their modest means. Business was booming in Europe, new needs and new means of satisfying them were flaunted before the bemused Beys who were two hundred years behind the times. The country was in bloody confusion, brigandage was rife, there were no roads and not more than 700,000 people in a land as big as England.

The French had been settled in Algeria since about 1830 and they did not look with much disappointment upon a neighbouring Tunisia obviously falling to pieces. After an 'International Financial Commission' had been set up, the French obtained railway and telegraph concessions.

Then the French consul began to complain that Tunisian subjects were raiding Algerian territory. As the Bey had no means of controlling his subjects, the French landed troops in order, it was proclaimed, to 'help the Bey to assert his authority'.

The French have been helping the Beys to assert their authority for just over seventy years; so the Tunisians, or some of them, maintain that, by this time, either the French are powerless to aid the Bey in asserting his authority, or that authority has been long since effectively asserted.

The treaties whereby the French established their protectorate were drawn up and imposed in the good old way. The treacherous natives had been taught a lesson. On 11th May, 1881, the text of a Franco-Tunisian treaty was laid before the ruling Bey, Mohammed es-Sadok. He was given until nine that night to signify his approval. Nowadays the Bey has stalled for weeks and refused to answer when the most pressing demands were made upon him for a reply.

The French Protectorate (established by treaty in 1883) was imposed by force—as were of course all 'protectorates'—and the French claims to control in Tunisia are based upon treaties concluded with an absolute monarch, for no parliamentary body existed in Tunisia either in 1883 nor has it at any time since.

A very great deal of the trouble the 'imperial' Powers are experiencing comes from the fundamental weakness that their juridical and legal rights proceed from pacts made with absolute rulers whose successors are no longer absolute. Can a people be bound indefinitely by agreements accepted by autocrats in the past?

Where do Tunisian loyalties lie? How was the Prime Minister disloyal? Even supposing that the treaties are of lasting validity, should a Tunisian subject of the Bey disavow and be treacherous to his sovereign because that sovereign's protector demands a different acceptance from that the sovereign wants?

Mysterious matters. Can one be loyal to two masters when they disagree. What is treason? Or let us say, what is a Tunisian traitor?

Delinquent, criminal, sinner? In the good old days no one had to pin a tag upon recalcitrant Tunisians. Now it is all so difficult. New words, if not new ideas. The Tunisian Prime Minister (his office and that of his colleagues are quite new things) in his communications with the French Resident-General, now writes, 'I have it in command from my August Master . . .'

## THE HOUSE OF EXILE

*Mon Hôte, laissez-moi votre maison de verre dans les sables . . .*
*L'été de gypse aiguise ses fers de lance dans nos plaies.*
*J'élis un lieu flagrant et nul comme l'ossuaire des saisons,*
*Et, sur toutes les grèves de ce monde, l'esprit de Dieu*
　　*fumant déserte sa couche d'amianthe.*[1]

The sands sigh. The palm-fronds whisper as they slide their leaves. Yes, it would be soothing to be able to live only in our private world, soothing but in the long run tiresome and crippling to the artist. But it is one thing to live in the world and not be entirely of it, and it is another thing to be uncomfortable in order to earn enough to go on being uncomfortable.

The world's slow stain.

When I went to bed the space between the two panes of my double-window was clean: when I rose in the morning there was a layer of sand an inch deep between them, and the table before the casement was powdered with grit. There are, they say, many sorts of sands, but these of Kebili are as fine as face-powder—not that ground nacreous and iridescent from cuttle-fish, but the finest *poudre de talc*. Saharan sands for ever sifted with the winds.

In the twilight of full morning we stand at the arched gateway and survey the dunes, which present a bulwark ten feet high. A Door on Dreams.

As we trudge to the track cut for the car, the surface of the sand-drifts is pitted as that of a sea-strand under rain.

The yellow haze still blurs and magnifies all outlines, the

[1] Saint-John Perse (Monsieur Alexis Léger, formerly Secretary-General of the French Ministry of Foreign Affairs and now exiled in the United States) is without doubt one of the most significant of contemporary French poets. His art is elusive and its secrets hard to pierce but his rhythmic invention and his substitution of internal harmony for external accord give his writings a form that is unique.

light, such as it is, tells us nothing. There is surely some reversal
of time, morning melting into night or evening into afternoon.
We move slowly onwards; the sand-mist lifts and drops as we
slip down on to the fossil shores of the dead sea. The salt curls in
little frozen ripples against a sandy beach. The sky is no more
luminous but has receded until it is high and dull.

## MIRAGE

A boundless plain, dazzling white, barred with a double
horizon-line; below, the solidified salt-marsh and above, a sus-
pended strip of mirage. An Indian mirage, you would say, one
of white-walled palaces, of pools with tree-tufted islands, a glimpse
of glittering Rajputana and its sacred crocodiles' tanks.

This plain is the lagoon of the ancient Igharghar flowing
north from the Tassili. For much of the year the *chotts* are a
crystalline expanse, though at any moment the tracks across may
weaken. On this June day, though no rains have fallen for months,
the way across the Chott-el-Djerid is out of bounds. We roll over
the eastern saline, the Chott-el-Fedjadj, as on a speedway.

The depression of the *chotts*, though it is desiccated enough,
is damper than it looks; the soil is moist enough to attract or
retain a world of beasts. Elephants lingered here long. Herodotus
tells that they flourished to the west of Lake Triton, that is the
Chott-el-Djerid, while Pliny says that they could be found in the
country around the Syrtes, that is the Gulf of Gabès in southern
Tunisia and the Gulf of Sidra in Libya. No elephants could
thrive, or even exist, in these regions now.

All round about where we are now there lived in ancient time
the half-fabled Psylli who, it is said, would throw their new-born
infants into a case of cobras so that it might be known whether
the babes were bastards or not. I forgot to mention this during
our Ghadames conversation on pride and prejudice.

From hereabouts come the cobras that the charmers charm
before the mosque gates in Kairouan; cobras with broken teeth,
of course, but anyway the African cobra is of little account
compared with the sand-grey horned viper slipping through the
sands, snakes whose bite is mortal unless you have snake-serum
ready at hand, and even then . . . However, the serum has bereft
the scorpion's sting of its horror, though this baleful creature is
an ancient inhabitant of the Sahara and yellow scorpions lived

in the desert before it was formed, right back in Tertiary times millions of years ago.

These living fossils, the most ancient arthropods known, need moisture and damp; they become dehydrated in the wilderness. It is the scorpion's dependence upon humidity that, it seems, excited the fond tale of the reptile's stabbing itself to death when caught within a ring of glowing embers.

Here and there a shapeless pale hut. Pot-bellied dark children naked. Men slumped in the miserly shade. A hungry land.

In the shadows you may watch the obscene and complicated conjunctions of the scorpions. The love-dance of the male while he deposits his seed within a calix, his shaking, shuddering ritual as he pushes the female on the calix . . . and much more, *l'amour chez les scorpions*.

## THE ROMAN WALL

The ground rises beyond the *chotts* northwards; you are in a different world. Turn round and look back over the sheen towards the grey smudge of the sands, they stretch for two thousand miles and span a third of Africa, for the Sahara covers nearly four million square miles. Quite a tract of land.

The road northward is a track, gritty, harsh and dry, a smear among the blotched ground on either side. It is difficult to think of this region as having been fertile at any time since the recession of the last Pluvial maybe ten thousand years ago. Still there are plants. Under the dull penetrating sunshine they look alike, though here or there will be a rarer herb, perhaps ephedra, whose roots as those of all the desert plants spread very far in search for damp.

What the wise women tell is true; if you rub a bit of ephedra-root on your forehead the headache will quit you. Useful in the desert where your head will sometime split.

When you see jujube-bushes there will be more earth than sand. The harsh, tough scrub needs nitrogen and most African soil is poor in this element. We are nearing Bir Oum Ali, the Well of Ali's Mother. An insignificant name, but it is a most significant place, hereby is a stretch of the Imperial Bulwark, the *limes*, the Outpost of Empire.

Another turn of the road and there, on the right, lain like a gigantic worm up the slope of the brown hill is the Wall.

This *limes* is a double line of masonry of which but a small stretch has survived. It clings to the slopes of the hill and quite apart from its physical appearance it is significant and impressive; it is the witness of an essential barrier, a man-made barrier if we will, but still one marking an extension of the human imprint upon the face of the world. There is always a strange sensation of finality when one walks through the gate of an age-old wall. I have strolled back and forth a dozen times in an hour through the great Gate of China on the eastern frontiers of Tongking. Each time I tried to persuade myself that the land, the countryside, the aspect of the world was just the same here and there; so it was, except that it was quite different. A photograph on one side and a photograph on the other look alike, but in the living scene all the assumptions, all the conventions are different, the air has not the same scent here and there, the rhythm of movement is other when you just walk through this Gate and then, after all, you change from a land with the oldest surviving civilization to one that shows but a mingled and blurred image of things Chinese mingled with things both barbarous and European.

When we come to compare Roman with Chinese we at once see how short-lived was the Roman Empire; it was not until about 146 B.C. that the Romans effectively occupied *Africa*, which was only a small part of present-day Tunisia.[1]

As established finally, the imperial Roman *limes* ran south of the Aurès Mountains (in eastern Algerian territory) and then round the north shore of the Chott-el-Rharsa and south of the Chott-el-Djerid (Kebili was an outpost) and then to the sea at the Lesser Syrtis, or Gulf of Gabès.[2]

The military set-up of imperial Africa was illuminating. Except during the pacification operations, there was never more than one legion (of about 5500 men or less than a division) stationed in the province. Moreover, at least from the 2nd century onwards, most of these troops were native Africans, some of whom

---

[1] This *Africa* was bounded by Scipio's Ditch running from Thabraca (Tabarca) to Thenae (Henchir-Tina) opposite the Kerkennah Isles. Julius Caesar pushed back the frontiers of *Africa* from Thabraca to Ampsaga (Oued-el-Kebir), so to *Africa Vetus* was added an *Africa Nova*, to which a coastal strip along the two Syrtes was joined.

[2] There were some isolated forts south of the Roman *limes* in, for instance, the Ouled-Naïl country in Algeria, but there was nowhere a line of forts right out in the desert as there was in Libya where the actual frontier ran about a hundred and fifty miles south of the Tripolitan *jebel* or plateau's edge that you see rising like cliffs when you get about thirty miles inland. Mizda was the hinge of the defence system in western Libya and Mizda is, roughly, on the same parallel as Bir Zar and only some hundred miles north of Ghadames.

were citizens when they joined up but most of whom received citizenship as a reward for service in the army. If we count auxiliary forces[1] the total number of Roman imperial soldiers did not exceed 27,000, which is a good many fewer than the French maintain today. Even if we add to the total the numbers of the native irregulars and of the Proconsular Guard, we still do not get anywhere near the effectives of the French. Secret of Empire?

After *Africa* was reconquered in Justinian's time, the Byzantine *limes* was, for much of its length, set a good deal farther north than the Roman wall. The desert dwellers were by now fully organized and equipped with camels. The Romans, for most of their time, held out against an empty desert, the Byzantines had to ward off incursions from a Sahara swarming with nomads. However, after Tebessa (in eastern Algeria) the Byzantine wall struck southwards to the shores of the Chott-el-Djerid and thence to the sea by Gabès oasis.

However, this humble little section of wall does mark the point from which, northwards, can be measured the greatest breadth of the Roman Empire. Its span comprised the lands and seas between this Wall here and that Wall in the north of the province of Maxima Caesariensis. In fact, here is our African edition of Hadrian's Wall in England. From the north of the Prefecture of Gaul to the south of the Prefecture of Italy, for Britain was a diocese of Gaul as Africa was a diocese of Italy.

The Wall at the Well of Ali's Mother is not tall, about twelve feet high, but it was, no doubt, set at intervals with watch-towers serving both as look-out posts and as barracks.

Northumberland and Tunisia. There is a break in the British story as brutal as that caused in the North African when the Moslems swept through. But there is no blank in the Tunisian record whereas after the end of the Roman domination (conventionally set at A.D. 410) there is mysterious darkness in Britain. Roman ways of life and even Latin as a learned speech may have lingered on even a century, but the cleavage is absolute. No connection can be traced between Roman London of the 5th century and Alfred's of the 9th.

[1] There were about 6000 *auxilia* in Numidia and some 15,000 in Mauretania. At first these were a mixed lot—British, Corsican, Dalmatian, Spanish, Gaulish, Parthian, Thracian and what you will—but from the 2nd century onwards they were all Africans. The Proconsular Guard, stationed at Carthage, did not comprise more than a cohort (of some 500 men).

No Tunisian Kipling to give us the Tale of the Southern
Roman Wall though it must have been exciting enough.

A bend in the road. A natural guardian of the South and one
of the most spectacular rock-formations you may see anywhere.
Weathered out of a mass of close-packed strata and jutting out
upon the wayfarer is a headland that is the forepart of a stupendous
saurian, a dragon of the wastes. The monster is in wakeful repose.
It is a petrified reptile of most archaic age. It must have been
carved by men's hands. But no. When the winds and the sand
and the weather can fashion such terrifying images, we may
wonder if men did not in their earliest art imitate such natural
sculpture rather than living models. We do know at least that the
natural sweep and form of the rock-face was often used to assist
the prehistoric painter. That curve makes a bison's back, that
concavity a horse's belly, that boss a bear's rump.

The great lizard of the imperial boundary.

The shapes of hills and crags now become more lively, the
highway curves and mounts. High above the road and upon a
cliff-ledge stands motioness the figure of a camel. No, this is a
smooth, shiny, slate-coloured camel apparently cast in metal. It
must be a camel for no other beast hereabouts has a hump, but
it is a very curious camel. He has been shorn close and tarred
against the ticks. Maybe he is enjoying his new ease and comfort,
for he stands quite still. No other living thing for miles. We are
in a land where we would say that it has never rained, yet the
soil is not all sand, though the rocks and hills show sharp contours
as though sand-blown. Often the tints are dark, sinister, putres-
cent, sometimes there are vast patches of green-grey marl, fossil
sewage, archaic excrement, somehow humid-seeming in the
shadows though the air is very dry.

The road is now fair though stony. We traverse a region
of wider views and set with strange hills. Some are most regular
in outline—they have weathered evenly in their nudity—others are
as architectural as man-made monuments. There are spectacular
knolls bearing upon their summits rectangular blocks of some
resistant stratum. The effect is that of an edifice set upon an
artificial hill. In fact, several of the mounds are surprisingly like
the temple-hills of pre-Columbian America and others again
resemble the tumuli of the Asian steppes, kurgans, or the grave-

mounds of ancient Chinese emperors on which were funerary shrines and sanctuaries. Fancies, literary phantoms, maybe.

The desert is a theatre of designs and contours and outlines shifting with every change of light, with every variation of luminosity. One thing is a hundred; a hundred different objects merge into one. You just have to dream in the desert, you must welcome literary phantoms, you must rejoice in the word made flesh, at the play of imagination, of a waking vision, the formless takes on form and the shapeless shape. You must create in the desert for there nothing has a name, a function, a significance except those with which we endow these shifting shapes. Either you allow the scene to stultify you—or you do not.

You rush along, the country seems at once very large and surprisingly small, there are in fact no buildings, no men to give it the measure of our proportion. Yet from the *chotts* to Gafsa we are traversing a stretch of country that is as wide as the width of Surrey and Sussex.

## BATS D'AF

In the sloping, shapeless streets a mauve forage-cap swaggering along. The hall-mark of the *Bats d'Af*, the *Bataillons d'Afrique*, famed in the factitious folklore of 19th-century France, though it is true before 1918, service in the disciplinary battalions was pretty harsh. Out on the Djebel Guettar range men rotted at the *corvée au bois*. They died with their boots on, in the sun.

Cranks and simpletons will tell us even now that French prisons and penitentiaries are cruel, though offences for which men were once relegated to Devil's Island were crimes which in many other countries would have been punished by death. However, the lads who got themselves into mauve caps were a tough lot and were treated appropriately; today the *Bats d'Af* are not so bad. Anyway, if our manners are not more polished than those of a generation or two ago, at least we are so humanitarian that crimes are now often laughed off as boyish pranks.

*Encore un ami de moins, quel soulagement!*[1]

Monsieur Macrosène recognizes an old friend, engages in conversation and when he rejoins us is not a little put out. Maybe

[1] Jules Renard.

". . . neatly framed in Diocletian's Arch we may observe the functional outline of a lofty derrick" *p. 162*

". . . the most obvious man-made objects remain . . . uprights . . ." *p. 164*

both of them belong to the rather large class of men who never get on well enough in the world to be able to say 'Go to hell' to old friends, but who, nevertheless, do get on well enough in the world to keep old friends. I venture to suggest there is a good deal of satisfaction to be derived from drawing a line and writing 'paid'. "One less friend, what a relief," as Jules Renard wrote when he quarrelled with Edmond Rostand. Monsieur Macrosène complains that *sacrés pions*, 'blasted ushers', are all alike. Know everything. Understand nothing. I hint that the teaching profession is highly respectable even in its less well-paid ranks.

Also I get him almost to agree that it is wise to keep one's own counsel regarding 'blasted ushers' who supply a not inconsiderable number of our present-day masters . . . what the ex-colleague told Monsieur Macrosène we shall never know. It was something wounding, but I dared not be inquisitive; may be that it had to do with our friend's queer travelling companions. Anyway, the blasted usher served one purpose. He vouchsafed that the least repulsive food in Gafsa was to be found at Serafino's.

Gafsa, the classical Capsa, is not more attractive today than half a century ago when Norman Douglas devoted four-fifths of his *Fountains in the Sand* to this ancient but not venerable town. It says much for Douglas's genius that he was able to set a charming book in so unpromising a framework. Gafsa is dusty, windy, colourless and now bears evident scars of war—it is a wonder that anything of so flimsy a settlement could have survived an hour's bombing—the *kasbah*, or citadel, a fairly imposing, medieval-seeming (but much restored) Moslem stronghold was blown out in 1942-43. Gafsa looks ready to sink at any time into its sandy soil.

However, Gafsa is an oasis; quite a fertile one. There is plenty of water, fruit-trees grow, crops ripen though there is little rain. It is a very good year when six inches fall in the twelve months, then the barren hills, for a few short weeks, in springtime, are covered with a tinted mantle of brilliant annuals. Eastward along the Gabès road is the first woodland you find on your way up from the south. It is the 'forest' of Bled Talah, straggling over more than sixty thousand acres. It is a strange forest with trees never less than twenty yards apart, so that as you drive through it you have the impression of exploring a bewitched orchard whose trees yield dust-apples.

K

Years ago, when first I passed through Gafsa and got out on the road to the enchanting oases of Tozeur and Nefta by the shores of the dead salt-marshes, when I saw before me desert-steppes befogged with sand, a vast waste blotched with reptilian tussocks of bitter scrub shivering in the stinging blast, then I thought I had plunged into the Sahara's heart. But no, the country around Gafsa is but a pale image of the wastes.

## Big Business

Serafino's somehow appears cheerful, maybe that is due to the smiling confidence of Serafino himself. He is a Sicilian, hefty and brawny. He sports two fine, flashing diamond rings and surveys his establishment from behind a combination radio, phonograph, pick-up and T.V. Comely Italian girls do his bidding. He is a reasonable Southerner, not sentimental, and would echo the sage Monsieur Léautaud's views on love:

> L'amour c'est le physique, c'est attrait charnel, c'est le plaisir reçu et donné, c'est la jouissance réciproque, c'est la réunion de deux êtres sexuellement faits l'un pour l'autre. Le reste, les hyperboles, les soupirs, les 'élans d'âme', sont des plaisanteries, des propos pour les niais, des rêveries de beaux esprits impuissants.

Serafino, though a man of the Mediterranean, has nothing of the 'Mediterranean' about him; his is not the slender, long-faced, long-headed type of the men who made the first civiliza-tions but who today seem to be among the less originative of mankind. We may well wonder if physical type has anything to do with capabilities; there are fools among negroes, and pink men. Great civilizations were invented by Mongoloids and Mediterraneans.[1] So what?

With his own hands Serafino served us some of his food, southern Italian. It is not the finest even Italy affords, but it is exportable to harsh Africa. With macaroni, lots of tomato sauce, unidentified meat and a bottle of Sicilian white wine we fared not too ill.

Serafino tells us he is now a French citizen, that he has a

[1] The largest block of 'Mediterraneans' in Europe is in the Iberian Peninsula. As a Catalan lady (not of Mediterranean type) put it to me not long since Spaniards' thoughts run this way: *pesetas, pesetas, y pues la familia y pues nada,* 'Money, money, then their family, then nothing at all.'

brother in Chicago, that although things are not so brilliant in Tunisia, they are much better than in Italy with two and a half million unemployed and as many Communist Party members. Of course, Serafino, as a personage of importance in Gafsa, is a natural conservative. He is almost, perhaps quite, in the rich *colon* category even if he is not of so much account as is his brother in Chicago. When he takes a trip to Sicily he can measure the extent of his good fortune, can Serafino. He is, in fact, possibly a trifle too prosperous for his profession; like wily Chinese *restaurateurs* he has a number of sidelines, any one of which is probably more profitable than slinging hash.

Maybe Serafino deals in chemical products, quite a considerable quantity of which passes through Sicily; not a little finds its way by the grape-vine to the United States where importation is effected by Italo-Americans, by Americo-Italians and by just plain Italians. That brother in Chicago handles, perhaps, the American end of Serafino's racket.

These chemical products are valuable and not bulky for their worth. In fact, a kilogramme of them sells for three kilogrammes of gold. The stuff comes, of course, from the north, the southerners handle but do not manufacture it. The Milan factories alone turned $20,000,000 worth in 1948. It is true that in 1952 a six months' ban was laid on manufacture, but so profitable a merchandise cannot be allowed to fail the Italian target or whatever it may be dubbed.

Little fishing-boats are handy for running the stuff from Sicily to Africa. The most widespread narcotic in general use in North Africa is hemp, which grows wild all over the *Maghreb*. The Tunisian and Moroccan tobacco *régies* still offer *kif*—that is hemp—for public sale as the British do opium in the Far East. *Kif* chopped fine and smoked in pipes with tiny metallic bowls is not a very powerful intoxicant and *kif* reefers are less potent than the marijuana cigarettes common in the United States. It must always be nice exercise in common sense to determine how much narcotic we need, how detached we must become. The trouble with *kif* is its extreme possessiveness; one does not smoke it because one needs it, but because without it we are unhappy and uncomfortable. Still, anything is better than remorse, regret and eating one's heart out. In North Africa where the climate is trying, where alcohol is forbidden, and where tensions snarl the nerves, it is hardly surprising that men have recourse to narcotics, and not just *kif* but the stuff that Serafino handles, heroin and the like.[1]

## STRANGE MEATS

That dreadful road Norman Douglas jolted over from 'Majen' (i.e. Bordj el Maadjen) to Gafsa, a highway deep rutted and procuring exquisite agony to the traveller, this track is but a memory. The Gafsa to Feriana road is the usual billiard-table, asphalt speedway the French have laid down all over North Africa. It is but forty-five miles to Feriana but you pull up to the high steppes.

In bygone days the Feriana region was famed for strange meats. Haïdra—where is a Byzantine fortress—about forty-five miles to the north-west, was the headquarters of a tribe James Bruce called the 'Welled Sidi Boogannim' who were 'immensely rich'. They achieved so enviable a situation because they paid no taxes either to the Bey of Tunis or the Dey of Algiers, or to anyone else. As we all well realize today, however optimistic we may be, people who pay taxes cannot get rich. The 'Welled Sidi Boogannim' owed their privileges to their habit of eating lion-meat—and doubtless also to their sturdy, independent character. Anyway, the tribe's gastronomic customs must have made for the disappearance of the king of beasts from western Tunisia. Bruce feasted with the highlanders and found a dish of broiled lioness not at all bad, but then the mountain air whets the appetite. The 'Welled Sidi Boogannim' did their work too well. They ate up the lions and when there were no more the tax-gatherer appeared. Wealth vanished and the poor 'Welled Sidi Boogannim' just were enslaved and ensnared into the inestimable privileges of good government.

They told me in Feriana that undoubtedly lions do linger in the wild region stretching westward into Algeria, but no one would vouch for any having been killed in recent years. Perhaps the beasts have become shy. The lion was hunted in the wooded hills of Khoumeria in northern Tunisia until the turn of the century, but there are no lions there today. They have dis-

---

[1] Most of the Egyptian supply comes, it would seem, still through Syria. The use of narcotics is, of course, frowned upon by the pious; the prescriptions of the Faith are, however, not clear. The Italian houses turn out a good selection of the new synthetic narcotics—pethidine, methadon, levorphan and the like—there are many of them.

appeared from Northern Algeria in the last fifty years, though they still linger in the Middle Atlas of Morocco. These are small, dark-coated creatures but undoubtedly lions, and, like the King of Beasts everywhere, rather timid.

## "FERIANA . . . CELEBRATED FOR ITS ROMAN ANTIQUITIES . . ."

Feriana, thought James Bruce, was the 'ancient Thala destroyed by Metellus in his pursuit of Jugurtha', but nothing is less certain. Feriana seems rather to be near if not upon the site of the ancient Thelepte. It lies nearly 2500 feet above sea-level and is not more than fifteen miles from the Algerian border, so the soft, sandy streets, the tall hedges, the fruit-trees and the greenery all suggest an oasis in a northern desert; indeed, Feriana is the last—or the first—of the oases. There are Algerians strolling about—you may know them at once by their tall, bulbous turbans such as Tunisians never wear.

On these uplands sheep flourish, fat woolly sheep and not the scraggy, wretched kind of the lowlands.[1] The evening sky contracts in cool colours. The breeze from the west is quite fresh. A tall, grave shepherd halts his flock and silences his fluffy dogs. The curved ram with sagging scrotum staggers to a halt. He is most like prehistoric engravings on the Algerian rocks.

The shepherd draws himself up, raises his arms in an attitude of antique adoration as though about to venerate the setting sun. Maybe he is a pious man, and although there is no muezzin's call, he will perform the evening prayer. But he does not sink to his knees, he bends down, picks up a handful of small stones, raises his arms again and chucks a few pebbles among the sheep. Up go his arms and as he lowers them he bows and emits a swishing, gurgling sound as the rush of waters through a tap or faucet. Two or three times he repeats his odd ritual. The sheep obey and stale.

A highland shepherd, a bony, free-seeming man, but you cannot say whether hired or master of his herd. He flings an arm forward, the dogs bark, nose and shove the sheep. All trail off into the gathering dusk around the fruit-trees; palms, figs, pomegranates and apricots.

[1] Sheep, say the zoologists, are not indigenous to Africa, but, then, neither are the destructive goats who frisk and frolic in the Saharan oases.

## FERIANA BROSE

The hostelry of Feriana is frankly European—no Turkish bath decoration, no hard settees, no gaudy rugs, no pseudo-oriental gimcrack brass and pottery. Here Victorian armchairs, mid-19th century, solid shiny furniture. The place belongs to Alsatians and the food they gave us was the best we struck in rural Tunisia. That, in itself, is not saying very much for Africa cures the gourmet of his virtues. Is there any restaurant in all Africa where food is served that would pass as absolutely first-class in France? Why, according to that most reliable of authorities, the *Guide Michelin* for 1952, there are but seven super-excellent restaurants in all France; only seven three-star marvels, and they are all, with the exception of two in Paris itself (the Café de Paris and Lapérouse), situated in the eastern regions of the country and in wine-producing provinces. Wine—well, of African wine it is best not to speak. The plutocrats in the Belgian Congo drink champagne.

The Sahara is a great breeder of colds and chills and coughs; I had brought a cold with me and was getting hoarse. The old Alsatian lady of the house prepared what may be called a Feriana brose compounded of brandy, apricot syrup and honey. The apricot, when eaten fresh, is to my way of thinking one of the most insipid of stone fruits; the Arabic name of *mishmish* is not a little appropriate, but apricots preserved or stewed can be delicious. The Feriana apricots, however, are richly flavoured when you eat them raw; the men of Feriana, indeed, claim that their apricots are the finest in the world. They are superb, but are not more luscious than those produced in the Roussillon of South-Western France, but then these apricots of the Pyrénées-Orientales are incomparable.

Still, the Feriana *mishmish* is ruddy and blushing, perfumed and fresh, orange-coloured and velvet-skinned.

The brose was comforting. I carried some off to my bedroom and filled a thermos flask with the splendid medicine. This brose is sovereign against all coughs, colds and hoarseness, but you must have the syrup of Feriana apricots, while only the *miel du Bey* will do, honey produced by the private bees of His Highness the Possessor of the Kingdom of Tunis. Otherwise, I am afraid the drink may be merely pleasant but devoid of all really curative properties.

THE TWO CASTLES

The Two Castles are two Roman mausolea. By a ford you cross the Oued Derb even when there is water; most often there is none and the course is just a gigantic rut. The ruins of Cillium lie about you, Cillium that was a *municipium* under Vespasian and in the 3rd century a *colonia*, a considerable place in a strategic position commanding the way down from the eastern Algerian highlands and into the steppes that lead into the heart of *Africa*. Among the remains is an Arch engraved *Colonia Cillitana*, and the mausoleum of one Flavius Secundus, which latter together with another ancient tomb makes up the Twin Castles.[1]

". . . the whole land, as far as the eye could reach, was covered with halfa-grass, leagues upon leagues of this sad, grey-green desert reed."

Norman Douglas's description of half a century ago is no longer true. The esparto grounds have been ravaged. The grass, like all else in this wilderness, grows slowly and there have been but few attempts at replanting. The best esparto is now upon the hillsides where the harvesting is expensive, but only twenty-five years ago, when I first knew this part of Tunisia, the esparto sprouted over huge tracts of countryside while, in places, the grass formed a thick mantle covering the barren body of the land.

This *stipa*, Spanish Grass, alfa or esparto, is still about the best substitute for linen-rag if one would make decent, durable paper for books. Now we see along the road great cubes of esparto tightly packed and bound with metal thongs. Elephants' fodder, you would say, for the roadside is also a railroadside, though we can hardly perceive the line. Anyway, it does not betoken business and bustle, it is just the modest little one-track railway built by the phosphate companies in order to convey their ore up to the eastern ports of Sfax and Sousse.

A KICK FROM VENUS

"Those bundles, Monsieur, the raw material, if I may say so, of literature."

[1] The Kasserine Gap figured much in the news of the 1942–43 North African campaign; here it was that the Allies were held up by Rommel's Germans. Kasserine would be a key-point in any future land-campaign in eastern North Africa, but it is doubtful if anything to the east of Kasserine would be defended, rather the position is a rampart of the Algerian and Moroccan 'redoubt'.

"Pretty expensive too. Tunisian export taxes are too high; I'm thinking about this Libyan esparto, payable in sterling, you know."

"Do you remember Paul Valéry's fable about the disappearance of all material that could be used for writing?"

"Yes, indeed, but he should have thought of T.V."

"By the way, while we are on literary subjects, what is, as a literary man, your opinion on syphilis?"

"As a literary man? Well, they do say that a single shot of flacillin 96 will cure syphilis, at some stages anyway, but we may have to wait a good time so as to see . . ."

"Yes, yes. Well, Madame Macrosène—and I'm very much inclined to agree with her—holds that the falling-off in literature is due to modern cures . . . people are always thinking up anniversaries, but the really significant dates are never mentioned. Now the most important thing that ever happened to Flaubert, for instance—you're surely an admirer of that superb literary artist?—was his receiving what may be called a kick from Venus at Beirut in 1850. It was, as you know, Maxime du Camp, Flaubert's officious friend, who invented the story that epilepsy was the writer's malady. Epilepsy! Why, that nonsense has become part and parcel of the literary legend and Flaubert's name is ensconced in the cranks' list of eminent epileptics. Now, Flaubert didn't go to Carthage until 1858 and there he invented *Salammbô*. Would he have given us this masterpiece had he not been enjoying the stimulus of syphilis? I think not. 1850 and no other is the critical date in the Flaubert story. Epilepsy, indeed."

Comment from Hilali: "Epilepsy can be very interesting. Many families have cause to praise God that they have an epileptic son; he can earn money, good money by throwing fits on the pavement. Onlookers are often generous . . ."

Bounded by barren hills, the land stretches empty and consolatory. The camels stroll and nibble as they please, for they are fastidious feeders; their pastures are most satisfying in clay hollows grey from salt-worts, glass-worts and flecked with mauve statice, sea lavender. Where you see the silvery-green bushes of striplex, that the Tunisians call *ktaf*, there the soil will not be so salt.

Indeed, through its veil you may read the arid African face of the country. When the rains fall, the earth hereabouts does not flush into colour as farther north; the slopes and steppes are not suffused with anemones violet and red, with the blood-drops scarlet or with the yellow and mauve of asphodels. However, when touched with moisture the steppe does soften, does relent, the crucifers bloom while the *harmel* flaunts its long white trails of blossom.

"I had hoped to wander for half an hour or so among the ruins of this ancient city of Suffetula," wrote Norman Douglas fifty years ago when, on the Tunisian steppes, he had been re-pelled by chill winter winds and cold dust. He was unlucky, for though Sbeitla lies over 3000 feet above sea-level, whenever I have visited it in autumn, winter or spring, the countryside has worn an attractive face. Nearly 200 years ago when James Bruce, accompanied by a 'French renegado and ten horse-soldiers', explored the Wild West of Tunisia, he thought Sbeitla "inde-pendent of its architectural beauties . . . situated in one of the most beautiful spots in Barbary embossomed in juniper-trees and watered with a charming stream which sinks into the ground and is seen no more".

The embossoming juniper-trees have vanished and the Oued Sbeitla's abundant springs are now diverted to the supplying of the Sfax waterworks on the east coast over a hundred miles away. But Sbeitla is a charming place and on this early June day the brilliant, clement sunshine was exhilarating and the sky all one shade of vivid gay blue.

You are suffused with a glow of ease. It is good to be alive.

The straight highroad seams the plain and skirts the ground-plan of old Suffetula but rather the Byzantine than the Roman. There are stumps of Byzantine forts, ruins of chapels and churches. With the exception of the Capitoline Temples the Roman things are vague, traces of Baths, of Theatres, the framework of a provincial city. On these steppes the grasses, growing short, hide neither ancient streets nor squares. It was here that Gregorius, the Byzantine representative, held out awhile against the on-slaughts of the conquering Moslems.[1] There is, however, but one sight at Sbeitla and that is the Capitoline Temples, luminous and majestic; they might be of alabaster and lighted from within. The Capitoline sanctuary dedicated to Juno, Jupiter and Minerva, an Eruscan trinity.

I unfold my painting tackle and prepare to daub a little.

[1] In A.D. 647.

Monsieur Macrosène opines the world would be a less tiresome place if there were more amateur painters; painting is a civilized, soothing occupation, *un grand délassement pour l'esprit*, but I fear he really despises subjective interpretations. When he has retired on some photography expedition I take up my quarters within the temples' precincts, a walled court into which you enter under the Triumphal Arch of Antoninus Pius opposite the frontage of the fanes. It was while encamped in this temple-court and admiring the 'extensive and elegant remains' that Bruce was 'incommoded by the Welled Ourran, a lawless, rapacious tribe'. He, his renegado and the ten men, held the compound, though the siege was farcical since neither side dared take the offensive. Bruce's forces and the rapacious Welled Ourran sat glowering at each other until the friendly Welled Hassan hurried up to feed the half-famished traveller and his companions. The rapacious ones beat a retreat when they perceived the loyal natives who used to figure in every traveller's tale but who, alas, are now so deplorably out of fashion.

The Roman Capitol stands out splendid and impressive, a majestic monument to imperial might. In one corner of the court is a tiny Byzantine chapel. Strange, one would have thought the temples would have served the new cult, or can the Christian shrine date from times when the official gods were still being venerated and adored in Sbeitla?

## FORTUNA ROMANA

The nature of the Roman Gods was confused and obscure. Roman religion was mainly cult and rite, though the ceremonies were not mandatory—the Gods could not be compelled—but rather conciliatory and businesslike. *Do ut des*, or in familiar language, 'I scratch your back and you scratch mine.' But if we look below the cold and ritualistic surface of classical Roman religion, we see, just as when we push aside the later trappings of Chinese cults and customs, clear traces of remote and sinister things, taboos and interdiction, totems, fetishes and an uneasy mingling of magic and religion in beliefs and ceremonies among which the cult of the dead loomed large.

Though these southern towns such as *Suffetula*[1] were of late

[1] *Suffetula* (Sbeitla), *Sufa* (Henchir Sbiba), *Ammoedara* (Haïdra), *Mactaris* (Maktar) and *Aquae Regiae* (*Cillium* or Kassarine) were all colonized at or after the time of the Antonines. The steppes southwards to the *chotts* were peopled by nomads.

foundation we may suppose that they were created with the same ceremony that the oriental Etruscans had employed when they made the Eternal City; for the transformation of humble hamlets on seven hills, their constitution into a town was the work of Etruscan conquerors. The shrouded, veiled priest, bearing in his hands the augural staff, after consultation of the auspices, traced with his wand a *templum* or sanctuary in the sky. The tell-tale flight of birds was watched. The confines of the city were marked by a plough drawn by a white ox and a white cow. In fact, all the complicated symbolism and magic which the legends show Romulus exercising when he created Rome. In Etruscan Rome, the royalty was invested with a primitive and sacred character. That meant the King was a perilous possession. The Romans got rid of him, and never again had a monarch until the divine ruler blazed forth in the brilliance of empire.

The Romans never lost their sense of the sacred forces dominating man, but with the Romans, to the end of their story, *sacer* was horrible, awe-inspiring, dangerous and to be averted. The whole Roman vocabulary of religious terms— *Contagio, Miracula, Religiosus, Prodigia* and the rest—is informed with an antique terror. However, not only did the Etruscans give to Rome much of the complex and ambiguous symbolism en-shrined in the incarnation of abstractions: *Pax, Salus, Fortuna*; the Etruscans furnished the Romans with most of the elements of their astounding fortunes, but it was a Roman achievement. There was, doubtless, a good deal of luck, *Fortuna*, and then there was the geographical situation, the way the internal social structure evolved and the Romans' ability to learn from the Greeks without becoming Greek.

The Roman achievement was so stupendous that the Romans themselves did not cease to be astonished at it and to attribute their good luck to some special genius—the *Fortuna Romana*. At critical times a Voice spake saving the City from destruction. The men of the City bequeathed to the Western world an obsession with predestined patterns, and such preoccupations, strengthened with an oriental, Roman and Roman-African religion, stay with us.

In later Republican Roman times, history was conceived to be an instrument of discipline. The official version of the Roman story, brought up to date, became sacrosanct. To question the tale was to be guilty of disloyalty, treason, blasphemy. In their vagueness lies the awful menace of these terms. Yet the traditional history of Rome before the early 4th century B.C., or even its middle, is a tissue of fables as fanciful, though hardly as strange, as the farrago of nonsense that passed in Japan as true until the bomb fell on Hiroshima. There is, of course, no wonder that old legends and chronicles are highly unreliable. There has always been some ulterior motive for their perpetuation or fabrication. Where we err is in a tendency to accept the written records and not to check them off by what remains of the past, by archaeological evidence.

When the Romans were strong and rich enough to look beyond their frontiers, there was the majesty of Greece. The Greeks had an ancient and glorious pedigree; the Romans had not. So the most successful upstarts the world has ever known set to work to fabricate their genealogy and very cleverly they proceeded. The most impudent falsifications are presented in grave, reassuring terms and in a language concrete, reasonable, dignified.

Its imperious voice was heard all through the Middle Ages and impresses us still. The so-called sense of history, the pattern of history, invented to mould the morale and flatter the national pride of the Romans, are things that hover over us still whether we like it or not. Moreover we have, at the present time, an abundance of historians each one of whom has his own key, pattern and explanation. The cyclical view expressed by such writers as Tacitus has doubtless done as much, if not more, to prepare and to smooth the path for the logicians of history, as has been done by oriental myths incorporated into the common stock of European prejudice.

I am inclined to think that the design- and pattern-purveyors suffer under the magic of false analogies and the fallacious reasoning of words rather than concepts. To seek design in the activities of human society is to be led astray by comparisons of a wood of trees with a group of men. Natural history is confused with history.

The philosophy or meaning of history?—that is, of a sum of human activities: we may as well demand what is the philosophy or meaning of football? The view that history repeats itself is generally confirmed either by a complex of doctrine it is sought to justify, or by what might be called just a preference for deductive reasoning.

History derived entirely from chronicles is highly suspect; history derived entirely from archaeology is confused. But archaeology and chronicles together may give us something worthwhile. "Archaeology," as an American writer has put it, "is the great retriever of history, it records and interprets what was never meant to be recorded and interpreted." History is a jumble of confused events quite incoherent. The historians select from the jumble and turn out a glib synthesis. Of course, Western historians are informed by the religious, social, economic and other conditions of their civilization area. Similar material if handled by a Chinese, Indian or Moslem writer will give something with another 'pattern' and 'logic'.

We may go a long way before we surpass the wisdom of the Chinese view of the Mandate of Heaven. In essence the theory of the Mandate is this: 'If you are lucky, you will have luck.' That is the sort of thing. Real, reliable prophecy.

It is difficult to escape the feeling that such pattern as may be found in history is to be discerned at epochs and in (comparatively small) areas where men affected to conform their lives and their thoughts to a whole complex of basic assumptions. When such a complex faded, men, looking round for a substitute to take the place of their former beliefs or tacit acquiescences, seized upon the idea of 'progress' measured in terms of machines, tools—perhaps even knowledge.

The historians dazzle us as they put order and meaning into past epochs, though we may say that the chroniclers do not go back quite far enough. What is the meaning, logic or pattern of European history during the last 100,000 years? If we ever recover from the verbal brilliance we may make bold to ask the historians to tell us what is going to happen next. We may find, to our dismay, that our guides are blind and as ludicrously wild in their predictions as we are ourselves.

However, they may reply, we are not prophets (though we may hold that if there's a pattern or a logic then the historians should be able to guess what the next bit is like without seeing it). All right: "Can we please be told what is the pattern of the times we are living in, of the immediate past, say, that of the last five years?"

Very rarely have contemporaries guessed at the real direction of the stream sweeping them along. Very seldom do we find a writer who can appreciate what is exceptional, what is essential in his epoch. So few historians are men of the world, of the great world. *Il leur manque d'avoir été mêlés à de grandes affaires.* They are bookish, ingenuous. Their presentation of men is not often informed with wordly wisdom, with knowledge of the motives that move men, and with experience of what really happens, and not of what is given out as having occurred.

Among the recent figures which still arouse interest and great curiosity is that of Hitler. Sometimes we have to receive interpretations of him, portraits of him and what you will, fabricated out of books and documents and the like. I had some opportunity of studying Hitler at close quarters; of having two fairly long conversations with him; of hearing about him from those who were or who had been about him. I cannot recognize Hitler in the complex of repressions, impulses and phobias the publicists display.

"They lack personal experience of great business and affairs," and, we might add, they lack experience of the formative, illuminating and sobering commerce and the favour of attractive, intelligent, unsentimental and worldly-wise women. Just that.

The bookish men with an axe to grind, with a theory to prove, their world is peopled with puppets and described by eunuchs. The chroniclers know well, however, the way to exploit fully the vague deterministic prepossessions cherished by most of us and either as obscure legacies of past beliefs or just as inherent in the language we use, or which uses us.

Here in this North Africa, on a soil arid of the arts, purged of informed intelligence, wrote, at the edge and fringe of the Sahara, the acutest and most sensible of historians, a man whose innate rigour of judgement was matched by his lively, keen, and perceptive mind.

He penned his marvellous book in a robbers' nest at Biskra across the Algerian border and at the Saharan face of the hills. He was living among the savage Hilali Bedawin 'hostile to all buildings', the scourges who stripped North Africa and destroyed the last vestiges of ancient order and organization. He had been a man of action before he took to writing; he travelled all his life, he knew and practised the art of living, *il savait vivre*, which is what the professional historian has usually no opportunity of learning. He is undoubtedly the leader of historians who wrote in the Arabic language; he is in the front rank of all historians who ever wrote in any language.

Ibn-Khaldun was a Moslem Spaniard born and bred and must take his place among the most significant of Spanish authors, though the Spaniards are only just beginning to acknowledge that—let us be indulgent—at least half of their valuable literature is written in Arabic.

Ibn-Khaldun saw a pattern in history. The pattern of climate.

Yes, painting is great ease for the spirit. History spills gently over one in the Roman Africa of Sbeitla.

## THE FLIGHT OF BIRDS

When I straightened up and glanced through the Triumphal Arch, I could see, a few hundred paces away, an elegant young man clad in a stylish robe of pale buff. He had a falcon on his wrist while with his other hand he held the bridle of a mettlesome Barb stallion. The falconer seemed to be attempting to mount, but the stallion, just pacing round and round in shapely curves, baulked the elegant young man.

Tunisia is on the direct route of the quail migration. It is not known how far south the creatures fly in autumn, but it is to some favourable clime, probably West Africa and particularly Senegal. It is astonishing that these clumsy, awkward birds do skim across both desert and sea. We all know how difficult quail are to shoot for they dart up from under one's feet and zig-zag about, but quail are poor stayers. In crossing the Mediterranean they fly from Cape Bon in Tunisia to Sicily and up north, or they head for Sardinia and Corsica or Spain. But they are careful and hang about on Cape Bon awaiting a favourable wind.[1]

[1] In the May migration-season if a stiff sea-breeze blows up, the quail—which fly only at night—get knocked about and scattered over the ground to the delight of the local sportsmen. When the quail come in from the south, they are thin and 'green'; when they return in late summer or early autumn, they are plump and toothsome, though by no means all the birds fly as far as Europe; some breed in North Africa. You find young quail in August and sometimes a plain will be covered with dying chicks, the parent birds having just flown off, possibly before the blast of a sirocco wind. Quail's usual food is grains, cereals and insects, but the 'green' birds are thought sometimes to be poisonous because they have eaten of plants venomous for man. So the 'quails from the sea' in the Bible, when eaten by the people, caused a very great plague. It is certain that migrating birds do spread diseases.

There is an international agreement whereby quail-shooting in springtime is forbidden in Tunisia. Therefore, Tunisian falconry is flourishing. The falcons used are the Barbary—or Tunisian—once a favourite in Britain, which is found in abundance on Cape Bon where the falcon-grounds are the property of a few families who jealously guard their rights. The trade in falcons is highly profitable, for the Tunisians do not keep their birds from season to season but catch and train fresh falcons each year.

There is a curious story that falcons which have been trained in Tunisia sometimes migrate northwards as far as the Caucasus and are there employed in falconry.

The falcons are snared with a living bait and a net controlled by a hidden hand. A dot in the sky, the snarer tugs his cord and the sparrows flutter, the falcon sweeps round and faces the wind, rushes down at lightning speed. If the snarer raises his net too soon, the falcon avoids it and pulls up steeply; if the net comes up the fraction of a minute too late, then the falcon is already far off on her way.

It is curious to sit at night among the falcon-dealers at the market of El-Hawaria. Torchlight; you drink mint-tea; the birds pass round from hand to hand. A glance is enough. The colour of the eyes, dark or yellow or rose. The pupils' brilliance. Shape and curve of beak, carriage of the head, the claws, the legs. Naturally, only the females are kept—and in all the hawk tribe[1] the females are larger and more ferocious than the males—the much smaller male falcons are given to the children who pluck and torture them as they will.

The falcon is fitted with jesses and attached to a short leash. All day long from morning to evening she is kept on the hand or the shoulder of her master. In a week she will know him, though if he leaves her alone for a couple of days she goes quite wild again. He excites her appetite by fasting, and her food—generally a sparrow complete with feathers—is given her by hand. When she is more or less tame begins the real training. It is not, it would seem, essentially different from the classical European method, though the Tunisian makes much mystery about his and claims family secrets handed down from father to son.

---

[1] In 1951 a good falcon was selling for 2000 francs or about £2—a considerable sum if one remembers that a Tunisian farm-labourer earns not much more than 200 francs a day in a country where the cost of food is not much lower than in France.

"The Trees of Life" *p. 171*

"... the fish between two cups. But it is something quite
other ..." *p. 186*

It may be that the elegant young man was trying out family secrets in a quiet place where he could be free of inquisitive onlookers, but why the stallion? Yes, he was probably a master-falconer. The first part of the training is done at home—the falcon is excited by a dead quail thrown down near her and little by little dragged away. After each lesson she may eat the quail which she holds in a claw and rends. It is a fine, cruel, glittering spectacle to watch. The falcon's cold precision.

Now comes the training on some open ground, far from interruption, on the spaces near the Capitoline Temples of Sbeitla, for instance. A live quail is tied to a string and the falcon pounces on it in the air. It is a ticklish business. Each movement of falconer and quail must be co-ordinated. There is the elegant young man's quail on a string, but why the stallion? Does he ride while hawking? Yes, surely.

When Monsieur Macrosène and Hilali arrive they are much intrigued. A man who cannot ride is ridiculous.

"Perhaps he cannot ride."

"Hilali, you may be right . . ."

"It's dangerous to mount if one knows not how to ride. Many are killed when flung from horses. Why do not bad horsemen carry loaded crops? Then if there is trouble a resounding thwack between the beast's ears will bring him up short . . ."

We suggest the remedy might be worse than the disease. But we are all puzzled. Why do we not settle matters by hailing the falconer? Well, that's one of the things that just is not done. No, not at all, falconry is a serious business, one of the more important of life's games. No, we cannot break in on falconry, that's the sort of thing that starts revolutions.[1]

A postscript from that admirable but little-known writer the late Elie Faure:

[1] The ordinary Tunisian falconer, the man of the people and not plutocratic cavaliers such as our anonymous young man of Sbeitla, set out on foot. The falcon is on the man's right wrist and in his left hand he holds a stick with which he beats the coverts. If a quail rises he throws the falcon after it and she darts straight to it, grips it and lands. The falconer walks up slowly and quietly, puts the end of his stick on the jesses, thrusts his hand between quail and falcon and jerks her on to his wrist. Each tenth breast is allowed to the falcon and she feeds her ferocity by pecking at a little of the breast-meat, but she must not get heavy and lazy. In the heat of the day comes the rest when the falcon drinks. A good falconer gets fifty birds a day, a crack performer may obtain a hundred. But it is a ticklish business, not a few sportsmen get home with no quail and no falcon; she has just flown away from a master she cannot but despise.

L

*Le gentilhomme, pour être un gentilhomme, doit connaître, en effet,*
*la vanité de tout et de lui-même, mais agir et se conduire comme si tout*
*n'était pas vain. . . . Le pessimisme est toujours à la base aristocratique*
*de l'esprit.*

## PRICE FIXING

It is six or seven hundred yards from the Capitoline Temples
and past ruins of Byzantine forts to the Arch of Diocletian. It
has been much restored but it is an imposing object that must
be about the latest in date of the Roman, as opposed to
Byzantine, remains at Sbeitla. The monument was set up at a
time when the empire was beginning to crack from economic
pressure. The crisis shook Roman Africa where the great private
domains were owned by men pretty indifferent to the welfare of
the workers or even to public weal in any sense.

The Arch was erected, indeed, at a time which has been held,
rather arbitrarily, perhaps, to mark the end of the classical world.
All during the 3rd century the winds of anarchy whistled while
the Empire was getting less and less Roman and more and more
barbarian. In A.D. 301, when the Arch was set up, Diocletian was
reigning as the first of the autocrats and the wearer of the
Persian-style diadem. In this same year he issued his price-fixing
*edictum de pretiis rerum venalium*, the Edict on Prices. Its provisions
were, of course, never observed, while the Edict itself soon became
a dead letter, but the decree marked the profound economic
disorder which heralded the break-up of the old Roman Empire.
Price fixing, debased currency, the collapse of old systems in new
conditions, there is something faintly familiar about all this.

Now, neatly framed in Diocletian's Arch we may observe the
functional outline of a lofty derrick. Prospection.

It is the world desert belt that is also the Moslem Zone. The
sort of country where, at least until yesterday, no account must
be taken of any Nationalism but that of autocratic sovereigns.
Oil, however, seems to favour only the eastern half of the Moslem
World. It would be reassuring to feel that the western, the
African half, were not neglected. It seems probable that there
are oilpools under the surface of Egypt, but the most promising
region would be Sinai, and that is Egyptian, but not African,
territory. Perhaps there is oil nearer to North-West Africa and
to the Moroccan Redoubt. Anyway, Tunisia is being actively

prospected and there looks as though there were a fair chance of finding petroleum. Some frivolous travellers maintain that the local mineral-water has a distinctly oily flavour. But there are more reliable indications. A good deal of natural gas has been discovered in the Sidi Abderrahmane anticline on Cape Bon. Concessions have been granted for the prospection of nearly all northern Tunisia; most of the capital, all the machinery, and the know-how are American.

Oil or no oil? Tunisia is no realm such as Sa'udi Arabia where the wily, one-eyed old monarch can still with truth say *l'état c'est moi*. Oil in Tunisia would add to the flame of agitation. How the Tunisian Nationalists would clamour for their share of the Black Gold, but His Highness Sidi Mohammed el-Amin Bey may be 'Possessor of the Kingdom of Tunis' but he does not own his country lock, stock and barrel as do the monarchs of Arabia, Kuweit and Bahrein.

The French are finding it hard enough to hold down things as they are. They glance round towards Morocco that has been thrown into a ferment by the construction of the American air bases, though these once built may not have so much lasting effect upon the economy and price structure of the Sherifian Empire. Oilfields in Tunisia would be quite another proposition.

Although the French in Morocco have insisted upon low wages for French and Moroccan workmen, it is American money that is rocking the Moroccan ship of State. The French workmen get from forty to seventy cents an hour if they speak a little English—less if they do not. Native Moroccans earn a little over a dollar a day. The *basic* pay of the American workman is $2.25 an hour—about 18s. in British money—so the American draws down in twenty minutes what the Moroccan gets for a day's work, while the French, at the best, get one-quarter of the pay of an American. If oil is struck in Tunisia and the land is overrun with hundreds of tough lads with anything from $200 a week pocket-money, the Tunisians may get very insistent indeed in claiming their rights.

Of course we may take the long view, may reflect that oil is capital and not income, that it is a wasting asset being rather rapidly used up. Water-power, solar energy can provide lasting assets . . . or, perhaps, Africa is the continent for atomic energy experiments. It seems a startling idea.

AFRICA FELIX

The steppes stretch northwards from Sbeitla, but they are bright and often brilliant green from the fields of prickly-pear planted as reserve fodder. When the land is parched the camels will nibble sprouts of the jagged, barbed opuntia, which if we so much as touch will leave our hands smarting and itching from a thousand invisible darts. The camel has a leathery mouth.

The countryside is attractive; there is something classical about it, cheerful and with some promise of fertility; the silvery sheen of the woolpack clouds, or cumulus, enlivens an azure sky washed and purged and occidental. The light is dispensed, not dispersed; you get joyful glimpses of distant bright sun-patches. After the desert and immediate luminosity you feel that this is the sort of place where you could sit down and make up a very plausible tale, put a good deal of order into your surroundings. Classical.

Here and there are goats as well as camels. There are the black, low tents of the nomads, Arabian tents, Asiatic tents, and always a little incongruous save in the sands, though you can find a real Bedawin-type tent right up to the Mediterranean's shores; I came across a clump of such near Utica some time ago. These friendly steppes might be cultivated, indeed the French have constructed dams and barrages on uncertain streams, but the land is hard to woo and the most obvious man-made objects remain worked stones, uprights like stelae and recumbent ones like sarcophagi; here and there a tumbled tomb, Roman witnesses to a time when this was part of *Africa Felix*, tended and cultivated.

It is true that the desert has gained since Roman times, the climate here is dryer and, above all, the land has been stripped of its trees, but it is also true that there was a cool phase of climate round about the Mediterranean basin between about 500 B.C. and A.D. 500. Much of the Roman story is a little clearer if we think of it as having been unrolled in weather conditions rather markedly different from those of Italy today. But it is well to keep a sense of proportion. When we hear stories of *Africa* having been the granary of Rome, when we see the stupendous amphitheatre of El-Djem, large enough to seat with ease 60,000 persons, when we discover, far beyond the range of today's cultivation, the traces of Roman olive-presses and farms, then we are inclined to say that Roman *Africa* must have been another southern Italy or Provence, but it is more than doubtful if the African population was, in Roman times, anything like as dense as that of areas of Italy or of south-eastern Gaul.

Pliny tells us that in Nero's reign six wealthy men owned half of *Africa*; even if we take this statement with a grain of salt, it is obvious that the economy of the province was a lopsided one. As time went on a great deal of the African landed property passed into the possession of the Emperors. The estates were run by stewards while the poor farm-labourers or tenant-farmers lived in huts. So, there were not many villages and Roman *Africa* consisted of a few towns separated by great stretches of countryside. In any case, when the Romans got *Africa* well in hand, Italy had no surplus population for export, or, let us say, there were not many citizens who would emigrate to *Africa*. The situation, indeed, was, in some respects, like that as between France and North Africa today.

What this steppe-land would best bear would be olive-trees, but there are already many millions of them in more fertile eastern Tunisia where so much olive-oil is produced that its marketing is not always easy. What a pity that some arrangement cannot be made whereby the British would take considerable quantities of Tunisian oil. It is, of course, no effective substitute for real butter as a cooking-fat, but oil is flavoursome and wholesome, and if it were more used British digestions would be eased—but then the patent-medicine mongers could not sell their digestive tablets so readily. Anyway, let us look at the matter from the, well, aesthetic point of view; streets and houses would not stink so much of vile greases, whale-blubber and 'substitutes'.

### Arcanum Imperii

"Muchtar," wrote James Bruce, "contains two Triumphal Arches, the largest of which is equal in mass, taste and execution to anything of the kind I ever saw," though when he visited Maktar Bruce had not much first-hand knowledge of Roman monuments. However, it must be admitted that the Maktar Triumphal Arch does make a brave show. It stands right in the middle of the town and is no battered and isolated ruin. Maktar, indeed, in itself and in its countryside, does evoke for us the confident days of Roman *Africa* before the economic, social, financial and spiritual crises that rocked it in the 4th century. In tombs and arches, mausolea and ruins of bridge and farm, we can see the image of the African provincial town where the contrast was often striking between the fine public buildings—closely copied from those of metropolitan Italy—and the mean little dwellings of the mass of the urban population. We get much the same effect whenever the dominant people import from their homeland the outward trappings of a life more sumptuous and solid than that in the 'colonies'. Maktar was as different from Milan as is Oran from Orleans. Despite the names they assumed, most of the Roman citizens in North Africa were not of Italian origin, though they revelled in the imperial official civilization and outdid the Italians in Roman patriotism. The middle-classes and those above them, were Latin-speaking—more Latin-speaking probably than the Tunisians are French-speaking—but everyone could talk one of the 'African' languages, Berber, 'Libyan' or even Punic.[1] The situation was akin to that prevailing in some classes of Russians or Rumanians a few generations ago.

But right until the last, the Romans possessed and exercised the secret of government, the *arcanum imperii*. They knew how to keep the people interested, obedient, respectful, hard-working and proud to become Roman citizens. This secret seems to have been lost. It may be questioned, indeed, whether any people, any imperial people, of later Europe, has known this secret; the Spaniards came nearest to the Romans. The *arcanum* has eluded the French and British—we need not consider the Dutch for their bagman's realm has faded without leaving a trace—or, at least, neither has mastered as did the Romans. It is easy to criticize, but circumstances must be favourable. To use the secret we must be strong, rich, unchallenged. Unchallenged, that is important, there must be no rival masters. Then there must be a culture, a civilization, a code of manners and of living, which are in themselves imposing, attractive, irresistible. Finally there must be assimilation. The Romans were not, of course, wholly successful; they failed in the end, but in their heyday they stood alone, their civilization was incomparable and they were prepared to open their ranks to any suitable candidate.

[1] However, the sister of the Emperor Septimius Severus (who was born in Libya and who died at York) had no Latin when she got to Rome. The Latin of Africa was certainly provincial and marked not only by an odd accent but also by peculiar words and even phrases. The funerary inscriptions are often marked by spelling mistakes and grammatical errors. No doubt, had there been no Moslem conquest, in North Africa would have been developed as original and special neo-Latin, 'Romance' speech as anywhere in Europe.

The sting for us lies in the last. Either the conquerors must take up the conquered and make the victors and the vanquished one, or the 'empire' will last only until the inevitable bad days press down on the imperialists. Then the subjects flick off the yoke. It does not matter what may have been the material or even spiritual benefits spread by the aliens, no memory of such things will serve to keep a subject people subject. Unless men have accepted it for their own, the foreign tongue, its images, its world, the reality it makes are all loathsome, as are likewise the manners of the overlord. The Romans made Roman the white men around the Mediterranean, the British could not make British the brown men of India and beyond, the French could make French the white men of North Africa if these were not leagued together by Islam. The black men of the Chad are not knit up by the Faith, but they will never look like Frenchmen of France. Quite a problem.

## THE GODS OF AFRICA

Late in 1951 there was unearthed near Maktar a stela that once adorned the tomb of a priestess who is, upon this upright gravestone, represented standing, clad in her sacerdotal robes between two candelabra and holding—with what seem to be ritual gestures—a caduceus and an ear of wheat. Above are serpents guarding sacred objects the like of which may be found on Greek monuments. Here, then, is a servant of Demeter, the Earth Goddess, and she is engaged in rites borrowed, doubtless, from those of Eleusis and the other Hellenic Mysteries. It may be that Aegean influence was felt very early in North Africa; as we have noted, horses seem to have been introduced into Cyrenaica from Crete and it is possible that the seat and centre of the first European civilization, that is the Cretan, entertained quite close relations with not only Egypt but other parts of the southern Mediterranean's shores. It looks as though immigrants from the Aegean Isles settled not only in Cyrenaica but also in *Africa* before the coming of the Phœnicians. In any case, there has been, all through recorded history, a stream of influence pouring into North Africa from the east, a stream from the civilization areas of the Levant in the first place. Maybe a prehistoric debt was being repaid in historic days.

Not only in the private houses, the shops and native shrines was a Roman African town exotic—and the climate alone would impose a way of life a little different from that in Italy—but the undercurrent of superstition, religion and custom was non-Latin. The oriental impress left by the Carthaginians was not effaced by the Romans, while from the 4th century B.C. Greek influence in *Africa* was marked. It was an amalgam of Punic, Greek and Roman traditions together with native Berber or Libyan elements which formed the North African religious and spiritual complex.

The contractual, frigid, ritual Roman religion hardly grew to a stature matching the material majesty of empire. The Romans never seem to have been clear about an after-life and a defined dogma of personal immortality has usually accompanied certain phases of political, social and economic evolution. The Romans got on too fast, their cults and beliefs could not keep up. But as the misery of the masses deepened, salvation religions flourished. The confused symbolism of the Asiatic Mysteries swept the Roman world. As early as Hannibal's time the Roman Senate had imported the cult of the Anatolian Mother of the Gods and her scarlet-clad, prancing, eunuch priests.

Augustus restored the temples but he could not restore their hallowed character. The imperial religion was just a Test Act or a Church Parade. Long before the Empire's evident decay the new personal, private faiths were poking their way into the imperial edifice and burrowing under its foundations. In Africa, Mithraism was a particularly favoured religion and there, as elsewhere, popular with the army. This Persian-inspired saviour cult was, indeed, for long the rival of Christianity which borrowed freely from the Iranian religion.[1] It was with a mind to restore a State Religion and cut out the subversive nonconformists that Constantine adopted the Church as cement for the State. It was; but the private religions were not subversive because nonconformist, they were nonconformist because subversive.

Before its promotion in the 4th century, Christianity had spread slowly. In a town like Maktar, 3rd-century Christianity, exclusively a religion for the poor and outcast, acquired a social significance it was never to lose until the Moslems swept away all traces of the Church.

The Christian masses of *Africa*, and even their clergy, were

[1] Sunday is Mithraic: the 25th December is the birthday of the Unconquered Sun. The trappings of immortality and the blaze of glory come all from Persia.

penetrated with Manichaeism, which indeed was regarded as another sort of Christianity. St. Augustine was a converted Manichee and his early unorthodoxy and dissolute life were long held against him, so Irish Pelagius dared to say *Quis est mihi Augustinus?* or "Augustine means nothing to me."[1]

It was the identification of Christianity with the lives of the poor and resentful, an identification prolonged in Africa where, in a colonial atmosphere, the conservatives clung long to the privilege of old ways, it was this identity of church and poverty that led to the Donatist socio-religious schism and revolt. If Manichaeism was crushed by the persecuting Vandal Arian heretics, if Christianity was crushed by the persecuting Moslems, the Donatist communistic social revolt whose leaders brandished religious slogans, had successfully undermined both Manichaeism and Christianity before the triumph of Islam.

Well, what about the pattern of history? We can often find it if we fiddle about with the labels. Shall we say 'Western Civilization' evicted by social revolt whose leaders brandish religious slogans and prepare the way for the triumph of . . . now we can all sit down and think what name.

## DISCRETION IN MAKTAR

The main hotel at Maktar is a sobering place, its hall is shiny and chromium-plated, modern and American. The food is, well, let us say, African. The hostelry is worth a visit for the student of manners and customs. The spacious dining-room is adorned with a considerable number of tall, two-leaved screens, red, green, or blue. These cumbersome objects are mounted on rollers and can be shoved about from one part of the room to another.

In theory the serving of alcoholic drink to Moslems is forbidden; in practice, any Moslem with the necessary money can repair to a European-run hotel and there drink what he likes. But the proprieties must be observed. When the grave Tunisians enter and sit down, one of the screens is hustled up and disposed so as to hide the customers from onlookers out in the street. The booze is brought in coffee-cups and everyone is happy.

The favourite drink with these Moslem topers as with the

---

[1] Many of the Church fathers were Africans, men from the continent of Egypt and black men, and masks and mystery. Athanasius was an Egyptian, Arius a Libyan, Augustine (who with Origen, the castrated Egyptian, was the creator of Christian orthodox dogma) was an "Algerian".

'colonial' is *pastis*, which may vary from a comparatively in-nocuous *anisette* to the connoisseur's good old-fashioned absinthe under another name.

It is said of the hard-bitten *blédard*, or settler in the 'bush', that he needs neither thermometer nor watch. He knows the temperature and the hour when he surveys the level of the liquid left in his bottle of *Pernod*. You will often hear that the 'colonies wear a man out' (*usent son homme*), and it is a fact that few settlers ever get really acclimatized save in the most clement parts of Africa. Second-generation North Africans are different, very different. However, the hobnailed liver is not due to the climate alone for most aliens in Africa feel they need alcohol—though, if they are wise, they will drink only after sundown in the hot regions. The generally most satisfactory stimulant is, apparently, whisky, regarded all over the world as the British major contri-bution to civilization. I am by disposition what might be called a sober man, despite a liking for good wines, and in any case I do not relish the taste of whisky; I drink brandy instead. Still, the African climate does play queer tricks.

Two or three years ago I had to spend a couple of days in Casablanca. The weather was already hot, damp and depressing in the unattractive commercial metropolis of Morocco. Walking along the main avenue, I was assailed by symptoms of approach-ing dissolution and I concluded, within the space of a few seconds, that I was poisoned, had sunstroke, was afflicted with coronary thrombosis and had been knifed in the bowels. I therefore sat down at the nearest café and consumed two brandies-and-sodas. Thank God for the French; none of this damned prohibition, or closing hours. Perhaps I was just dehydrated. Dehydration does make you feel as though you had every known disease of mind and body. When you die of thirst in the Sahara you die in con-siderable and prolonged agony. Never wander off the track. Still, Casa is a bit far north for dehydration, but one never knows.

Very slowly and with some dignity, I wandered along the avenue and stopped at every café-terrace on my side of the road. At each pub I drank a brandy-and-soda—just one. After four hours of this treatment I felt much better. I was, indeed, cured and was enabled to survey with equanimity the commonplace scene.

.      .      .      .      .

Hilali takes on a far-away look, affects not to notice the clandestine boozers of Maktar. It is a small town and what will the neighbours say? Monsieur Macrosène is indignant, not that he would deny alcoholic refreshment to Tunisian Moslems, but he is shocked at the hypocrisy. He would like to see the men drink their *apéritifs* out of glasses in full view of all-comers. Thus the absurd prejudices of the Moslems would be turned to ridicule. Monsieur Macrosène is, at times, a little old-fashioned and ingenuous in his views of life and morals.[1]

"Let him drink and forget his poverty and remember his misery no more." So is preserved for us in Holy Writ the saying of sapient King Lemuel, verily a wise man and a chieftain among his fellows.

## THE TREES OF LIFE

Sometimes they are white, sometimes they are blue. I have never seen the Trees of any other hue, but I do not think that there is any significance in the colours; white or blue may be cherished by Moslem or Jew. The Kairouan Trees were white and fresh.

The trees not only adorn walls but also the skin and bodies of women in the Algerian South, in many parts of Morocco—and in Ghadames, we may remember.

It is often said that tattooing is forbidden in Islam. If this means that a prohibition is to be found in the Koran, then the statement is not true. It is a strange thing that the Koran is often referred to by non-Moslems, but rarely quoted.[2] After all, it seems that there are now in the world more Moslems than Roman Catholics, and as the Koran is more widely learned, scanned, read and chanted than is the Bible, we may conclude that the Koran is the most-read book of any.

---

[1] It is commonly said that the drinking of 'wine' is forbidden in the Koran, but the precepts are not clear. In the crucial passages the word *khamr* is used and this may mean the fermented juice of any fruit or plant and may in Mohammed's day have signified palm-toddy. The word has been interpreted to cover all intoxicants. Islam has not escaped the tendency more marked still in Christianity to create new sins. Still, gambling and usury are forbidden in Islam. What would 'Western Civilization' be without the one and the other?

[2] Islam, however, though simple and unburdened with ritual and sacerdotal organization, does (in most orthodox sects) acknowledge other guides to faith and morals than the Koran alone. There is a rich vocabulary of Moslem exegesis. A *Hadith* (or saying attributed to the Prophet) does contain various condemnations of tattooing which, curiously enough, seem all to refer to women and not to men.

The only text the commentators have been able to find that relates to tattooing is this:

"And verily I will lead them astray . . . and bid them that they may slit the ears of cattle and bid them that they may alter the creature of Allah."[1]

It has needed all the cunning of exegetists to twist this text into a condemnation of tattooing, though the expositors can always find in Holy Writ support for their burdensome precepts. How much ingenuity has been expended in justifying from the Bible political and economic injunctions?

It is generally accepted in the House of Islam, however, that the only two 'alterations of the creature of Allah' are dyeing of the hair and circumcision, though the latter barbarous mutilation would certainly seem to be covered by the condemnation of this Koranic text.

I have often asked what the Trees of Life and other tattoo designs 'mean', though, of course, when confronted with anything so ancient, so venerable and so sacred, even, as these symbols, it is rather silly to ask for 'meanings': such emblems transcend verbal descriptions and are part of a heritage that is felt and not thought. The answers I have got are usually that tattooing is 'customary', or 'lucky' and even, in some out-of-the-way districts of southern Algeria and of Morocco, that the patterns 'distinguished True Believers from Jews'.

In North Africa tattooing is disappearing everywhere, it is hardly ever practised in the towns, and is confined to the poorer classes in the country—they need luck anyway. The Ouled-Naïl are naturally conservative, professional harlots generally are, and even they are ceasing to be tattooed, though some of the older women have their legs, thighs, bellies and arms covered with strange designs of rich, elegant and archaic appearance, but I have not examined such pictured ladies for the last fifteen years and the Ouled-Naïl I looked at then were middle-aged.

Several of the tattoo-designs resemble patterns on the painted rocks and cave-shelters of Spain. There are 'trees' also scattered among the naturalistic paintings of the French prehistoric caverns (as, for instance, at Niaux in the Pyrenees). The Spanish red-ochre

[1] Chapter IV, verse 119.

figures and symbols are found on rock-faces over a large area of eastern, southern and central Spain. These mysterious signs are mostly neolithic but some of them may be more ancient. Many of the figures are clearly recognizable as those of human beings or of beasts. A great many more can be recognized as stylizations only because there is a series leading from the realistic images right up to symbols which, at first glance, appear to have no connection at all with any form of naturalistic art. For instance, there are the semi-naturalistic animals at the site of Los Letreros (Velez Blanco, Almería), here we can behold ibexes merging into 'combs', very surrealist. At La Piedra Escrita (in the Sierra Morena) are dead women without heads, suns, combs, animals upside down, human couples highly stylized, their legs apart, and there are Trees of Life.

The Trees of Life you see on Tunisian walls consist of a long median line from which extend, on either side, three 'branches' in the form of angles or hooks. The trees have nothing to do with tree cults (though plenty of traces of these still survive in Tunisia) but are painted to celebrate weddings. The Trees are emblems of good luck and therefore ensure and attract it. It is difficult to say how long the Trees have been limned on Tunisian walls; maybe for a very long time indeed. The innocent-seeming geometrical pattern survived under the jealous eye of Islam so intolerant of idols that little Moslem girls can never have dolls. We can be sure, however, that the lesser Trees of Life tattooed upon North African women are magic emblems from a mysterious past. They are, in fact, fertility symbols, each set of 'branches' is the conventionalized representation of a sitting woman, her legs wide apart, as we may see them on the Spanish Spirit Rocks.

Magic symbols. Designs, not naturalistic presentments of living things; designs that are not what we should call writing. But are we so sure? A script is composed of symbols with fixed values. But writings fall into two classes: those with symbols to recall ideas, objects and so forth, and then symbols in another group, those to recall the sounds employed in pronunciation.

There is a nice little battle of words always waiting to be fought between those who consider that a script such as the Chinese (which recalls concepts and percepts) is of more, let us say, intellectual nobility, than a writing such as we employ which evokes the sounds of words employed to define concepts or percepts. Well, well. Anyway, pictures are a sort of writing, they convey a meaning, but, we may object, they are not writing because the meaning is not fixed and will vary according to the spirit and mind of the onlooker. True enough—for us, but it may well be that the stupendous and awe-inspiring art of the palaeolithic men spoke to them in uncertain terms. We can let our fancy roam.

But here is something more definite. The checkers, comb-shaped, roof-shaped objects, the scrawls and squares, and springs and prongs and all the hundred and one nameless and un-identifiable things appearing on the walls together with the pictures of huge bisons, wild oxen, of bears and mammoth and cave-lions, of horses and rhinoceroses, these conventionalized symbols must be something very like writing in the widest sense of the term.

There is every reason to think that the three fundamental components of the prehistoric schematic art are masculine figures, feminine figures of human beings and zoomorphic or beast-signs. The three are these:

The pectiniform or comb-like signs are found, as we have seen, on the great naturalistic pictures of southern France and northern Spain; the signs occur all through mesolithic and eneolithic times and remain a fundamental motif, though modified and complicated, of eneolithic schematic art.[1] In 1900 there was discovered at the Romanelli cave near Otranto in southern Italy a limestone block covered with five lines of 'writing' comprising the three fundamental symbols: man, woman and beast. The 'writing' is most probably palaeolithic, of Old Stone Phase times, that is more than ten thousand years old. A distinguished Italian archaeologist has not hesitated to call this 'real primitive sacred writing'. Why not? It certainly faded away and writing was rediscovered, reinvented in Sumeria about five thousand

[1] The Mas d'Azil painted pebbles (doubtless lucky and magical) carry signs which include our three fundamentals, but the resemblance of these signs to Latin and Greek letters cannot be anything but fortuitous.

years ago. Then representational art faded away from Europe, and the world, it seems, and appeared again. Well, that is the question, when?

Anyway, the Kairouan Trees of Life blazon forth one of the three fundamental designs, that of women, and the symbols are just read as 'luck' or not read at all, but heedlessly accepted.

We have to get a large truck shifted before we can photograph the arrogant fertility scrawls. Monsieur Macrosène, being French, and, as he puts it, *cent pour cent laïc*, cannot resist some light-hearted banter. *Les jambes des jolies femmes je les écarte*, he hums as though he had invented the witticism. Hilali shows no signs of complicity. What can one do with a people who, as is well known, are just *pourri de vices*, lousy with vices, and are so sly and hypo-critical they won't see the point of a healthy *gauloiserie*? What indeed?

## JIHAD

Kairouan was reputed once a Holy City, whatever these words may mean, though as it was the foundation of the Moslem Conqueror of Africa maybe there was some immanent virtue stored within the walls. The Kairouanis are not in appearance fanatical, though I have often found them less urbane and polished than the inhabitants of other Tunisian towns, but the dwellers in cities of shrines and pilgrimage are often both grasping and sceptical.

The Kairouanis, however, just as most other Tunisians, know there is a sort of cold war being waged by Moslems. A cold war or a holy war? Well, this word *jihad* has passed into our language, and our dictionaries give as its explanation 'religious war of Mohammedans against unbelievers', but, as a matter of fact, *jihad* does not signify 'war' at all but a 'struggle in which one puts forth all one's strength' just as much in a cold as in a hot contest. There is a *jihad* on.

In most Moslem communities today the people, to a greater or to a less degree, suffer from a sense of inferiority provoked by Western ways and machines and *not* by what we call 'Western civilization'. Even those who do not know what is hitting them, so to speak, feel the pinch of modern methods applied in social and economic conditions quite unsuited for such methods. The Moslem world is in a ferment, because Western ways have cruelly disturbed poverty-cursed populations; but the House of Islam is also heaving because agitators, Nationalist and Communist, are encouraged by the manifest weakness of Britain and France and by their obvious dependence upon the United States reputed to be favourable to the cause of subject States. And, above all, the local native Moslem régimes cannot or will not give what the countries need and must have if they are to escape Communism; that is, not bogus democratic systems, but social and economic revolution under the direction of a commanding and ruthless leader such as was Mustafa Kemal Atatürk.

Atatürk weakened, though he could not destroy, the influence of Islam in and among a people pious enough but hardly so identified with Islam as are the inhabitants of the Arabic-speaking lands. There are no signs that any leader from Morocco to Iraq would dare to combat the Faith even covertly. Indeed, a by-product of the discontent in Islam is a revived Faith, not perhaps in the sense of a spiritual renaissance, but in that of a challenge to the social and economic standards of the Western world. The Cairene crowds which fired Egypt's capital in 1952 were moved by a complex of motives, but their fanaticism, their hatred and their fury expressed themselves in Koranic formulae. Islam is in its essence, if not a religion of simplicity and poverty, still one, in theory, opposed to usury and ostentatious display. Few movements, we may think, are more disturbing to the privileged than a revolt directed against the fabric of society rather than against just the form of a régime.

Islam is, in fact, a Party, although it is not the only one offered to Moslem peoples. Still, not a few Moslem Communists affect to profess the Faith, and this seems paradoxical enough but not incomprehensible. If there is no such thing as 'Western civilization' and has been no such thing as 'Western European civilization' since the Reformation, 'Moslem civilization' does exist in the sense that there is a peculiar area in which certain conventions and ways of life are maintained by custom, law and religious sanction. As, alas, in these degenerate days, the last of these supports of society is perhaps the weakest, we find Moslem leaders identifying themselves with Nationalist movements, not only that some of the violence and resentment and hate may lend their strength to religion at the same time as to nationalism, but

". . . fat amorous bull-frogs are reposing from the heat
of the day" *p. 188*

". . . Ksar Lemsa has a familiar outline . . ." *p. 192*

also that a road-block may be thrown up against the advance of the Other Party.

## SUCCESS

Over the Plain of Kairouan, brown and bright. Distant horizons heat-hazy. Through the necropolitan outskirts of the city, for the suburbs are graveyards dotted with white tombstones and the domed cubes that are the last resting-places of holy men proved to be such by the luck that dogged them, by their illustrious descent from the Prophet through his daughter Fatima, or by common consent. By dreams.

The holy man, that is the blessed man, can hand on, can communicate his virtue and, after his death, his remains are beneficent. Just as contact with saints' relics were salving both to the living and the dead of medieval Europe, so in North Africa not only do men seek to touch a holy man, but the dead are buried in the company of the saints. When the time comes it may be possible to follow up in the saint's train.

A 'good' man is not one who might be so termed for any of the reasons current with us—playing the game, benevolence and what we will—or even for his compliance with divine law. It is all too obvious that what we most often see are the success of knaves, the calamities of fools and the misfortunes of those led, as Lucian put it, into a belief in the discretion of fortune. A good man in Islam is a man God has marked with His favour. How do we recognize that favour? Well, not necessarily by what we should call success. No. Your North African knows that you are not likely to win a prize in the lottery if you don't secure a ticket; he does think, however, that winning a lottery prize is quite as respectable and indeed religious way of getting money than scheming and fighting and lying and killing for it. Very quaint and primitive.

As Monsieur Macrosène says, we can learn a lot about what we impudently call our thought if we compare the ready-made phrases we deal out in French or in English, let alone Arabic. *Il n'est pas très réussi* emphatically does not signify 'He's not very successful'. Even when we speak the subtle speech of the matter-of-fact French, when we mention a successful man we must indicate how he is successful. Oh for the blessed haze of English!

M

## THE GREAT MOSQUE OF FROISSART'S AFRICA

This Mahdiya or Mahdia, founded by the Fatimid ruler of Tunisia, Ubaidallah el Mahdi or the 'Guide', was built upon the site of a Phœnician factory and a Roman town; Mahdia was Froissart's 'Africa'. Often a prize disputed between Moslems and Christians, the overgrown village is now a raw, white, decayed place with, it seems, ten thousand inhabitants. Its interest lies in the treasures of its sea and in the beauty of its mosque. Three miles out, beyond the lighthouse, sank in ancient times a galley from Athens. For five years after 1907 divers brought up from the hulk the splendid bronzes and marbles, gnawn and pitted by the sea-salt, which are now in the Tunis museum.

Art is reality. Because of the Moslem ban on representational art (a ban, we may remember, which was imposed, like the Jewish ban, so that idols might not be created) the creative art of the men in Islam was swung into one majestic channel, that of architecture. The architects of earlier times gathered into themselves, it would seem, the invention, the artistic skill, the sensitiveness and the imagination which in other societies have been dispersed and scattered among different sorts of artists.

This Great Mosque of Mahdia has a superb porch, in itself worthy of the pilgrimage to old *Africa*, a porch so like all the trivial, mean, blighted and gimcrack arches and porches of modern *style arabe* and yet a portico so entirely different. As you gaze at it you may measure how feeble and vulgar are imitations of it and also how noble is this entrance-gate, horse-shoe shaped, niched, linked in spirit both to Mesopotamian buildings whose pedigree reaches right back to Ur of the Chaldees, and akin in inspiration also to Roman Triumphal Arches, the most common monuments of domination still surviving in North Africa.

Sometimes the Mahdia mosque may be visited on very rare occasions with special permission and with little publicity, for all the mosques of Tunisia have been photographed, and not always by Moslems, but those of the whole country, with the exception of three in Kairouan, are supposed to be shut except to the Faithful. Anyway, this Tunisian mosque was the model of the famed mosque of Al-Hakim in Cairo, also built by the Fatimids, and after they had conquered Egypt,[1] and Al-Hakim's

---

[1] The Fatimid dynasty of Caliphs was, if not of Tunisian origin, Tunisian in its early history.

edifice, one of the most splendid in Islam, while owing, of course, as did, and as does all Moslem religious architecture, much to Syrian prototypes, is clearly an Egyptian version of our Mahdia mosque whose monumental entrance is reproduced in Cairo.

## JUSTINIANOPOLIS

The bold, grey walls stand still intact save at the north-west corner, though the bombardments of the late war changed considerably the appearance of Sousse. When the Emir Ziyadat-Allah refashioned the Byzantine ramparts which had girt Justinianopolis, he set up those swallow-tail crenellations just a year after Ecgbert had secured a vague primacy over England while the Norse sea-bandits were beginning to harrow his country and France.

We drive round the foot of the towering walls, first from north to south, following the road dividing the Old Town from the new shapeless, nondescript houses and streets lining the port; we swerve westwards, still with the walls to our right and reaching up high above us, then we are at the city's kernel, the mass of the citadel forming a projection beyond the walls' alignment. The frontage of the *kasbah* is Byzantine and Mesopotamian. Constantinople and Ctesiphon. The twin sources of Moslem architecture.

Through a court white, high-walled and then into the halls and apartments. Ninth century. Where are the 9th-century British palaces? There never were any on the scale of old Sousse and of its citadel-palace, luminous, spacious, gravely gay.

Sousse, of course, before being Byzantine Justinianopolis or Roman Hadrumetum, was Phœnician, Punic, but of this Sousse there are but few remains. The Romans abolished their predecessors sometimes with kindness, for there was here no such harrowing and ploughing as sterilized the site of Carthage. Still, it is quite possible that the Phoenicians had a factory here 3000 years ago, 1000 B.C.: that is ancient in the history of North Africa, in its written history, let us say.

## THE SIGN OF TANIT

There are not many Punic things in the *kasbah* of Sousse, but there are enough to remind us that although we know a good deal about what the Romans wanted people to think concerning the Carthaginians, we know nothing about what the Carthaginians wanted people to think about the Romans. There can be no doubt that the Carthaginians taught the Romans much; it is said, among other things, the art of making roads. Punic art may seem so disappointing because so little of it has survived, above all because we have no Carthaginian architecture.

Here at Sousse are some pointed jars from tombs, jars identical with those of the Levant and very like those found in Spain; there is a Throne of Baal and a stela with the Sign of Tanit and invocations to Tanit, Baal and Hammon in that neat, legible, workmanlike script the Phœnicians invented, their alphabet; no elaborate ligatures, curls, whirligigs, diacritical marks and the like. A script so clear, so simple that a dullard can learn it in a day or two.

I have been lately to revisit Utica and Carthage, the one so desolate and the other commonplace. I had been promised revelations and, indeed, there is a good deal to see that was not there fifteen years ago.

You stand on rising ground overlooking the wide and melancholy plain of the Bagrada (the Medjerda, as it is now called) which has pushed the sea away for miles since the time, three millenia since, when the Phœnician merchant-venturers came hither on their ships from Tyre and Sidon.

In places the mounds have been cut down to reveal the Punic cemetery. The pits are deep; at the bottoms lie massive stone sarcophagi. Below them is nothing, nothing of man's handiwork. On the hard floor, sterile of all art or craft, are the witnesses of a complicated civilization. There is always something startling about this fade-out in daylight, so to speak. We like origins to be lost in mists. But there are, indeed, no dark ages in *Africa*, except those of prehistory. History in this North-West was imported ready-made. The Phœnician, Punic, Carthaginian things bear no relation at all to what preceded them.

In this graveyard of Utica many of the monolithic sarcophagi lie in the damp of the river's seepings, and these sarcophagi seem not to have been placed where they are but to have been hewn out of the death-pit's rock. There is a curious place in Burgundy where you may see half-finished Merovingian coffins roughly cut out of the stone but never finished or removed—an ancient undertaker's workshop.

As you hop from edge to edge of the masonry blocks which line the walls of the subterranean mausolea, you are in a ruined necropolis. All around the poor, harsh, salt soil sprouts coarse grass. There are a few black Bedawin tents, some stone huts, nothing more but some men in tatters and noisy, troublesome woolly Berber dogs. What is a civilization? The scene at least must look less 'civilized' than 3000 years ago.

There is a new little field-museum that is really an archaeological laboratory: grave-gear, terracottas, lamps and small mass-produced articles giving little hint of artistic creation. Probably the Carthaginians did not waste valuables down with dead men in coffins. Maybe we can get a better idea of what Punic *Africa* may have been if we stroll through the crypt of the Louvre where is displayed a superb collection of objects from Phœnicia itself.

At Carthage (that was until the 7th century B.C. subordinate to Utica) there is nothing affording a fresh revelation of Punic Carthage; the dusty collection in the museum of the *Pères Blancs* is still the most considerable exhibition of Carthaginian arts and crafts.

What has been cleared since the war is a large area of the Roman town; it is below the hill of Carthage and quite near the sea-cliffs. As a show it is disappointing. There are huge, clumsy remnants of market-place, forum and temples; massive, provincial, marine. The significance of the assemblage lies in its foiled destiny.

We do not always remember that Carthage might have become the Byzantine capital. During the critical years of the birth of Islam Heraclius was Emperor; his reign was a long struggle against the Persians by whom he was so sorely defeated that he proposed to transfer the capital of the Empire to Africa and to make Carthage the Newest Rome. However, Heraclius decided to have one more try, he pulled himself together and inflicted a crushing blow on the Sasanian realm, a blow, indeed, from which it never recovered, for so enfeebled was it that the Moslems encountered relatively little resistance when they attacked Persia.

The fatal year for the Persians was A.D. 629. The Empire at Byzantium lasted more than eight centuries longer. The Newest Rome at Carthage might have stayed the Horsemen of Allah. Logic of history?

As you stand among the stupid stumps of Roman Carthage, there, a mile or so to your right, is the conglomeration of white cubes that is the New Palace of Carthage. His Highness Mohammed el-Amin would not have his summer residence, as had his predecessors, at La Marsa to the north of Carthage headland, for at La Marsa the French Residents-General keep their country house.

Tunisian architecture, however, even of the most flimsy and uninspired sort, is never quite so treacherous to its prototypes and models as are some Western architectures to theirs. You do not get in North Africa those really hair-raising abominations created, you would say, by drunken barbarians who having seen photographs of the Medici Chapel, the Panthéon, the Grand Palais and the Salon d'Hercule, could not remember which was which.

## THE PIT OF TOPHET

Though there is nothing more to be seen of Punic Carthage, there is a Punic site excavated in recent years. It is quite near Tunis at the little suburb by the sea, Salammbô, so called after Flaubert's book which owed so much, it seems, to its author's physical misfortune. There are some shapeless depressions which, one is told, mark the emplacement of Carthaginian docks. Then, passing through surroundings for all the world like those of one of the southern Paris suburbs, say Fontenay-aux-Roses or Sceaux, you pull up beside a rock-garden and are soon on a path between two pits roughly circular at the surface of the garden but then narrowing to an almost pointed bottom. Little craters, in fact. Dotted about the pits' sides and all about you at street-level and among Alpine plants, or rock-plants, are hundreds of small terracotta or stone boxes shaped somewhat as were the incense-altars of the Romans, boxes with horns at the top corners and incised on the front with a stylized figure of Tanit, the Punic Goddess, with hands and with crescents. Hands of Fatima and Crescents of Islam a thousand years before Mohammed. Hands of Fatima you will find everywhere as trinkets or on house-doors. Magic hands, stylizations of the mysterious stencils on the walls of caverns fifteen thousand, twenty thousand years ago.

Under and beside the Punic symbols are several lines of matter-of-fact Phoenician script.

These are the Pits of Tophet. These the cinerary urns that

held the ashes of children offered up in sacrifice to Baal. Sacrifice of infants induces fertility of the soil, the blood is lapped up by the hungry earth. The Phœnicians brought with them a mass of soil- and earth-cults and a preoccupation with blood, fecundity and death, the religion of an agricultural community whose mysteries and rites were so sharply different from those of hunting and food-gathering folk as were perhaps still the mass of the native North African Libyans even if they were perforce settling down.

The sacrifice of infants also keeps the population stable and checks the growth of numbers, so much more a menace in an agricultural than in a hunting society.

In ancient *Africa*, as elsewhere in the world, more female infants would be immolated than males: the gods get what is good for them, and if that is not always the most precious of men's possessions, why, such a state of things merely shows that there are always, as the practical French say, *des accomodements avec le ciel*—ways of fixing things with Heaven. So, the ancient Romans averred that no sacrifice to some gods, at least, was more pleasing than that of a pig, much less expensive than an ox.

It is not, of course, certain that all the multitudinous cinerary urns contained the ashes of victims to Baal, maybe some of the remains were those of children who died a natural death and who were dedicated posthumously to old Baal-Hadad, the ancient divinity of the Syrian highlands and Lord of Rains and Storms. The Semitic-speakers found him when they came up from their drying deserts of Arabia and sought out the fertile coast-lands of the Levant. In the saga of Baal-Hadad, of his sister Anat and in the legend of Danel (preserved in the tablets from Ras-esh-Shamra in Syria) the Great God El himself after having ripened the ears of corn, kisses them with his divine lips and renders the wheat fit food for Men and Gods. He has de-sacralized the grain and removed from it its awful and ominous character. In the Syrian myths runs a preoccupation with blood, life, death, human sacrifice, fecundity rites and worship of the spirits of the earth. In fact, here are the beliefs and practises of communities whose religion and whose magic and whose art were so opposed to those of the hunters who created in our Europe the first paintings and drawings.

The Romans very quickly wiped out not only Carthaginian

monuments, but also Punic culture, administration and fashions. The Carthaginians had kept the natives segregated, or at least, *Apartheid* was the State policy. The Romans offered assimilation. For the trade economy of a privileged minority—the imperial economy of a commonwealth; for a provincial civilization—an oecumenical one. Punic religion, however, and Punic language, lingered on. There is no proof that the Romans exerted pressure to ensure conformity. However, after the destruction of Carthage in 146 B.C., Hadrumetum, that is Sousse, rallied to the Roman cause and was declared a free city, so remaining until Trajan's time when it became a *colonia* or colony.

The representational art of North Africa. There are the anonymous and magic paintings and engravings on the Written Rocks. Of Punic art little remains. Roman art stands alone. Since Roman times the mask of Islam has lain upon the land.

The relics of Hadrumetum are imposing; triumphal chariots, vacant but impressive statues and the superb, unrivalled, multi-coloured pageant of the mosaics revealing a civilization even in this provincial version, sophisticated, clear-eyed, articulate; little that is silly or childish.

It is the Roman things; for there are some Byzantine but so few; they are mildly interesting but of no great aesthetic value; they are oriental in spirit and execution.

Yet even the Roman things are tinged with un-Latin pre-occupations, or it may be that we find these un-Latin since we have been taught to keep our eyes fixed upon the Golden Age in Italy itself and not to peer at the Silver Age in the colonies where there are too many strange things waiting to puzzle and edify us.

Here is a Virgil and the Muses, but in the 3rd century when this was made to adorn some rich provincial's villa, the poet's image indicated no literary preoccupations on the part of the business man. Literature does not seem to have flourished much more in Roman *Africa* than it does in French Tunisia. Once he gets free of metropolitan trammels the indomitable barbarian makes little pretence at respect for culture. No, the Virgil of Hadrumetum was already a mystical, prophetic figure, almost medieval in significance, *sortes Virgilianae*, Virgilian Lots. The poet is placed between two panels showing Bacchanals. Mysteries. The Car of Neptune displays a huge magic trident.

But the classical scenes are a little mechanical; perhaps, with few exceptions, mass-produced; in fact, they are decoration, but significant decoration, almost protective or magical. There are Tritons and Nereids, a Rape of Ganymede very like one unearthed at Bognor in Sussex, the Four Seasons, the Toilette of Venus, Apollo and the Muses; even these mythological subjects have an African tilt; Leda and the Swan, Orpheus and his Lyre.

Some things are more exciting, a Triumph of Bacchus very classical, the God's chariot drawn by leopards as in Tintoretto, all the trappings here of the 3rd-century Dionysiac cults. There is a charming design of Satyrs and Bacchantes; it looks like a *toile de Jouy* wall-hanging and the *motifs* are for all the world those you see on Moustiers faience and earthenware. Here is a hunting scene, perhaps interpreted in oriental and un-Latin way as a parabole of the Trials of the Soul.

There is a fishing scene with an Egyptian background done doubtless by Alexandrian Greek artists come to Hadrumetum in the 2nd century. A delightful mosaic of Pygmies, aquatic plants and hippopotami—no, it is not some marvelled vision of an earlier and more fertile Sahara, it is a view of the Nile delta where the hippopotami lingered until a thousand years ago.

An anchor, very cruciform and entangled in fish, that may be, no, doubtless is, Christian; though the picture may mean no more than that in the medley of African cults, mysteries and rites, a cross was as prophylactic as a fish or a hand.

Now for the sporting side of life. The horses. Roman *Africa* was a racing man's country. Here are the four winners, the stallions that carried off all the prizes one season about A.D. 240. Nicely groomed, in good condition, tails plaited and tied, horsecloths on, forelegs bound, out for a walk with the stable-boys. Sorothus was a well-known owner. Here's a view of his stud: stallions, mares and foals, Barbs, no doubt, but well-trained, handsome Barbs, remote ancestors of Tulyar and Monsieur Boussac's cracks. But the finest sporting print of all is the double medallion of heads; perhaps it was let into the wall of a stable. The fine, delicate noble beasts live, their eyes follow you about the room.

Yes, a sporting community. A sporting community enveloped in strange preoccupations and survivals.

A most superb scene, immensely impressive. The Sea God at the bottom of a basin in the Bath—the mosaic was found with the lead pipe still in place—he is none other than Baal Hadad, protector and guardian of Phœnician sailors in the western seas, old Baal by whose favour and grace the Punic navigators skirted Africa right round to the Cameroons, and who knows? maybe farther still.

The God's head is of majestic gravity, his visage noble. Crawfish claws clamber from his hair, aquatic plants and leaves are intermingled with his long tresses and beard. It is a dream of greens and blues and mauves. From the corner of his eyes, from his nostrils and the ends of his mouth, trickle streams of waters, imperial tears for mankind.

A master artist and a master craftsman designed and executed this vision of Hadad the old Storm and Rain God of the Syrian highlands, Baal-Hadad. After this, a magnetic-eyed Medusa seems almost insignificant.

The Evil Eye surrounded by two serpents and a fish. Fish are plentiful on these African Roman pictures, the fish passed as a Christian symbol and an acrostic was woven from its Greek name. There are fish today on the Tunisian Italian ice-cream vendors' carts. And there are fish on the mosaic thresholds, magic thresholds at Sousse. Nothing is more sacred than a threshold, nothing can be rendered more salutary and magical.

Here is one of many. O CHARI reads the inscription, the fish between two cups. But it is something quite other, the fish is a phallus and the cups female symbols. The great power of nakedness and sexual conjunction that protects, wards off and counteracts. Trees of Life, magic pictures. Which things, maybe, are an allegory.

## The Road Through the Almond Trees

We are on our way from Kairouan and hope to strike an uncharted defile through the mountains that lead, we hope, to Ksar Lemsa. Monsieur Macrosène deplores that the Tunisians are now so hostile to the French. I feel that it is impossible to gauge the importance of any public opinion. It is easily twisted and moulded. In 1938, for instance, if you walked down the avenue Jules-Ferry in Tunis at dusk, you would be surrounded by crowds of jostling, insolent louts, smart and sporting Fascist buttons. These young men were the politically conscious *Italianissimi* who, as they served in neither Italian nor French army,

could well afford to be bellicose. Today, it is almost impossible
to imagine that such creatures can ever have existed at Tunis. One
sees no one even remotely resembling them; it is true they are
nearly fifteen years older—they are, also, most of them now,
naturalized French.

"I should say that in the French overseas possessions, the non-
European populations have got a deeper French imprint than
British-controlled peoples have a British imprint. . . . We've
only to think of India . . . where Hindi, they boast, is entirely to
supplant English by 1965 . . ."

"You saw that, with the exception of Chandernagore . . ."

"And that's a suburb of Calcutta . . ."

"Quite true, with that exception the French colonies in India
have voted to stay French; their capital is Paris, not New Delhi."

"Of course, but there are practically no French *colons* running
French India, the French Indians are masters in their own house,
the smuggling's good and there is no tiresome Prohibition. . . ."

"And we French take life as it comes and even when we treat
people like dogs, we don't insist they should come smartly to
attention and snap out, 'Thank you, sir,' as I've heard happens
in some places."

We have been told to drive on until we get to a clump of
almond-trees and there to ask the way to what our informant in
Kairouan picturesquely called *trik el-luz*, the Road of the
Almonds. Near the trees is a group of men, peasants, perhaps,
fairly prosperous and pleasant mannered, subtle, for they are
Tunisians, egalitarian because they are Moslems, but not very
communicative even to Hilali. We begin to rise from the dusty
plain and to engage among foothills which, as they close in upon
us, disclose on either side and on the lower slopes, bushes and
clumps of vagabond heather, of rosemary, cystus and ashy broom.
Here and there is a holm-oak or an Aleppo pine. These hillsides
could be easily reforested, it is a dry land but one knowing a
succession of seasons. The native African thuya would do well
here, holding the soil and attracting the moisture.

We come to a stop on a clearing; across the little freshet and
among the trees is a tall building, a sort of antique barn, perhaps
forty feet by twenty. One side is scored with three arches bricked
up and from this edifice emerges the man whom Hilali was told
to find and to question.

Always polite, Hilali hails him:[1]

"The blessing of God be upon thee, where is the track through the hills?"

"Ah, the track; I live in the Roman's House and by the Well of the Frogs, as you may see."

We do, just near us is a deep well on whose low waters fine fat amorous bull-frogs are reposing from the heat of the day. We stroll round the Roman House; it might be some Byzantine chapel, botched and patched and rebuilt, or at least it may stand upon the site of some Byzantine structure. *Dar er-Rum.* The House of the Romans. *Rum* is a word all Moslems know. There is no reason for wonder that the poor countryman uses the words and that Hilali picks them up. 'The Romans' is the title of the Thirtieth Chapter of the Koran, and although there is not very much which is particularly specific and detailed about the Romans in the Holy Book, still all Moslems who have any education at all have learned the phrase 'The Romans are vanquished' in this same chapter of the Koran. Of course, in the Moslem scriptures and perhaps in the mouth of an Arabic speaker today *Rum* signifies 'Byzantine' and not what we call 'Roman'.

Hilali and the Man of the Roman House converse. Question and answer. Ask the way and get it pointed out. Then find, when you have followed the road, that you are not at all where you had hoped you would be. But more sophisticated conversation is often as disappointing and barren. Arabic, nevertheless, is a language in which phrases generally mean something, though possibly several things at one and the same time. However disappointing may be the spiritual and intellectual treasures revealed to those who take the trouble to learn literal Arabic, we may reflect with satisfaction and thankfulness that *Gone with the Wind* fitted into an Arabic dress of forty-four pages in rather large print.

All about us are tall tufts of rosemary, here more insolent and upstanding than in our northern climes. This Tunisian rosemary is a violent herb, *klil* they call it. We pluck sprigs and roll them in our hands. The perfume is rich and vivifying:

---

[1] When he asks any question or inquires for information Hilali says *barak' Allahu fik*, which is just 'please' in Arabic; one does not nowadays hear the formula as often as one should.

"And hence some Rev'rend Men approve
Of *Rosemary* in making *Love.* . . ."

Tunisian rosemary, indeed, yields an essential oil forming a
base of stimulating and provocative odours suited to the African
air, so often neutral but not seldom hospitable to perfumes. The
scent of *klil* hangs about the gold-speckled Venetian phials and
lace-glass stoppered bottles and vessels in the cabin-shops of the
Perfumers' Row. It is pleasing to reflect that something, at least,
of African sweet odours is a gift of the country and not imported
from Basle, Geneva, Milan or Stuttgart.

Hilali is perturbed at the thought of the solitary life of the
Man of the Roman House. Perhaps he has known misfortune?
We should say that he is still well acquainted with it. About a
third of the Tunisian population is unemployed or is employed
only for part of the year. There is a sort of farm-pool made up
of shifting, migrant, unhappy men.

We offer a mite. I was taught to give to beggars and it was
impressed upon me as a child that not only was alms-giving
honourable and decent, but also that mendicancy is one of the
most arduous of professions. I like the company of chapmen,
seelys, bancrofts, baxters and others whose names have become
respectable with capital letters, but of them all the cheapjacks
are my favourites. . . .

Alas, the Man who has known Misfortune is also more or
less a halfwit, but whether his halfwittedness has been assumed
as a protection or imposed by misery, or is a curse from before
birth, we do not learn.

"His hand does not restrain," murmurs Hilali. The man
himself appears bemused. Charity bestowed edifies the bestower.
Should he, in folly and impiety, seek gratitude, he invites and
deserves disappointment, and chagrin.

A road rutty, uninviting, still a road, and beside clear,
shallow running waters that darken soon into a muddy line of
puddles while the road fades into a track that looks and feels
like a dry torrent. We swing and slither along, twist, turn, rise
and dip, but, on the whole, we seem to be pulling up between
hills that approach but never form a gorge. In the shade the air
is cool but laden with warm scents. A whiff of Provence. The glen
is full of scrub and shrubs. The view expands; we swerve right

and find ourselves on a fine main thoroughfare, asphalt-surfaced, beautifully cambered, part of the scene, but if we look back we cannot see how we came, the hills present an unbroken face. We keep on towards the north. The country, though empty, is much less dusty and dry than the land around Kairouan on the other side of the hills. Here and there a farm, or rather a more or less European-style house surrounded by trees, sure signs of the settler or *colon*. This one we are coming to now, it has red-tiled roofs and is on a knoll overlooking broad fields, it may be the home of one of the richer *colons*—the men who are the real rulers of this so-called Regency of Tunis.

The French in Tunisia number about 150,000 but many, if not most, of them are French of recent date. The real hard core of *colons* is made up of some six thousand men who own fully half the arable land in a country with about three and a half million inhabitants. No French representative in Tunisia and no government in Paris has hitherto been able to run counter to the will of the *colons*. They are the men with the money. They are tough and they know what they want and they know what they do not want and that is any sort of Home Rule or real autonomy for the native Tunisians, for these would inevitably bring about the destruction of the *colons'* privileged position.[1]

Monsieur Macrosène is not a *colon*. He is one of the 144,000 odd French outside the charmed circle of the big bosses. He is a civil servant and he is, by temperament, rather anti-settler, he is Leftish and the *colons*, the big boys anyway, are conservative to the core whatever may be their origins and affiliations. He looks on *colons* as social reactionaries and bloated capitalists but he cannot go Tunisian-Nationalist. Indeed, under Home Rule, maybe he would find himself on the retired list and not very sure of his pension. He is, in fact, one of the people who cannot choose. He is just forced to stay where he belongs and most of the spice of life is tasted where one does not belong.

Some seventy years ago the French found about 700,000 Tunisians and the population is now, roughly, three and a half millions. Pretty good going. Outdoes the record of India where in 1852 there were, as *The Times* journalist put it, "one hundred

[1] Not only can the *colons* of Tunisia make their influence directly felt in Paris but they have also the support of the parliamentary group of the Algerian *colons* who realize very acutely that everything happening in Tunisia has repercussions in Algeria.

and fifty millions of people whom *Providence* has committed to our care."[1]

Since 1900 the world's stock of men has increased by about 50%. Every day there are some 75,000 more human beings. The world's population now is probably five times what it was in 1652. If the merry rates keep up, in a generation, thirty years, we shall be a nice little family of three and a half billion, in a century there will be nearly four billion more. Looks as though one large, long-lived, greedy mammal has got out of hand. Atomic warfare? New contraceptives? Where's the remedy?

We are almost certainly on the eve of a discovery more momentous for mankind than that of atom-splitting—until we split the globe and make an end on't—supersonic air-travel, antibiotics and what you will. It is the discovery predicted a short time ago[2] by Dr. Conant, President of Harvard University.

## THE ORAL CONTRACEPTIVE

Take pills and keep the population down. Of course, though no doubt the people who will swallow the pills will be just the people whose groups do not much increase. The spawning myriads of Asia and elsewhere will, most likely, continue their reckless proliferation.

The face of Tunisia was changed and the number of Tunisians boosted not principally by the French administration. It was the *colons* who made the country as it is today. They were encouraged to settle in the Regency and to sink their capital in the soil. It is hard to repress a good deal of sympathy for the *colons*, as a whole, even if not all of them may arouse, individually, much spontaneous goodwill. Why should they?[3]

*La plupart de nos erreurs viennent de la réalité que nous donnons à nos idées d'abstraction.*[4]

[1] The area of British India was not in 1852 as great as in 1939 when, however, the population was over 300,000,000. In 1900 there were in Tunisia about 80,000 Italians (most Sicilians) and only some 800 or 900 *colons*. The French all told were not more than 20,000.

[2] Early in 1952 Dr. E. D. Goldsmith (of the New York Academy of Sciences) announced a drug which arrests pregnancy in mice. Pregnancy is not prevented. The foetus is resorbed.

[3] The tax-figures tell their story. There are, say, 2,900,000 Moslems and 72,000 Tunisian Jews. These two groups together pay one-third of the taxes. The other two-thirds is contributed by 150,000 French and 70,000 Italians. And *colons* are not given to paying more taxes than they can help.

[4] Buffon.

Most of us have a secret castle in our memories, one we clambered up to long ago while we discovered it was the scene of half our fairy-stories; or it may be a fortress where other tales were lived, a castle pale grey under a clement sky, gracious and a theatre for Sleeping Beauties. Then there will be another, less magical, perhaps; we can all recognize it. Here we are, we've just secured a seat, have eluded travellers brandishing British passports but who have not yet quite learned their native language; we have resisted the siren-call of the Voice assuring us that a nice cup o' tea is awaiting us in the dining-room on C-deck. We are happily ensconced beside fellow-citizens who might be but are not, profitably engaged in studying "How to forget", well, let us not be offensive, but you know what I mean "in Three Months". Our gaze lingers lovingly upon the rather grubby White Walls of Old England and upon their crown, a slightly dingy castle which, the guide-books inform us, is a Norman Structure, that it certainly is not, at least externally. It may be a Norman foundation but its appearance may owe to Sir Jeffrey Wyatville, architect to the First Gentleman in Europe, what it does not to bluff King Hal.

The scene is transformed, here is now a castle both northern and gracious. We are strolling over dry, stony ground, yellow ochre, sprouting grey-green scrub, patches of sharp grass and an occasional wild olive. The soil is parched but there is no dust, no sand. When the sparse rains do come that low, worn range of rounded hills shows quite green against the high, pale powdery blue sky. The air, though fresh, has not the exhilarating tang of that blowing through the steppes. There is nothing here but Ksar Lemsa. It is rich red-ochre in the shadows and where the sun strikes, golden. But Ksar Lemsa has a familiar outline, it is that of Dover Castle seen from the Channel packet. Ksar Lemsa is a square with a rectangular tower at each corner. Even its workmanship recall things rather north than south of the Channel. The masonry blocks are large, the execution, though massive, coarse.

One curtain is down, that facing us, though save for this demolished wall the castle is a well-preserved shell. Each of the towers, some forty feet high, is crenellated, as also are the walls in whose thickness you can trace passages, while in the towers are marks where the floors were fixed. There are loopholes and small doors. Here are the things we have been induced to people with medieval knights, pages and fair ladies—all the romantic furnishings of 19th-century gimcrack Gothick. It is all rather exciting, unexpected, even startling. Is this a relic of some unnoted European domination? Can the place be Sicilian or even Spanish? It looks so new: it cannot be more than a few centuries old.

At the foot of the left-hand tower facing us lies a dead donkey, swollen and dust-covered. Dead asses bring, it is said, good luck to those who touch them. This dead donkey, at a gentle prod, opens one eye, wriggles as we scratch between his ears and then composes himself to more slumber.

The castle is not large—about a hundred feet square. In its courtyard is a wild fig-tree shading a russet-fawn foal and a shapely bay mare with sweeping tail. Monsieur Macrosène trots off to peer and squint through filters and view-finders, for, he says, Ksar Lemsa is an unrecorded treasure and no photographs of it exist.

As soon as I am alone a countryman emerges from one of the corner towers; he is sturdy and not so tattered, no *bedawi*, no man of the South who has straggled up hither because times are bad. You would spot this man for a Tunisian anywhere in North Africa. Nothing negroid, a Mediterranean, though one with a face less mobile than those of most of his European fellows.

After a few vague phrases and no indiscreet questions he proposes to sell me the foal cheap. He assures me that it can be folded up and stowed away in the car. I reply this may be so but that it will not fold up in the Air-France 'plane from Tunis to Marseilles. What is that gossip-writer's phrase that sings in my head? Oh, I know. Referring to the present Lord Cardigan, some stalwart wrote 'Love of horses runs in his family for his ancestor led the Charge of the Light Brigade'. Of course.

Despite the hard living, horses hereabouts are not degraded into the sorry, starved nags of the towns. Every now and again you come across a splendid beast out in the country. No room in the car for the foal, but it is a charming little creature.

Hilali comes strolling up. Ksar Lemsa does not surprise him, does not interest him, though he is too well bred to affect contempt for what he does not understand just because he does not comprehend it. Perhaps he does understand, though.

N

"I see this also is the work of the *Rum.*"

And so it is. Ksar Lemsa was a Byzantine fortress and by no means the only one that Justinian's servants set up on the high plateaux behind the imperial frontier. There is a fine Byzantine castle at Haïdra five or six miles this side of Algeria and far away to the west of us, while across the border is Timgad, whose fortress is more than 300 feet square and is set with eight towers. This last is probably, in its origin, what we should call Roman and was refashioned by Byzantine times for there was no break in the tradition of military architecture. What castles the Romans erected are now muddled ruins though here and there—as, for example, at Jublains in France—we can, with a little exercise of the imagination, visualize how the imperial legions' citadels appeared nearly two thousand years ago. Indeed, these buildings resembled Byzantine castles or our own Western ones after the Crusaders had brought back with them plans of fortresses so much better and more effective than the Europeans' own. Roman architecture lasted longer, much longer, in North Africa than it did in Gaul or Britain, for the medieval buildings of the Moslems are, in great measure, lineal descendants of Roman models.

Ksar Lemsa is entirely Byzantine. I should say that there has never been any restoration at all. By dead-reckoning we can set the date of its erection at about the middle of the 6th century. I should be inclined to narrow the dates and say that Ksar Lemsa was made in the decade from 533 to 543.[1] The place may look new but it is about fourteen hundred years old. It is true that the castle seems so modern because it stands alone and isolated: no stumps of columns, no blurred outlines on the ground, no slabs of paved road, nothing to evoke the provincial Roman township.

Let us say that in A.D. 540 Britain was plunged in darkness, or at least it seems so to us, for we know really nothing of the island's story after the withdrawal of the imperial administration at the beginning of the 5th century and the emergence of the Saxon kingdoms much later. In 540 Clotaire was well on his way to dominion over an expanded Gaul bounded by the seas, the Pyrenees, the Alps and the Rhine. There is no break in the French —or the Tunisian—story. But Britain and Gaul were touched by

---

[1] The Vandals occupied *Africa* in A.D. 439. Belisarius brought back the province to imperial rule in the years 533 and 534. Ksar Lemsa was built, no doubt, as part of the net of communications, walls, castles and forts designed to protect *Africa* from attacks by the desert nomads.

the grace of Roman civilization only a matter of centuries before 540. *Africa*—that is Tunisia—had when Ksar Lemsa was built a connected history of more than sixteen hundred years of civilizations—Punic and Roman and Byzantine.

The Work of the Romans. No doubt, though directed from Constantinople, the Empire still kept Latin as its official language when Ksar Lemsa was set up, and if, a generation later, imperial edicts came to be issued in Greek, what we call Byzantine was Roman for both Christian and Moslem alike until the end of the Empire in 1453.

## A CROWN OF WILD OLIVE

A tree-shrub of wild olive, incredibly knarled, tough and bristling with horrid thorns. Olives of all sorts, despite the legends, will thrive quite far from the sea. Though they love marine breezes what they like even better is a limestone soil. Gypsum kills the olives and there is plenty of this in North Africa. However, any light earth will suit these beneficent trees, but the richer the soil the poorer the tree and its fruit. The Romans grew olive-trees, it seems, in this part of Tunisia, so this stunted, hardy bush may be the descendant of tamed ancestors which formed a grove around Ksar Lemsa. If this be so, the wild olive has reverted very thoroughly to type. I try to wrench off a branch in order to plait a crown of wild olive. I must twist and tug and twine for long minutes. How did the ancient Greeks fashion a wreath of wild olive and how did any victor wear such a garland? If bereft of its spikes and thorns the branch makes but a chaplet of bent twig. It may be that the famed tree Kallistephanos, brought back by Hercules from the land of the Hyperboreans, was less prickly than the wild olives of Tunisia. Still, it seems to me that a Crown of Wild Olive must be a Crown of Thorns. Some allegory, maybe.

The valley is shadowless and affords no hint of the hour. Living things are still though there is a gliding hawk in the skies, but on the ground all is motionless. You cannot even notice those delicate, desert-coloured, hopping horned birds that strut warily upon the roadways farther north.

But vehicles do use these excellent metalled roads. Here is something that was not there when we stopped to explore Ksar Lemsa. In the middle of the road, two or three hundred yards

N*

away, is a lump. Cars are so few that the woolly Berber dogs have not learned how to dodge quickly enough. The beasts have not been conditioned. As Monsieur Macrosène remarks, that compact bundle of fluffy fur is proof positive of maladjustment. How right he is. Those dogs will survive which have found the knack of getting out of the way of oncoming vehicles. What other qualities the beasts may possess will be subordinate to that of car-elusion.

The countrymen's dogs will get fit, fit for taking avoiding action.

## IDEAS NOT THINGS AT ALL

"... *ce sont les idées et pas du tout les choses qui restent dans le moi, et la rigueur de langage exige Je me souviens de tel acte de mon esprit par lequel j'ai perçu cet objet, par lequel j'ai déduit cet axiome, par lequel j'ai admis cette vérité.*"

That is it. The old-fashioned compilers of literature-histories would assure us that *Bouvard et Pécuchet* showed Flaubert's sad decline into nonsense; as a matter of fact this last book is worth all the rest and is full of insight.

"... what stay within us are ideas and not things at all. Strictly speaking, language demands that we should say 'I remember such and such an act of my mind whereby I perceived such and such an object, whereby I deduced such and such an axiom, whereby I recognized such and such a truth'. ..."

Monsieur Macrosène wants to show me a strange and peculiar landscape. He also wishes to photograph it. The strange and peculiar place is the Oued-el-Kebir barrage. A barrage does not sound exciting and the Oued-el-Kebir, despite the identity of name, resembles not at all Guadalquivir in far-off Spain.

The barrage one sees not, but the waters of the Oued-el-Kebir are dammed into a great expanse of shallow lake, its surface turquoise-blue. There is a lateral spaciousness about the scene. In the foreground are yellow sands sprouting lilies. The lake is bordered by low hills set against a distant background of ranges so lofty that their peaks are lost in the pale, vivid blue of the sky.

To the right the waters touch sand-slopes patched with the dark green of firs or pines. Before us, and to the left, the shores are broken into splits and tongues. The whole is stepped back in planes like theatrical scenery.

No house, no dwelling, no man or beast. Africa is still empty, thank God, and may it long remain so. Some imperceptible haze from the lake's surface must soften the colours and contours. The diaphanous and delicate picture is not North African, harsh, immediate, forthright; it is a view with overtones and undertones.

This might be one of the fabled pools of Turkestan, a central Asian landscape.

Monsieur Macrosène is doing transformation tricks. We look at Oued-el-Kebir through red filters and orange, through blue and pale yellow. He is going to photograph the place with infra-red rays filtered through a special screen, and then with ultra-violet rays; with a sodium lamp, with a mercury lamp, and he is even going to experiment with a solarization effect.

It seems that young ladies photographed in infra-red light look younger still, and that in ultra-violet light old ladies appear older still. Perhaps so, we shall see; but the colour-filters do their horrid work at once. We have a Oued-el-Kebir, very African indeed, harsh, stripped, matter-of-fact. As Hilali says, "What to believe?" Maybe we should drop belief altogether.

## BOUKHA

*Boukha.* That's the stuff. We are sitting at a Jewish café. The Moslem ones serve nothing all these long Ramadan days. Before us, on the table, are grey mullet's eggs, *poutargue de thon*—dried and pressed tunny roe, tunny caviar if you will—and *boukha* that is a powerful, headache-inducing alcohol distilled from the juice of ripe figs. It is not too disagreeable to the taste, a sort of mocking African vodka, and it goes well enough with bogus African caviar.

We will take off tomorrow. Fly from the businesslike and imposing El-Alaouina field so magnificent compared with the friendly old Kheireddine runway and hydroplane base. We will be leaving a Tunisia which at every turn, even for those who like it as I do, and who cherish delightful memories of Tunisian days, seems to remind one that its foundations are sand. The once well-disguised tensions of alien domination now hum in your ears. What should be the modern *arcanum imperii*, secret of dominion?

Perhaps a return to the Roman. Offer them a new earth rather than a new heaven, sweep them up into the family, no class-distinctions, no colour-bar, no native scale of pay. Hilali's adventure in Europe led him to think that the Soviets are winning right now, so he tells me in an aside before I leave, consolidating their empire and ruining us. The French know a rival faith the Romans did not know, the French have to meet an Islam when the Romans could ignore the religions of the masses, and the French, like the British, are weaker than before, while the Romans seemed strong for very long.

A stirrup-cup of *boukha*. Out on to the avenue and past the French Residency guarded by chubby little black boys armed with Sten guns. Black Africans to keep White Africans in order. Who will keep the Black Africans in order? We may have soon to pretend that they are keeping themselves in order. What did Monsieur Hormone Banana—that, I think, was his auspicious name—deputy from Senegal, declare upon a memorable occasion? "Remember, please, that we are French citizens."

## WU TAOTZU'S CAVE

This Monbazillac is remarkably good. As satisfying in autumn as in springtime; as delightful after a meal as before it. A very noble, polyvalent and generous drink.

The swallows and the house-martins and the swifts are swirling. They are getting ready for Africa. Its mirage has by now faded a little from my eyes, for I have been moving rather rapidly and with some discrimination through our own Western European scene.

Among more majestic of the Pyrenean prehistoric painted sanctuaries, none, however, surpassing great Lascaux, not far from here, or superb Altamira in Spain, though, what are we thinking of? Frontiers and such inventions. The northern Spanish Cantabrian Mounts are, of course, but the western portion of the Pyrenees; how our minds are tied in time.

There is stupendous Niaux a mile long and in places taller than any cathedral made by hands, Niaux with superb black outlines of bisons, aurochs, and wild horse here pierced with arrows and there only menaced. Yes, arrows, for some, feathered, are shown separately. Bows and arrows ten thousand years and more ago? Our remote European ancestors were either remarkably inventive or most cunning in adaptation. No, inventive; they did not adapt their art from anywhere, no, surely not. At Niaux, too, are mysterious signs and symbols; abstract or geometrical art or rather primitive script? The signs meant something that could be read.

And you may see how a curve will serve a bison for a back, how a hole in the rock-face was crowned with antlers and makes a ghostly stag. Some of the astonishingly fresh-looking paintings are covered with thin scales of calcite, proofs of great age, but the finest pictures are in a remote recess where temperature has been constant for millenia, where there is no humidity, no draught, and the air is more scentless, sterilized and neutral than at far-off Ghadames.

Scribblings attract pictures, pictures attract scribblings; some of the subterranean halls and passages have been known for long; there are scores of signatures—but not, alas, prehistoric—some dated to the 17th century. It is impossible to tell if they are bogus; if not touched they may remain fresh for 5000 years and more. There is a signature, or the written name, of Louis Bonaparte. I think it is a fake, but wiser men than I hold it to be authentic and remind us that the King of Holland did take the waters of Ussat quite nearby and that, indeed, these waters proved so restorative and invigorating that they were largely responsible for the spurt of vitality that lead to the generation of him who was to be Napoleon III.

Prehistoric paintings and Second Empire.

This hill-country of the Ariège is delightful, castles perched on mountain-tops; Montségur and memories of the last stand of the Cathars, the western Manichees, Albigensians, followers of a faith St. Augustine once professed. They say that the Cathars, the Pure Ones, left a great treasure. Men still affect to seek it. It is as evasive as the buried riches of Captain Kidd or the wealth of the Cocos Islands. Vain fumblings. The Cathars' Treasure was not gold or gems. It was knowledge, perhaps knowledge of how to make a world with words, a world satisfying man's needs born of implements, objects, machines.

There is a nip in the air though the mellow sunshine is reassuring. The Monbazillac goes well after the local Dordogne wines you get for luncheon; good, wholesome beverages that trickle in fat tears as you swirl your glass; pretty heavy, as the

French say, pretty full-bodied, perhaps 14% of alcohol. Strange, I could never get stuff like that from my vines at Eyssal or Fayolles. Poor old Fayolles, the damned Boches burned it out during the latter part of their stay in France; its walls now stand stark amid the delightful undulating countryside on the borders of Dordogne and Gironde, a most clement and occidental scene. No, we used to import Cahors wines for ordinary use. Dark crimson, fruity, a little vulgar maybe, but that's how we liked them, though our main standby was claret. The nearest claret country, Saint-Emilion, was not more than ten miles away from Fayolles; moreover, Saint-Emilion, they say, is the Burgundy of the clarets and I think all archaeologists and prehistorians should be Burgundians. The sovereign vintages of the old Duchy are comforting and allow one to view with equanimity the march of time in the past.

Yes? the Ariège. The famed caverns of Les Trois-Frères and the Tuc d'Audubert, the one with its prancing, masked wizard amid a world of magic, and the other with its marvellous Magdalenian models of clay bisons, all on the estate of the veteran *comte* Bégouën, gourmet, trencherman, prehistorian and nonagenarian. We've been with the discoverer of the mysterious Montespan cave, wherein, beyond a subterranean lake, are sanctuaries and the headless model of a bear that served some strange rites a hundred and fifty centuries ago, maybe. Ancient bear-rituals borrowed, is it possible, from the trolls of prehistory, the Mousterian men makers of the most venerable religion of which we have any note? Bears, great grinning bears, ten feet high, awful divinities of cavern-temples.

We have explored Gargas, much smaller in size than mighty Niaux, but one of the most impressive places of our Europe, yes, just that. Oh, it's not complicated or immense. It is a grotto of stalactites and stalagmites but the walls are stencilled with hands. There are hands everywhere stretched out towards you from the remote past.

Scores of them, red and black, black or red, strange when you peer at them. Viewed from afar, and illuminated as they are with indirect lighting, they are hallucinating. Scattered over many prehistoric pictures are hands, but in no French cave are they so numerous as at Gargas; they have nearly always one or more joints missing. It is impossible, if the fingers be intact, to produce what appears to be the stencil of a maimed hand. No doubling, folding or lifting will convey the impression of mutilation.

Hand-stencils are found in many parts of the world and some of these imprints are quite modern. Well, if we do not know just why the votaries of Gargas hacked their hands about, we do know what the Papuans of New Guinea mean when they chop off a finger; the sacrifice is a sign of mourning, but it is something more. The old Plains Indians of the United States would cut off a finger-joint in order to propitiate the supernatural Powers. *Do ut des*. Simple, archaic, Roman. "Here's my finger, give me good luck for it."

Have a glass of Monbazillac. They're so small, just thimbles. The flight of birds, the darting swallows sweep and swerve and swoop. Nice birds; family feeling, moral sense. They wait for their children and take them with them to Africa. But how do the young cuckoos find the way? Have they in their consciousness not only a pattern for throwing hedge-sparrows out of the nest, but also a chart of the airways to Africa? I must ask someone who really knows.

Hands. Signs of possession, signs of power say some of the sapient archaeologists. But just what concepts, helped out by words or formed by words, of a hunter-artist, a hunter-wizard of fifteen thousand years ago can we dare to translate by the pale abstractions 'possession' or 'power'. Possession, yes, possession by devils. Power, yes, the power in the arms and claws of the cave-bear when he hugs you. Awful and bloody caricature of amorous embraces. What do we see dimly up there in the American north-west coast where there is bear-magic too, for it has lingered round about the northern parts? the parabole of the *vagina dentata* and the dream of a gold mountain perceived on awakening to be compounded exclusively of excrement.

Fifteen thousand years, did we say? Why, yes, since now for the first time we have, and have had for a year or two, indications of our first art's age. The radio-carbon tests applied to charcoal from beneath the soil of Lascaux's crypt, or lower gallery, yields a date of about 16,000 years ago for the time when the charcoal ceased to be living wood. The figures did not surprise. More or less, less or more; maybe the ancient engravings on, say, the walls of La Mouthe, are not less than 20,000 years old, more or less,

less or more. We are awaiting the indicator for our African mirage and its pictures.

Magic hands? Well, early art. Art is religious in its origin, yes, if we do not ask too closely for a definition of the word 'religious'; let us say that art reflects the feelings of its makers and, in a measure, mirrors its epoch. Maybe it is no mere coincidence that most of contemporary art is confused, inept, impotent, frustrated.

In the middle of the 1929 slump a buyer called on a surrealist painter and said:

"I want a picture, four feet by three, representing a woman sitting on a bench and kissing a crocodile. To her right is to be a reflection of the moon in a bucket. To her left a bird-headed cat. The painting must be ready the day after tomorrow."

It was delivered with the bill:

| | |
|---|---|
| 1 crocodile | 350 francs |
| 1 bench | 125 francs |
| 1 bucket | 20 francs |
| 1 bird-headed cat (very rare) | 400 francs |
| Woman and moon | gratis |
| Raw materials | 50 francs |
| Total | 945 francs[1] |

It was an excellent piece of work. The artist needed the money.

Picasso is the artist of our epoch, the holder-up of the mirror. Art is a mirror of ways of life, thought, belief.

In his *Libro Nero*, published in 1952, Giovanni Papini described a visit to Picasso when the artist delivered himself as follows:

*Dans l'art, le peuple ne cherche plus consolation et exaltation, mais les raffinés, les riches, les oisifs, les distillateurs de quintessence cherchent le nouveau, l'étrange, l'original, l'extravagant, le scandaleux. Et moi-même depuis le cubisme et au-delà, j'ai contenté ces maîtres et ces critiques, avec toutes les bizarreries changeantes qui me sont passées en tête, et moins ils les comprenaient et plus ils m'admiraient. A force de m'amuser à tous ces jeux, à toutes ces fariboles, à*

[1] i.e. about £10 in those days.

*tous ces casse-tête, rébus et arabesques, je suis devenu célèbre et très rapidement. Et la célébrité signifie pour un peintre ventes, gains, fortune, richesse. Et aujourd'hui, comme vous savez, je suis célèbre, je suis riche. Mais quand je suis seul à seul avec moi-même, je n'ai pas le courage de me considerer comme un artiste dans le sens grand et antique du mot. Ce furent de grands peintres que Giotto, le Titien, Rembrandt et Goya; je suis seulement un amuseur public, qui a compris son temps et a épuisé le mieux qu'il a pu l'imbecillité, la vanité, la cupidité de ses contemporains. C'est une amère confession que la mienne, plus douloureuse qu'elle ne peut sembler, mais elle a le mérite d'être sincère.*

The statement is important enough but will not probably be too much advertised, though some of us may still know when our legs are being pulled despite the humbug of art 'critics' and merchants.

"In art, the mass of the people no longer seeks consolation and exaltation, but those who are refined, rich, unoccupied, who are distillers of quintessences, seek what is new, strange, original, extravagant, scandalous. I myself, since cubism and even before, have satisfied these masters and critics, with all the changing oddities which passed through my head, and the less they understood me, the more they admired me. By amusing myself with all these games, with all these absurdities, with all these puzzles, rebuses and arabesques, I became famous, and that very quickly. And fame for a painter means sales, gains, fortune, riches. And today, as you know, I am celebrated, I am rich. But when I am alone with myself, I have not the courage to think of myself as an artist in the great and ancient sense of the term. Giotto, Titian, Rembrandt and Goya were great painters; I am only a *public entertainer* who has understood his times and has exhausted as best he could the imbecility, the vanity, the cupidity of his contemporaries. Mine is a bitter confession, more painful than it may appear, but it has the merit of being sincere."

Some would have it that the sense of the Sacred has been abolished. Others, that men are no longer conforming to an Absolute. I am not quite sure that I know what is meant by these brave and solemn words. Still, some men do ask themselves the old question, "Are we not acting in a peculiarly, specifically and uniquely human way when we affront the absurdity of the universe and make sense of it?"

Man's new role. A noble one, a majestic one, but I'm not so sure that the part makes much sense when we begin to act and to spout the lines. The First Player is called by a fine Greek name ΑΝΘΡΩΠΟΣ ΘΕΟΚΤΟΝΟΣ, the Second Player by a sonorous French one, *l'homme déicide*, the Third Player bears a homely English name, the God-Killer.

They all stare at the Dead God's face.

And each one beholds his own visage.

Where were we before we began to get too prophetical and magisterial? Oh yes, Gargas and its hands. Well, nearby, quite nearby, are two other sights. One is just a cave peopled with phantoms; the other is the glorious Gothic shrine of Saint-Bertrand de Comminges on its hill—no, that suggests the hill is crowned by the cathedral, but not at all, the little mountain is just a stand for the sanctuary.

The cave, two or three hundred yards from Gargas, is full of ghosts, ghosts of bats. Monsieur Norbert Casteret, the speleologist, so worried the bats—I hasten to say in the interests of knowledge and science—that they have now forsaken their old haunts, but before they left they let him into a number of their secrets, though one he could never pierce. All the bats were females come hither to give birth. In fact, the cave was a lying-in hospital for bats. But they did tell him how they use their radar, so never to collide though in pitch darkness and hundreds flying in a small space. They did show him how, when they were sent off by post to places hundreds of miles away, they found their way back readily and quickly, always travelling at night. But they did not tell him whether they went to Africa for the winter. What's the whole end of bats? Why, very much like that of scorpions or quails; keep alive, propagate their kind; no concepts, no, none at all.

Nice, useful, harmless beasts, bats. The butts of ridiculous superstitions; why, not so long ago in rural France, in this leafy Dordogne, and perhaps still, they used to crucify bats on barndoors and let them die slowly of thirst and hunger. Sacrifice. Kill someone else. I always had difficulty in preventing my home-farmer at Eyssal from burning rats alive. Old faiths, old habits. Peasants are cruel. They have to be; if they're not, they don't remain peasants very long, they come down in the world and have to get jobs in the civil service or go into practical, professional politics.

Here in France the context of life is rich, richer than in any land I know save possibly China. Here is the raw material of complicated, delicate, subtle and exciting art at your reach. But only the raw materials, unless we are tuned for the manifestations and their satisfactions. There, beyond the ground-plan un-covered of a Gallo-Roman town, and framed for us in fruit-trees, is Saint-Bertrand-de-Comminges. Linkage. One just has to try to be intelligent. There's a faithful miniature view of Saint-Bertrand on some of the French postage-stamps.

How well Monbazillac suits one's digestion after a Péri-gordian luncheon. Alas, the Pyrenean food is nowhere very memorable. Not memorable like that in our Dordogne, more hallowed than any Holy City, any Kairouan, if it be that sacred-ness grows with age.

Take the regular meal at my inn—on special occasions we exercise greater ingenuity, inventiveness, and we reserve a more vigorous appetite. Melon filled with port wine; truffled omelette; *tournedos à la Périgueux*, the local beefsteak which sits upon a crisp sofa of toast impregnated with truffled sauce and is crowned with an unctuous diadem of *foie gras*; two or three slices of *foie gras de canard* served with cold chicken breast-meat and certainly with a salad called 'Friar's Beard', or, less picturesquely, endive in Britain and chicory in France. Down in our prehistoric Dordogne the duck-liver is as succulent as the goose-liver. I am, indeed, inclined to hold that a really prime *foie gras de canard*—prepared, naturally, from the liver of a runner duck, may, on occasion, exceed in savour and delicate, rich perfume the *foie gras* of the goose. Anyway, you never are in the Périgord presented with the dull, leaden slabs of *foie gras* which the taverners of Toulouse and the Pyrenean and pre-Pyrenean region do dare upon occasion to set before unsuspecting strangers. . . . A choice of cheeses and then some wild strawberries and clotted cream.

The woodland fruits last long in this favoured countryside, though I have not tasted wild raspberries of the Périgord. I think they love the heights; anyway, I never plucked, or even ate,

any more delicious than those I used to hunt as a youth in the
Black Forest even when the cool breezes were quivering the
silvery sides of leaves up on Schauinsland or towards the
Feldberg's grassy alp.

But let no patriotic Pyrenean feel that we are belittling the
ancient art of his mountains. Not only is his prehistoric patrimony
rich, not only have the Pyrenees and their western prolongation,
the Cantabrian Mountains, been for many millenia sacred and
magical, but there is always something new to set one's imagination to work. A few months ago I was able to examine a
Magdalenian propulsor handle, but obviously it never served on
any weapon, it is rather a toy or an ornament of marvellous
quality. We must move up to the heights of classical Greek, of
T'ang China and of Renascent Italy, before we can find a peer
to this little carving of a reindeer fawn. Its age? Well, I should
say not less than 12,000 years.

After such masterpieces, art did die away in western Europe;
and why not? As Valéry sharply phrased our thought, "We
civilizations know that we are mortal." Argument from design?
Well, not quite that way, not from a design of the world, but from
the design of an art; yes, fair enough. Most of us have dangling
in the background of our minds a rope which, if pulled, rings a
bell that clangs out insistently, "Sticks go up and never fall down,
it will be still better next time, there are no bounds to our
credulity."

Bear-cults, hunting-magic, the medieval Way of Saint James.
In our day a Pyrenean grotto has become the most revered
pilgrimage-place in western Europe. Yes, faithful Périgordian
though I be, I must admit that, in some ways, the Pyrenees
have it.

Ah! Swallows and house-martins revolving; yes, here they
are, the swifts too. Exercising, trial flights; one day soon they
will break the ball, the circle of their gyrations and, with no
hesitation or fumbling, dart right out.

It seems that what makes one feel hungry is low sugar-
content in the blood. It's an hereditary condition, part of one's
inheritance, they tell us. It's what you eat and not how much
you eat; maybe. I certainly have an hereditary low sugar-content.
Let's stock up on some sugar. Years ago, when touring some
coalfields of northern France, my guide was an extremely

wealthy and philanthropic mine-owner. We pulled up early one morning and, with fine, democratic ease, took our breakfasts at the counter of a pub. Moved to expostulation by the sight of workmen swallowing glasses full of white wine at seven in the morning, prosperous mine-owner asked one fellow why he drank so at such a matutinal hour. *Pour tuer le ver.* "To kill the worm," came the time-honoured reply. "Well," answered the magnate, "you can do that just as well by munching lumps of sugar." The workman looked my host steadily in the eye and said, "*On voit que Monsieur est également sucrier.*" "Anyone can see, sir, that you have also interests in sugar manufacture."

Let us stock up on some sugar. Another tiny glass of Monbazillac on this clement, autumnal afternoon.

I walked up to the Font-de-Gaume painted cave this morning and looked again at the battling reindeer and the red rhinoceros. Rhinoceroses in this Dordogne, well, 15,000 years or so ago, not so long, and these pachyderms were hairy and cold-resisting. After all, it is easier to imagine a rhinoceros at home in the Vézère Valley than in the Oued Djerar of the Tassili n'Ajjer. You walk away from this French grotto, you cross the little Beune valley, turn back to admire the cavern's entrance most like a skull. Into the main road, past a cottage radio blaring and a woman looking peevishly up and down the road. She's seeking her man. He's late, of course.

That's a charming house, a *château* they call it still. It beseeches you to take it and restore its lost youth for it is elegant and noble still. The *via sacra* of the Vézère.

"The whole is a riddle, an aenigma, an inexplicable mystery."[1]

What is a man? Why, a creature that, through speech, substitutes his word-made world for the absurd world of the senses. A man is a being that with his skilled hands can make things both to serve and to dominate him. Since men alone can form concepts, why should we complain that the world is unjust and absurd? But the extension of the field of knowledge, the developments of sciences and the increase of the puerile good sense characteristic of the technician and scientific worker have

[1] Hume.

weakened sadly men's power to create, and if man does not create in art then he is less than human and, worst of all, he loses control of his inventions.

Increase in knowledge is, of course, quite useless as a substitute for artistic creation, which alone can set man at ease in his surroundings. So we have a throng of wailing intellectuals and impotent artists, who, because they have rejected old views and not found new views, howl that the universe is a bottomless pit, quite meaningless and absurd. So why not jump out of the window at once? Even in a world revealed less desperate than ours someone was found to declare that without the authority of Revelation few would guess that death was a punishment.

Though Monsieur Malraux's poetical syntheses and mystical imaginings are sometimes beyond my comprehension, he seems to me to be the most acute and intelligent of art-critics now living among us. Surely he hit the right nail on the head when he wrote:

> Le plus grand mystère n'est pas que nous soyons jetés au hasard entre la profusion de la matière et celle des astres : c'est que dans cette prison nous tirions de nous-mêmes des images assez puissantes pour nier notre néant.

"The greatest mystery is not that we are cast haphazard between the profusion of matter and that of the stars; it is that in this prison we can draw from within ourselves images powerful enough to deny our nothingness."

To deny our nothingness. Art is the name of those images. Science is the description of the profusion of matter and that of the stars.

Images on remote Saharan rocks. The heavens above us on the old Turkish Fort at Ghat.

Art does not imitate life which is shapeless and inimitable. Life conforms to art. Great God, now we have some inkling of why we are so uncomfortable.

One lap of my roundabout way northwards from the Pyrenees was an exploration and a pilgrimage potological and gastronomical too. We were introduced into the heart and body of the Armagnac country and to days of experiment. One bounteous morning stands out majestic in memory. At each cellar and *chai*

were glasses and bottles and flagons, but not even a dry biscuit
to munch. When I hinted that something to nibble was needful,
smiles and deprecatory gestures silenced me. Let us make no
invidious comparisons. The Armagnac liqueur is overwhelming.
It is not brandy, it is not *fine champagne*, it is something quite
different and I think, if not nobler, at least more virile, more male.

The modern men of Armagnac are an honest lot; none of
this 150-year-old brandy nonsense. Armagnac is very venerable
when it is forty. The taste is coloured, the colour tasty. A deep
golden taste, a metallic, meaty, ravishing colour. We drank a
great many drops at the bottoms of balloon-glasses. It says much
for the clean-living, uprightness, sincerity, frankness and nobility
of the lot of us—we were five—that between the savouring of
these elixirs and the partaking of a sumptuous, rural luncheon
served in the fashion of the Béarn of Henri IV and at a place I
should like to reveal as Luppé-Viollès, we were in a fit condition
of mind and body to revel in the revealing beauty of what must
be, I think, the finest Romanesque painted sanctuary in Gascony.
The place is called Panjas. The large, humble, village church is
dusty, lofty, luminous and adorned with interesting and provincial statues. The illuminated apse is covered with frescoes
which you may read as though they were enlargements of
miniatures, most majestic and exciting MSS. of the early 12th
century.

Romanesque wall-paintings which were, in our impoverished
West, substitutes for the sumptuous mosaics of Byzantium and
the East; wall-paintings, nevertheless, most moving and evoca-
tory for us in this land where painting and drawing were invented
it may be 20,000 years ago and more; arts that faded and were
reintroduced from the East to us.

The sanctuary of Panjas; bold saints, apostles robed; a vision
of world creation, salvation, damnation; a whole image of a
universe. A painted cave.

From my seat under the trees you can see the fine, white,
wispy trails of mist beginning to curl in the valley that will soon
have vanished. There is an odour of walnuts and new wine while
the migrant birds shoot off to sanctuary in Africa. . . .

Our invention is our salvation which comes not only from
informed intelligence but also from informed imagination . . . the
story of Wu Taotzu is edifying:

Wu Taotzu lived in the reign of Hsüantsung in the T'ang dynasty and he executed a painting upon a wall of the imperial palace. The artist kept his picture veiled until the Emperor and his Court came to inspect the work, then Wu pulled aside the curtain and revealed a wondrous scene of forests, high mountains, of clouds and vast perspectives, of men upon the hills and of the flight of birds. A magic world. As Hsüantsung gazed enraptured,

"Look," exclaimed Wu, "in a cave at the foot of this mountain there dwells a spirit."

He clapped his hands. The cave's door flew open.

"The interior is beautiful beyond all words; deign to permit me to show the way."

So saying, he passed within. Before anyone could move or speak the door had shut behind him.

There was nothing but the bare wall and no man ever again saw Wu Taotzu.

# INDEX

## A

Africa, A Private, 106–9
Africa, Roman, 141, 142, 165–7
Africa, The Sum of, 110–12
Aïn-el-Frass, The False Fonduk of, 22, 23
Alcohol and Islam, 169–71
Americans and Finger-Rings, 126–8
Art, Invention of, 62–4
Art and Life, 202 et seq.

## C

Cabrerets, The Curiosities of, 16, 29
Cancer in the Sahara, 23, 24
Carthaginian Art and Life, 179–82 et seq.
Chad, The Approaches of, 92, 93
Chad Province, 109–10
Chotts, The, Great and Small, 139–40
'Civilization', 99 et seq.
'Colonies', 128–30

## D

Djerba, The Island of, 121–4
Djerba, The Jews of, 123–4
Douirat, 119–21

## E

Education, French, in Black Africa, 95–9 et seq.
Egypt, The Sum of, 88–92
Erg, The, 37, 38

## F

Feriana, 150 et seq.
Fezzan, 115–17
Fort-Lamy, 93, 94, 105

Fort-Saint, 38, 39
Foum-Tatahouine, 118
French and North Africa, 162 et seq., 190, 191

## G

Gabès, 124 et seq.
Gafsa, 144 et seq.
Ghadames, 19, 23, 33–7, 112, 113 et seq.
Ghadames, Roman, 115, 116
Ghat, 54 et seq., 77–9

## I

Islam Today, 175–7

## J

Jihad, 175 et seq.

## K

Kaid of Ghadames, 24, 25, 32
Kebili, 130 et seq.
Ksar Lemsa, 192–6
Ksour, The, 118–19

## L

Language, 97–9
Law-abiding British, 29
Libyan Kingdom, 25, 30–2
Limes Romanus, 140–3

## M

Mahdia and its Mosque, 178, 179
Maktar, 165, 169
Man, What is a?, 58–62

Mathematics and Reality, 12
'Meaning of History', 156–9
Middle Ages, The End of, 12
Monbazillac Wine, 11–13, 17, 198
    et seq.
Money and Value, 34–6
Mosaics of Sousse, 184–6

N

Negro Music, 53–4
Negroes, Now and Then, 52–3

O

Oases, The Prehistoric Art of, 72
Oil in North Africa, 162–3
Ostrich Eggs, 22, 42, 43
Oued-el-Kebir and its Transforma-
    tions, 196
Ouled-Naïl, 20–22, 172

P

Pech-Merle, 15, 16
Pedigree-Mongering, 27
Prehistoric Painting, 13, 14, 63–6
Pyrenean Prehistoric Painted Caves,
    198 et seq.

Q

Quail Adventures, 159 et seq.

R

Religions in North Africa, 167–9
Roman Fortune, 154–6

S

Saharan Climates, 40–2
Saharan Dances, 18–21
Saharan Prehistoric Art, 69–72
Sbeitla and its Temples, 153 et seq.
Script and Writing, 173–5
Slaves, 48–52
Sousse or Justinianopolis, 179 et seq.
Southern African Written Rocks,
    85–8
Spanish Prehistoric Art, 66–9, 172–4

T

Tassili n'Ajjer and its Prehistoric
    Pictures, 55–7, 73–7
Tattooing, 171 et seq.
Tibesti and its Art, 79–82
Tools of Early Men, 43–6
Tophet, The Pit of, 182
'Treason', 133 et seq.
Trees of Life, 171 et seq.
Truman, Mr., and 'American Suc-
    cess', 125
Tuareg, 113 et seq.
Tunisian Story, The, 136–8

U

'Uwenat Prehistoric Art, 82, 84

V

Voltaire and Monsieur du Châtelet,
    28, 29

W

Wu Taotzu, The Edifying Legend of,
    209, 210